An Application of the Linear Regression Technique for Determining Length and Weight of Six Fish Taxa

The role of selected fish species in Aleut paleodiet

Trevor J. Orchard

BAR International Series 1172
2003

Published in 2016 by
BAR Publishing, Oxford

BAR International Series 1172

An Application of the Linear Regression Technique for Determining Length and Weight of Six Fish Taxa

ISBN 978 1 84171 540 7

BAR Publishing is the trading name of British Archaeological Reports (Oxford) Ltd.
British Archaeological Reports was first incorporated in 1974 to publish the BAR
Series, International and British. In 1992 Hadrian Books Ltd became part of the BAR
group. This volume was originally published by Archaeopress in conjunction with
British Archaeological Reports (Oxford) Ltd / Hadrian Books Ltd, the Series principal
publisher, in 2003. This present volume is published by BAR Publishing, 2016.

Printed in England

BAR
PUBLISHING

BAR titles are available from:

      BAR Publishing
      122 Banbury Rd, Oxford, OX2 7BP, UK
EMAIL   info@barpublishing.com
PHONE +44 (0)1865 310431
FAX   +44 (0)1865 316916
      www.barpublishing.com

ABSTRACT

The detailed estimation of the original live size of faunal specimens from archaeological assemblage provides a particularly useful, though generally under-employed, tool for zooarchaeological analysis. Though a variety of methods have been employed in the generation of such size estimations, statistical regression provides perhaps the most accurate estimations of the original live length and weight of fish specimens found in archaeological contexts. Such estimations are useful for the reconstruction of diet and the investigation of past environments. Furthermore, detailed size estimations can contribute to a refinement of other methods of faunal quantification, such as the calculation of minimum numbers of individuals (MNI).

Statistical regression was applied to the comparison of skeletal element size and the live length and weight of six fish taxa: Pacific cod (*Gadus macrocephalus*), Walleye pollock (*Theragra chalcogramma*), Atka mackerel (*Pleurogrammus monopterygius*), Greenling (*Hexagrammos* sp.), Rockfish (*Sebastes* sp.), and Irish Lords (*Hemilepidotus* sp.). For each taxon, a selection of skeletal elements were measured from comparative specimens and these data sets used to generate regression formulae which compared the known live length and weight to specific skeletal element measurements. This resulted in the creation of a easily applicable tool for the estimation of the live size and weight of skeletal specimens from archaeological contexts.

This methodology was tested in the context of a case study involving the analysis of fish remains from five archaeological sites in the Aleutian archipelago. Specifically, this included two sites on Adak island, a single site on Buldir island, and two sites on Shemya Island, providing a sample that spans the central and western parts of the Aleutian chain. In the assessment of the relative contributions of the taxa under consideration to the diet of the prehistoric inhabitants of these sites, the regression approach was shown to produce superior results to those obtained through traditional meat weight calculations. The results of this analysis also provide insight into temporal changes in the local environment and ecology.

TABLE OF CONTENTS

LIST OF TABLES

LIST OF FIGURES

ACKNOWLEDGEMENTS

This monograph is based on my M.A. thesis from the University of Victoria, Victoria, British Columbia, Canada, which was completed in the summer of 2001. The published version that is presented here has been only slightly modified and updated from its original state. A number of people provided support and encouragement during the preparation of the original thesis. My interest in archaeology I owe largely to my M.A. supervisor, Dr. Quentin Mackie, who provided invaluable support and countless hours of editing throughout my masters program. Susan Crockford and Becky Wigen are responsible for my interest and experience in zooarchaeology. In addition, this thesis project arose out of a much smaller project that was placed into my lap by Susan Crockford, and throughout the preparation of this thesis her insight and expertise were greatly appreciated. Debbie Corbett provided the Aleutian Islands archaeological materials and site information upon which much of this thesis is based, and graciously endured my countless e-mails requesting further information and clarification of this material. The Department of Anthropology of the University of Victoria provided access to comparative specimens and laboratory space for analysis. The National Marine Mammal Lab, National Marine Fisheries Service, Seattle, provided the remainder of the comparative fish specimens and financial support for the analysis of many of those specimens. The members of my thesis committee, Dr. Quentin Mackie, Dr. Leland Donald and Dr. Tom Reimchen, as well as my external examiner, Dr. Gay Frederick, read various drafts of my M.A. thesis, and their comments and suggestions aided in preparing the finished product seen here. Dr. Peter Stephenson encouraged me to publish my thesis, and Dr. Quentin Mackie furthered that encouragement and suggested BAR as a venue for publication. Financial support during the preparation of this manuscript for publication was provided by a Social Science and Humanities Research Council of Canada Doctoral Fellowship and a University of Toronto Fellowship.

Finally, I would like to express my immense gratitude and love to my parents, Kerry and Leona, and my brother, Jeff, who have supported me unconditionally throughout all of my endeavours. And to all my family and friends, for all of your love and support and for providing a break from the academic grind whenever it was needed.

CHAPTER 1. INTRODUCTION

The understanding of trophic relationships or dietary regimes, both of humans and non-human animals, is a particularly interesting area of scientific inquiry. A number of techniques have been applied to such study, including direct observation of predator-prey relationships (Reimchen 2000; Bertram and Nagorsen 1995; Breen et al. 1982) and isotopic analysis of bones (Cannon et al. 1999; Heaton 1995; Chisholm et al. 1982). Perhaps one of the most interesting approaches involves the analysis of the physical remains of the food items of the animals under consideration. For non-human animals, this has taken the form of the analysis of stomach contents or of scat samples (Yang 1999; Merrick et al. 1997; Olesiuk et al. 1990; Dwyer et al. 1987). In the case of past human populations, this has typically taken the form of the analysis of faunal remains from archaeological sites (see Chapter 2).

One of the major themes in recent years in the study of the Holocene human occupation of the North Pacific region, has been that of maritime adaptations (Erlandson et al. 1999; Ames 1998; Veltre 1998). This has particularly been important in a number of recent areas of study, including renewed interest in the possibility of a Pacific coastal route for the initial human colonization of the Americas (Fedje and Josenhans 2000; Dixon 1999; Sandweiss et al. 1998), studies of the development of Northwest Coast social complexity (Ames 1994; Croes 1992; Matson 1992), and environmental reconstruction through archaeological deposits (Orchard 2001; Mackie et al. 2001). The establishment of the degree to which a people were adapted to a maritime way of life is closely tied to studies of resource use and diet, and thus to the types of faunal analysis mentioned above.

In analysing faunal remains from archaeological sites, a variety of techniques and methodologies have been applied, such as the construction of species lists, quantification in the form of the number of identified specimens present (NISP) or the minimum number of individuals (MNI), and the determination of the meat weight represented by different faunal taxa present in an archaeological assemblage. Only rarely, however, have faunal remains been analysed beyond these basic levels, despite the wealth of information that is available from more advanced methods.

Detailed estimations of the original live size of faunal specimens, for example, hold great potential for contributing to several aspects of archaeological interpretations. Dietary reconstructions are generally dependent on estimations of the meat weight contributed by the various faunal taxa represented in the archaeological material. Detailed size estimations of individual archaeological faunal specimens provide a far more accurate reconstruction of the relative meat weight of the various taxa than can be obtained using more general approaches. More specific size estimations also have implications for technological interpretations. Different sizes and species of fauna require different technologies or approaches to harvesting them. Such technological requirements may be deduced from the results of detailed size reconstructions. Finally, generating a fine grained reconstruction of the size of individual faunal specimens from archaeological sites provides a picture of the local ecology and biology of particular taxa in the past. By comparing this to modern biological data and to data from archaeological sites of different ages, an understanding of changing environment and population structure over time may be obtained.

Statistical regression provides a particularly useful technique for the generation of such detailed size estimations. By comparing the size of modern comparative specimens to measurements of their skeletal elements, regression formulae can be generated that allow for the estimation of one variable from the other. Archaeological skeletal specimens may then be measured using the same variables, and their original size estimated using the generated regression formulae.

In this thesis, I have tested this methodology by applying the regression approach to the analysis of fish remains from the Aleutian Islands. In particular, comparative data were gathered for six taxa of fish that are particularly common in Aleutian Islands archaeological sites, and these data were used to generate regression formulae. These formulae were then applied to the analysis of archaeological specimens from five sites in the central and western Aleutian archipelago. Aside from providing a basis for testing the regression methodology, this case study addresses a relatively unstudied aspect of Aleut prehistory, and thus also provides unique insight into the culture history of the study area.

Chapter 2 reviews the quantitative methodologies that have commonly been applied to the analysis of faunal remains and examines some of the problems and advantages of these various methods. Simple techniques such as the generation of species lists, and the calculation of the number of identified specimens present (NISP) and the minimum number of individuals (MNI) are examined. In addition, various techniques that have been applied to the estimations of original live size are discussed. This includes a basic introduction to the regression approach, and a comparison of this approach with other techniques.

Early historic, ethnographic and archaeological sources on the Aleut are reviewed in Chapter 3. The chapter begins with a brief description of the Aleutian Archipelago itself, particularly in terms of its unique isolation and environment. This is followed by a discussion of the history of Russian contact in the islands, and the maritime fur trade that accompanied this contact. Ethnographic information on the Aleut is summarized, with emphasis on subsistence practices and particularly the use of fish resources. Finally, previous archaeological work in the islands is discussed, and in particular the faunal analysis that has been done to date is reviewed.

The thesis problem, identified in Chapter 4, combines the major issues from Chapters 2 and 3. The chapter begins by summarizing the problems of the methods typically applied in previous faunal analyses, and the prospects of statistical regression for accounting for some of these problems. The Aleutian Islands case study, in particular the five archaeological sites from which faunal material is being analysed, is then outlined in more detail.

The methodology defined to address this thesis problem is outlined in Chapter 5. The chapter begins with an overview of the methodology, and the six fish taxa selected for analysis are discussed. The regression approach is then generally described, and the specifics of the current application of that approach are outlined. The generation of comparative data is addressed next, along with a description of the available comparative specimens. This section also includes a detailed description of the osteometric measurements that are defined for each taxon. Finally, the methodology for the archaeological application of the thesis is outlined.

The results that were generated through this methodology are outlined in Chapter 6. This chapter is divided into two sections, addressing the results of the generation of regression formulae from comparative data, and the archaeological application of that data. In addition to presenting the general results of the regression of comparative data, the first section addresses some specific methodological problems that arose during the application of the methodology. Archaeological results include a variety of levels of quantification, including NISP, MNI, and the estimated lengths and weights made possible by the regression approach. In addition to relatively brief written descriptions of the results, they are presented in tabular and graphical form.

Chapter 7 presents a discussion of the results and outlines the major conclusions of the thesis. The chapter is divided into three sections, addressing the methodology, Aleut culture history, and Aleutians biology. The first section discusses and assesses the methodology, as well as its limitations and a number of potential sources of error that exist. The implications of the results for Aleut culture history are outlined in the second section, including an assessment of Aleut diet and the implications for subsistence activities and resource harvesting technologies. The final section of the chapter provides a brief discussion of the implications of the results for understanding changes in the biology and ecology of the study area.

The final chapter, Chapter 8, provides a summary of the thesis and highlights the major conclusions. First, the thesis process and results are briefly summarized. Then, drawing on the conclusions that were introduced in the previous chapter and the discussion of the results in general, the major conclusions and implications of the thesis as a whole are reviewed. Specifically, through a comparison with previous methodologies, it is shown that the regression approach provides a more fine grained technique for reconstructing meat weight. In addition, Pacific cod are found to be particularly important in terms of prehistoric Aleut subsistence, and in terms of assessing biological changes and impacts.

CHAPTER 2. PROBLEMS AND PROSPECTS OF QUANTITATIVE ZOOARCHAEOLOGY[1]

2.1 Introduction

Subsistence and resource utilisation form one of the central themes of archaeological inquiry, and these issues are often addressed through the collection and analysis of faunal remains from archaeological sites. Though faunal analysis has most commonly been applied to studies of subsistence, the detailed analysis and quantification of faunal remains has also contributed to a number of other interesting areas of inquiry. These include studies of the seasonality of site occupation (Ford 1989; Bernick and Wigen 1990), settlement and social relations (Acheson 1998; Hayden 1997; Lepofsky *et al.* 1996), and environmental reconstruction (Lyman 1996; Reitz *et al.* 1996). The basis for these varied questions or research topics, however, lies in a similar program of detailed faunal identification and quantification. It is these underlying methodological considerations that form the basis for the following chapter, though I will return to a brief consideration of the interpretive aspects at the end of the chapter.

Though it is useful to analyse all faunal remains, the importance of fish as a dietary source on the Pacific coast of North America, as well as elsewhere in the world, makes the analysis of fish remains particularly important. Despite the importance of fish remains, however, these have often been given less consideration than other remains, particularly in North America. Detailed analysis of fish remains can contribute much to archaeological interpretation:

> Fish remains can tell us something about the former distribution of a species, the time of introduction and/or the extinction of a species, palaeoclimates in general, and especially something about food preferences of the inhabitants of prehistoric and early historic settlements, the environment of their settlements, their fishing methods, the season in which the fish was caught, and the domestication of certain species (Clason 1986: 1).

The extent to which such interpretations can be made, however, is largely determined by the methods of faunal analysis and quantification that are applied.

Daly (1969) identifies two problems which have, in the

past, limited the widespread use of detailed faunal analysis. Specifically, she indicates that "there is...a tendency to regard animal remains as being of second-class status, ranking well below stone tools and potsherds in potential cultural significance," and furthermore "the excavator often feels that the difficulty of actually getting any specific information out of his faunal material is very great" (Daly 1969: 146-147; cf. Chaplin 1965; Casteel 1976: 72). The first of these problems can be alleviated only through a change in the attitude of archaeologists towards faunal remains. Faunal material must be treated with the same attention and detail that is afforded other material remains (Uerpmann 1973). The second problem can be lessened through a better understanding of the methodologies and potential of faunal analysis. Though faunal analyses are now commonly applied to archaeological material, the problems identified by Daly more than 30 years ago are still present in the field of archaeology. This chapter addresses these issues to some degree by exploring a number of the methods that have been employed in the analysis of faunal data.

2.2 Identification of Faunal Remains

In order to generate data that are useful in making interpretations about archaeological material, the treatment of faunal remains should extend far beyond the simple collection of skeletal materials (Reitz and Wing 1999; Wing and Brown 1979). Taxonomic identification of skeletal remains is a necessary first step in any faunal analysis, and though published guides for such identification do exist (e.g., Rojo 1991; Cannon 1987; Leach 1997), an extensive reference collection for comparative identification is generally considered essential (Reitz and Wing 1999; Wing and Brown 1979; Coy 1978; Wheeler 1978; Uerpmann 1973; Olsen 1971; Chaplin 1965). This is particularly stressed by Casteel who states that "it cannot be stressed too greatly that the comparative osteological and squamatological (scale) collection is at the heart of any attempt at identification and further work with fossil or sub-fossil fish remains" (1976: 7). Even having access to such a comparative collection is not always adequate, however, as Coy states that "small mammal, bird and fish identifications are a specialist task" (1978: 143). Even a specialist with access to an extensive comparative skeletal collection is generally not able to identify all of the skeletal elements or fragments present in an archaeological assemblage. It is this differential identifiability of skeletal elements that poses the greatest problem at the preliminary stage of faunal analysis. Minimally, the identification of faunal remains leads to the generation of a simple list of species present in the archaeological material, often termed the "laundry list" approach (Olsen 1971; Yesner and Aigner

1. Significant portions of this chapter have been presented elsewhere as Orchard 2000.

1976; cf. Grayson 1973; Daly 1969). The generation of such a list should only be considered a first step in any faunal analysis, however, and "interpretation, rather than identification, should be stressed as the final goal of bone examinations" (Olsen 1971: 1). In order to provide a basis for making interpretations, an attempt should be made to estimate or quantify the relative amount of remains of each taxonomic group (Horton 1984; Reitz and Cordier 1983).

2.3 Quantification of Faunal Data

A number of approaches or methodologies have been applied to the quantification of faunal data. The three most common are (1) the number of identified specimens present (NISP), (2) the minimum number of individuals (MNI) of each taxonomic group, and (3) the estimation of the original size of the animals recovered or their meat weight (Reitz and Wing 1999; Mitchell 1990; Grayson 1979, 1984; Lyman 1985; Wing and Brown 1979). Though additional methodologies have been used (Lyman 1985, 1994; Ringrose 1993; Fieller and Turner 1982; Gilbert and Singer 1982), the three basic approaches listed above will form the bulk of the discussion that follows.

The most basic method of quantification typically involves a simple representation of the amount of bone present at a site. This generally takes the form of either a count of the bones represented by each identified taxa (NISP) or the weight of bone represented by each taxonomic group (Driver 1993; Grayson 1978, 1984). Reitz and Wing (1999: 191) indicate that NISP represents a form of primary data. Lyman refers to such primary data as "observational units," and he defines these as "empirical manifestations that are easily observed general properties of phenomena; they are easily experienced with one's senses and can be directly measured" (1994: 37).

Despite the primary nature of NISP, however, a number of problems arise from its use in the comparison of relative frequencies of different taxa (Grayson 1979, 1984). One of the most commonly cited problems with the use of the NISP value is that of the varying number of identifiable bones found in different species (Driver 1993; Ringrose 1993; Grayson 1979, 1984; Payne 1972; Perkins and Daly 1968; Shotwell 1955). Daly, for example, indicates that "pigs have nearly twice as many identifiable foot bones as do deer and sheep, and carnivores have even more" (1969: 149). Clearly, when calculating NISP values, such variations will bias the results in favour of taxa which have more identifiable skeletal elements. This problem has long been understood, and some analysts have thus employed a corrected NISP value which attempts to account for the variation in the number of identifiable elements found in different taxa (Shotwell 1955; Gilbert and Singer 1982).

The second major problem that arises from the use of NISP

involves the differential treatment or butchery of different taxa (White 1952, 1953a; Driver 1993; Ringrose 1993; Gilbert and Singer 1984; Lyman 1985; Grayson 1979; Payne 1972; Perkins and Daly 1968). As Grayson indicates, "differences in specimen counts per taxon may simply reflect the fact that some animals were retrieved from kill sites whole, while others were butchered on the spot with only selected portions retrieved" (1984: 20). Differential preservation (Lyon 1970; Casteel 1971) and differential recovery of skeletal elements may also cause similar biases in NISP results (Grayson 1979, 1984; Wheeler 1978: 71; Perkins and Daly 1968). Morlan (1983) also identifies a related problem, indicating that it is generally impossible to identify all specimens in a faunal sample, and thus only some specimens are expressed by NISP.

The most important problem that exists with the use of NISP involves the potential interdependence of the faunal specimens that are counted (Grayson 1973, 1979, 1984; Morlan 1983; Lyman 1979; Payne 1972). Grayson states that there is "no known way of demonstrating which bones and bone fragments necessarily came from different individuals across an entire faunal assemblage" (1979: 202). It is thus inappropriate to apply to NISP values statistical methods which assume that all elements are independent. Despite these problems, NISP is one of the simplest and most transparent means of quantifying faunal data, and the use of NISP is supported by a number of analysts (Cannon 1991; Driver 1993). Grayson, for example, states that "although the number of these criticisms is impressive, it is clear that few are truly fatal to the use of NISP as a measure of taxonomic abundance" (1979: 201).

An alternative to the use of NISP is the calculation of the minimum number of individuals (MNI) which are represented by an assemblage of bones from a given species. Such a determination is possible through a comparison of the archaeological bones with the known set of bones represented by a living individual (Driver 1993: 86-87; Grayson 1984; Perkins and Daly 1968). The simplest form of MNI calculation is that employed by White, whereby he "separate[d] the most abundant element of the species found...into right and left components and use[d] the greater number as the unit of calculation" (1953b: 397). Though such an approach was previously used by palaeontologists (Grayson 1973; Morlan 1983) and by Russian archaeologists (Casteel 1977a,c), White is generally credited with introducing this methodology into the North American archaeological literature (Grayson 1973, 1979, 1984; Nichol and Wild 1984; Wild and Nichol 1983a; Horton 1984; Lyman 1985). MNI, in this simple form, is a very conservative figure, and the "minimum number of individuals" must not be confused with the "number of individuals" (Uerpmann 1973). This extreme conservatism is stressed by Allen and Guy, who further indicate that "the central problem with the MNI is that it says nothing about the numerical distance between itself and reality" (1984: 41).

In order to better estimate the true number of individuals, slightly more advanced versions of the MNI calculation have been suggested (Krantz 1968; Bökönyi 1970; Allen and Guy 1984). One of the simplest alternatives to the approach advocated by White was the "Grand Minimum Total" of Chaplin (1971) which accounted for the fact that not all of the left and right specimens of a given skeletal element necessarily form pairs (Horton 1984; Wild and Nichol 1983a). This realization results in the following formula:

$$GMT = L + R - P$$

where L and R are the number of left and right specimens and P is the number of identifiable pairs (Horton 1984: 259-260). Rather than seeking to estimate the minimum number of individuals in an assemblage, Chaplin's formula attempts to count the actual number of individuals or "those having at least one member still surviving" (Wild and Nichol 1983a: 338). This method, however, makes the assumption that at least one member of each of the original pairs has survived in the site deposits (Horton 1984). Clearly this will often not be a valid assumption, as taphonomic processes will affect left and right bones equally and many complete pairs will be lost from an archaeological site (Lie 1980). Krantz (1968) proposed a solution to this problem, by "recognizing that the proportion of pairs in a sample was a direct consequence of the amount of bone lost from a site" (Horton 1984: 261; cf. Wild and Nichol 1983a). Krantz (1968) argued that given this relationship, the original number of animals (N) could be determined by the following formula:

$$N = (L2 + R2)/(2P)$$

Wild and Nichol support Krantz's approach, indicating that it "is the only method in the literature that shows any promise for estimating in the presence of decay" (1983a: 344; cf. Wild and Nichol 1983b). A slightly simpler formula:

$$N = LR/P$$

was derived by Fieller and Turner (1982) and independently by Allen and Guy (1984), who argue that it better represents the original population size. As indicated by Morlan (1983) and others, this latter formula is analogous to the Peterson index that is used in biology to estimate the size of populations through capture-recapture techniques. Horton indicates that "if the numbers of lefts and rights are equal, then the two formulae will give identical results; if not, however, Krantz's formula will give higher figures" (1984: 262). The utility of these more advanced methods has been questioned by some authors (Nichol and Wild 1984; Lie 1983; Casteel 1977a). Horton, however, argues that much of this criticism comes from "a misunderstanding of the difference between [minimum number and original number] estimates," and he goes on to state that minimum, original and actual number estimates "are valid when used for the purposes for which they were intended" (1984: 265).

Regardless of the validity of these various approaches to the estimation of numbers of individuals, they are still problematic. One problem that arises from the use of such calculations results from the effects of sample size. Specifically, small sample sizes tend to yield exaggerated MNI values when compared to results from larger sample sizes (Grayson 1978; Casteel 1977a; Perkins and Daly 1968). Payne, for example, states that "use of [MNI] tends to exaggerate the importance of rarer animals" (1972: 69). This also applies to actual number and original number calculations, and Horton indicates that:

> The main drawbacks are that minimum and actual numbers tend to be overestimates when only a proportion of a site is excavated. Actual and original number estimates are very dependent upon the accuracy of pair identification, and original number estimates tend to fluctuate greatly depending upon the proportion of the site excavated (1984: 265-266).

Grayson, in fact, argues that rather than providing the expected quantification of faunal data, NISP and MNI simply detect "differing sizes of the samples from which the measures have been derived" (1981: 78; cf. Casteel 1977c). The varying effects of sample size limit the ability to compare MNI values or other number estimates from samples of varying size. This problem is particularly emphasized by Turner, who indicates that by taking different sample sizes "one simply achieves a different estimate of abundance for the same number of originally deposited bones" (1982: 200), and as such he argues that MNI indices may not be worth calculating at all.

Casteel (1976) criticises the fact that White's method of calculating MNI does not make allowances for differences in the sizes of individual animals within a species. This is equally true of the other methods that have been applied to number estimation, though the technique of pairing to some extent relies on size to pair left and right elements. Given that there are numerous methods that allow the estimation of the size of individuals from skeletal remains, as discussed below, Casteel argues that the estimated sizes of archaeological specimens should be used to aid in the identification of individuals from a faunal sample for the purposes of MNI calculations (1976: 31; 1974c).

One of the greatest problems arises from the fact that a variety of terminologies and methodologies have been employed in minimum number calculations by different analysts, making inter-project comparison of results difficult or impossible (Grayson 1973, 1978; Payne 1972). The use of varying terminologies in the literature is a problem which plagues both NISP and MNI, and Lyman (1994: 48) identifies 17 terms which are basically synonymous with NISP and 11 terms which are basically synonymous with MNI (cf. Casteel and Grayson 1977). A specific case of the use of varying methodologies involves the definition of the units of aggregation, or clusters, of faunal remains within archaeological sites which are used to calculate MNI. The use of different aggregation units will result in different MNI values, and these differences may occur differentially across taxa (Grayson 1973, 1979, 1984; Casteel 1977a; Reitz and Wing 1999; Horton 1984). Ringrose, however, argues that "not all...levels of aggregation are likely to be sensible, so that the problem is perhaps less than it might seem at first" (1993: 128).

Despite the numerous problems and critiques that have been levelled against the use of MNI, it has often been argued to be a means of dealing with the problems presented by NISP, particularly the problem of the interdependence of specimens (Ringrose 1993; Gilbert and Singer 1982; Grayson 1979, 1984; Payne 1972). This has been debated by others, however, and Driver states that "there appears to be no justification for using MNI as a way of dealing with problems caused by NISP or bone-weight calculations" (1993: 87). Cannon (1991), for example, uses NISP as a measure of relative abundance, as MNI is argued to be too problematic. The use of NISP as a preferable measure of relative abundance is also supported by Lie, who argues that it is not only valid to assume that each bone in an assemblage represents a different individual, but that in fact "the enormous reduction of the occupation material between the time of its deposition and its excavation...could mean that many individuals are no longer represented in the excavated material" (1980: 25).

An additional problem that arises from the use of both NISP and MNI is the general failure of these values to account for the actual contributions of the various fauna to the diet of the people under study. One common solution to this problem involves the estimation of the original live size of the animals represented in a given archaeological assemblage (Grayson 1984; Wing and Brown 1979; Uerpmann 1973). This approach will be discussed in detail in the following section.

2.4 Size Estimation of Faunal Remains

The estimation of the original live size of archaeological faunal specimens, most commonly in the form of meat weight calculations, can provide further insight into the diet and means of resource acquisition of the people under consideration, as well as revealing temporal changes in the

utilisation of faunal species. Casteel (1976) outlines five major methods that have been used for the estimation of fish size from archaeological remains (cf. Wing and Brown 1979). These include the single regression method, the double regression method, the proportional method, White's method, and the Cook and Treganza method (Casteel 1976: 93-123). The latter two of these methods constitute the most basic of the meat weight calculations. Both methods have the advantage of requiring very little in terms of background data or reference collections, though their accuracy is relatively poor, and more precise methods provide more useable data.

The simplest method that has commonly been applied to meat weight calculations, often referred to as the weight method, involves weighing the recovered bone and multiplying this weight by a factor which represents the ratio of bone weight to meat weight (Uerpmann 1973; Grayson 1984; Lyman 1979; Wing and Brown 1979; Casteel 1978). Casteel (1976) refers to this as the Cook and Treganza method, attributing its first use to those individuals (Cook and Teganza 1950). In this application, Cook and Treganza treated all recovered bone as a whole, making no taxonomic distinctions, and multiplied the weight of this recovered bone by a factor of 20, under the assumption that the relationship of dry dead bone to original fresh weight was 5:100 (1950: 245). They further recognized the fact that the bone recovered from the sites under study likely represented only a fraction of the original animal material brought to the sites, and assuming a preservation rate of 50% they increased their multiplication factor to 40. This was intended to account for the fact that some of the bones "could have been used for industrial purposes, thrown away at random, or carried off by animals" (Cook and Treganza 1950: 246). Finally, in order to estimate the meat weight represented by the site as a whole, the proportion of the site that was excavated was multiplied by the total site area.

The advantage of the Cook and Treganza approach to meat weight estimation lies in its simplicity. As Casteel (1976) highlights, the approach requires a minimum of data in that no comparative specimens are required and no taxonomic distinctions or identifications need to be made. Unfortunately, the simplicity of this approach is also reflected in the accuracy and thus the utility of the weight estimations. In comparing the five approaches listed above, Casteel (1976: 122-123) ranks the Cook and Treganza method last due to the very high degree of error associated with such size estimations. A variety of other criticisms have also been levelled against this approach by other researchers. The approach has been criticised, for example, on the basis that the relationship between bone weight and meat weight is exponential, and not linear as is assumed by the weight method (Casteel 1978; Grayson 1979, 1984; Lyman 1979). Furthermore, when dealing with large quantities of bone, this method calculates meat weight based on the assumption that a single, impossibly large individual is represented, rather than multiple individuals (Mitchell 1990; Grayson 1984; Casteel 1978). A final problem arises from the fact that buried bone has been known to change weight, thus making the use of modern comparative material impossible (Uerpmann 1973).

A second relatively basic method for the estimation of meat weight is that introduced by White (1953b; cf. Driver 1993; Mitchell 1988; Grayson 1984; Wing and Brown 1979; Daly 1969). Like the Cook and Treganza method, White's approach involves very little in the way of background data. A single value is used for each taxonomic group, preferably species, to represent the average size of an individual of that species (Casteel 1976: 117). This value is then simply multiplied by the calculated MNI for that species to give an estimation of the total meat represented by each species in a given archaeological assemblage (White 1953b; Casteel 1976: 118).

As with the Cook and Treganza method outlined above, the simplicity of White's method is reflected in an inaccuracy of size estimations. As Casteel indicates, "while this method has minimal data requirements and, as such, is appealingly simple to apply, the estimates derived from its application are highly inaccurate and entirely insensitive to variations in the actual sizes of the animals represented in the bone samples" (1976: 119). The use of such standard size estimates for individual animals of various species has been further criticised by others as being inaccurate or highly imprecise (Reitz and Wing 1999; Stewart and Stahl 1977; Orchard 2000). In describing the application of such an approach, for example, Chaplin indicates that this method "has no claims to precision and is used only to give an indication of the relative quantity of the different meats consumed and an impression of the magnitude of this" (1965: 209). Another difficulty with this approach is that it simply ignores all of the problems inherent in the calculation of MNI as discussed above (Grayson 1984; Lyman 1979; Uerpmann 1973). In a series of simple experiments, for example, Driver has demonstrated that meat-weights calculated from NISP may in fact represent a better estimation of the relative contribution of faunal species than those calculated using MNI (1993: 89-90).

The proportional method "is based upon the assumption that there exists a linear proportional relationship between bone size and fish size" (Casteel 1976: 104; cf. Casteel 1977b). Assuming that this assumption holds, it is possible to estimate the size of an unknown or archaeological fish specimen by directly comparing the size of its bones with modern specimens of known size. This is done through the simple formula $l^1/q^1 = l^2/q^2$ which simplifies to $l^1 = q^1l^2/q^2$ where l represents fish length and q represents bone length or width (Лебедев *et al*. 1961 as translated in Casteel 1976:

105-106; cf. Schuck 1949).

In testing the proportional method, Casteel (1976, 1977b) indicates that the assumption of a linear relationship is not always justified, with bone length and fish length in reality representing a curvilinear relationship. As such, the proportional method only provides accurate size estimations when the comparative specimen is exactly the same size as the archaeological specimen (Casteel 1976: 106). Thus, though such an approach is theoretically sound, it is "hardly practical as it presumes a collection of comparative material of infinite variety of sizes and species" (Wheeler 1978: 72; cf. Casteel 1976, 1977b). Nevertheless, the proportional method is useful in some contexts. Colley (1983), for example, utilized a modified form of the proportional method to group fragmentary and thus unmeasurable material into rough size categories through comparison with specimens of known size.

The regression, or allometric, approach "[relates] the size of a whole animal to the dimensions of a part" (Reitz and Wing 1999: 70). This methodology is applicable to a wide range of faunal remains including those of mammals and birds (Wheeler and Reitz 1987; Purdue 1987; Reynolds and Karlotski 1977), but it has most commonly been applied to the analysis of fish remains (Casteel 1974a, 1974b, 1976; Enghoff 1983; Noe-Nygaard 1983; Rojo 1986, 1987; Hales and Reitz 1992; Barrett 1994; Owen and Merrick 1994a; Smith 1995; Desse and Desse-Berset 1996a, 1996b; Leach and Davidson 2000; Leach *et al*. 1996; Crockford 1997). The regression approach relies on the assumption that the sizes of the skeletal elements of a fish are highly correlated with the live size of the fish, an assumption which has been widely demonstrated. Noe-Nygaard, for example, obtained a "highly significant relationship" with an r-value of 0.9 (r-squared = 0.81) when performing a regression analysis on pike (Esox lucius) in Denmark (1983: 130). Similarly, in a regression analysis of snapper (*Pagarus auratus*) bones, Owen and Merrick found that "each of the bone measurements has a high correlation with fish length," with r-values ranging from 0.926 to 0.987 (r-squared = 0.857 to 0.974) (1994a: 5). The r-squared value is commonly used as a representation of the degree of correlation in regression calculations (Johnson and Bhattacharyya 1992; Rojo 1987), and is described by Casteel (1976: 96) as a measure of the variance in the original data that is accounted for by the calculated line of regression. High levels of correlation have been further demonstrated in a number of additional projects, including those of the author (Orchard 1998, 2000; Smith 1995; Desse and Desse-Berset 1996a; Hales and Reitz 1992; Rojo 1986).

The simple regression approach involves the generation of regression formulae that compare the length or weight of a fish to specific measurements of skeletal elements. These formulae represent the mathematical description of the line which best characterizes the relationship between the two variables being compared (Johnson and Bhattacharyya 1992). Application of such formulae enables the estimation of the length and weight of fish from measurements of individual skeletal elements. An alternative to the direct regression of weight from skeletal elements involves the use of a second regression formula which compares the estimated length to the live weight of the specimen. This comprises the double regression method discussed by Casteel (1976), and such an approach has been argued to provide results which are comparable to a direct regression of weight from skeletal element size (Desse and Desse-Berset 1996a). Although it is possible to estimate the weight of archaeological specimens using techniques similar to those applied to length, weight fluctuates even in fish of identical length, and thus weight cannot be estimated with the same degree of accuracy as length (Wheeler and Jones 1989: 139; Rojo 1987). That aside, regression does provide a useful tool for the estimation of the weight of archaeological specimens, and it allows for much more precise estimations than are possible using more traditional meat weight approaches.

As with the other forms of quantification discussed above, criticisms have been levelled against the use of meat weight calculations in general. Wheeler and Jones, for example, caution that "[t]he simple expression of weight...is not a useful guide to the weight of protein available from a fish" (1989: 148; cf. Lyman 1979). This reflects the fact that only certain parts of fish, and other animals, are useful in terms of subsistence, while other parts do not contribute to the diet. Mitchell, however, argues that as there is "a subjective aspect to the decision of what is edible and what truly inedible," and as conversion factors exist for very few species, there is justification for using whole animal weight in such analyses (1988: 254). Driver further states that "live weights do not, of course, represent the amount of usable meat, but they provide a rough estimate of relative importance based on the size of the animal" (1993: 89).

Casteel (1976: 122-123) concludes that the regression approach is the best method for estimating the size of archaeological fish specimens, with the single regression method faring only slightly better than the double regression method due to greater ease of application. Rojo also supports the use of regression for the estimation of fish size and indicates that it is the only method "with sufficient accuracy to give an estimate of the alimentary value of animals used in human consumption" (1986: 330). He also states in a different publication that "a further advantage of using the regression method is that it will yield the best estimate of fish size for which the 95 percent confidence intervals may be calculated" (Rojo 1987: 214). The greater utility of the regression approach can also be seen in a simple comparison of the methodology and results of Mitchell (1988) and Orchard (1998). Table 2.1 compares the results of weight estimations for Pacific cod specimens from Shemya Island using both the traditional meat weight approach and the regression approach. This example demonstrates that the use of average meat weight values for a species derived from modern data may not always be applicable to archaeological specimens, as the mean estimated weight using the regression approach (4.61 kg) is more than double the mean estimated weight using modern averages (2.27 kg). In addition to a more precise estimation of the live size of individual archaeological specimens, the regression approach provides an indication of the range of sizes of fish that were harvested (1.43 to 6.69 kg; from Table 2.1). Such information is not attainable using the traditional meat weight calculation.

Table 2.1 Comparison of Average Meat Weight versus Regression methods for estimating the weight of archaeological fish samples. Data involves Pacific cod specimens from site ATU-061 on Shemya Island in the Aleutian archipelago (from Orchard 1998). The set of specimens listed below were selected as they represent a typical set that may be used to calculate the MNI of the site. The variation between the weights estimated using the two methods are clearly seen in the results listed below.

Specimen (from Orchard 1998)	Element	Standard Weight Estimate (kg) (from Wigen 1980, as used in Mitchell 1988)	Regression Estimated Weight (kg) (derived from Orchard 1998)
A11	Premaxilla	2.27	6.69
A12	Premaxilla	2.27	5.74
A13	Premaxilla	2.27	6.30
A14	Premaxilla	2.27	1.43
A15	Premaxilla	2.27	3.05
A16	Premaxilla	2.27	5.26
A17	Premaxilla	2.27	6.69
A18	Premaxilla	2.27	2.63
A20	Premaxilla	2.27	3.71
Mean Estimated Weight (kg):		2.27	4.61

2.5 Interpretive Aspects

The detailed size estimations possible through the use of the regression approach can allow for a much more accurate assessment than available through other techniques of the relative role of various taxa in the subsistence of a population under study. The potential of such techniques, however, goes far beyond purely dietary considerations. An integration of the more detailed size estimations possible through the regression approach with present day and historical knowledge about the biology and ecology of the faunal species under study can further contribute both to archaeological analysis and interpretation and to an understanding of the prehistoric biology and ecology of those species. Changes in the size of a species over time is one conclusion that may be drawn from such a synthesis of archaeology and ecology. Casteel, for example, found evidence for a large reduction in the size of sturgeon in the Soviet Union, likely as a response to intensive harvesting by humans (1976: 130-132). In a slightly earlier paper, Casteel (1974b) used a regression approach to estimate the size of Pliocene salmon specimens which were considerably larger than modern specimens. Similarly, a study of Pacific cod remains from archaeological sites in the Aleutian Islands (Orchard 1998) revealed that the average size of cod harvested by prehistoric Aleuts on Shemya Island was significantly larger than modern cod, with some specimens exceeding modern published size limits. Other information that may be gathered from a comparison of detailed archaeological results and modern biological and fisheries literature include changes in species distribution or changes in the presence or absence of a species in a given area (Casteel 1976). Wheeler, however, cautions that modern distributions of fish are often the result of recent intensive harvesting, and as such distributions in prehistoric times may have been quite different (1978: 74).

Similarly, it is often possible to make conclusions, through ecological data and estimated sizes of archaeological specimens, about the methods that prehistoric people must have been using to harvest a given species or several species of fish (Greenspan 1998; Desse and Desse-Berset 1994; Owen and Merrick 1994b; Balme 1983). The large size of Pacific cod remains from Shemya Island, for example, was taken as an indication that Shemya Island fishermen were selecting, whether intentionally or inadvertently, for larger fish (Orchard 1998). This may be a reflection of the technologies used for harvesting the fish, as differences in the types and sizes of traditional fishing hooks are known to dictate the size of fish caught (Stewart 1982; Balme 1983).

2.6 Summary and Conclusions

The use of allometry or regression does not eliminate all of the numerous problems that exist with other methods used to quantify and analyse faunal data. Weight cannot easily be estimated for all of the individuals in an assemblage, for example, as the problems of interdependence or aggregation described above for NISP and MNI are not eliminated (Grayson 1984). Grayson indicates, therefore, that although "the methodology has the important potential of providing accurate meat weights for individual animals whose weight is of interest, it does not provide a means of accurately assessing total meat weights per taxon in a faunal assemblage" (1984: 173-174). Lyman (1979) also indicates that preservation conditions and cultural treatment of skeletal remains may inhibit the accurate measurement of the skeletal dimensions required for regression analysis. Despite these problems, however, the regression approach provides a means of obtaining far more precise estimations of the size of specimens represented in the faunal assemblage than is possible using simpler meat weight calculations (Casteel 1978). As described above, such precise estimations of the live size of faunal specimens can enable biological and archaeological interpretations that would not be possible using less precise techniques. The regression approach is discussed in more detail in Chapter 5.

The major disadvantages in the use of regression involve the need for large comparative samples from which regression equations can be generated, and the time investment required for the generation of those equations. Fortunately, this problem is remedied through the preparation of comparative data sets and regression formulae for various taxa that may then be applied relatively easily to the analysis of archaeological samples from a number of different sites. Such data sets have been prepared for a number of taxa in areas of Europe (Desse and Desse-Berset 1996a; Smith 1995), the South Pacific (Leach *et al.* 1996; Leach and Davidson 2000; Owen and Merrick 1994a), and the western Atlantic (Rojo 1986, 1987). The area of the Northwest Coast has seen relatively little in the way of such comparative data sets, though this thesis and related projects (Orchard 1998) will help to remedy this problem.

CHAPTER 3. CASE STUDY: ALEUTIAN ISLANDS

3.1 Overview

The Aleutian Archipelago is a particularly interesting study area as it presents a relatively unique set of environmental conditions. This is emphasized by McCartney, who states that "it is the uniqueness of this island chain which makes it a valuable cultural laboratory" (1975: 288). Collins provides a good general description of the Aleutian area:

> The islands of the Aleutian chain form a continuation of the Alaska Range of mountains extending 900 miles or more westward from the tip of the Alaska Peninsula. They include 14 large and about 55 small islands in addition to innumerable rocks and islets...The climate is oceanic–wet and cool–rather than boreal, and the islands are ice-free and open to navigation the year around (1945: 3).

It is this unique environment that structures many aspects of the lives of the Aleut people (see Black 1981). As Yesner and Aigner indicate, "[t]he Aleuts are found entirely within a sharply delimited ecosystem" in which "there are no significant terrestrial resources" (1976: 92). This is also reflected by Corbett *et al.*, who indicate that "[c]ultural isolation has long been a paradigm of Aleutian archaeology" (1997a: 459; cf. McCartney 1975; McCartney and Veltre 1999). Lantis (1984) calls further attention to the environmental uniformity that occurs throughout Aleut territory (cf. Laughlin and Aigner 1975). Despite this general uniformity, however, the Aleutians are also subject to the relatively frequent effects of earthquakes and volcanoes, which have been shown to have devastating, though non-permanent, effects on the people and the environment of the Aleutian region (Black 1981; McCartney and Veltre 1999). The extreme degree of the marine base of subsistence for Aleut peoples is also stressed (Corbett *et al.* 1997a; Veltre 1994; Dumond 1987b; McCartney 1975, 1984; Black 1981; Laughlin 1963b; Ransom 1946). Collins goes so far as to state that "no people were ever more dependent on the sea than the Aleuts" (1945: 21). In particular, Aleuts relied for their subsistence upon marine mammals, invertebrates, migratory and resident birds, and fish, "especially marine fish such as cod, halibut, sculpin, and greenling" (Dumond 1987b: 67). According to Lantis, "life in such a situation, dependent on only local resources, required special adaptation, producing from a general Eskimo base the Aleut culture" (1984: 161). Within this unique and relatively harsh environment the Aleut people were immensely successful, and at contact the Aleutian Islands were one of the most densely populated areas of the New World (Collins 1977).

3.2 History of Non-Aleut Contact in the Aleutian Islands

The history of non-Aleut contact in the Aleutian Islands is long and varied. Russian merchants and explorers were responsible for the re-discovery[2] of many of the Aleutian Islands in the second half of the 18th Century. Makarova (1975) and Berkh (1974) provide extensive accounts of many of these early discoveries. Although the specific details are not clear from Makarova's account, she indicates that on the return voyage of the navigators Bering and Chirikov in 1741 "they discovered several islands which were later to become known as the Aleutian Islands" (1975: 36). This appears to have been the first non-Aleut discovery of the Aleutian Islands despite several earlier voyages in the Bering sea which sought to verify the existence of a strait between the Pacific Coast of Russia and Alaska. The success of early voyages to the Bering Sea and Aleutian Islands, and the large quantities of furs that the early voyagers gathered, sparked the interest of increasing numbers of *promyshlenniks* [fur hunters] (Makarova 1975; Berkh 1974: 1; Coxe 1970: 21). In a search for such furs in 1745 and 1746 a voyage under the command of Mikhail Nevodchikov discovered the Near Islands of Attu, Agattu, Shemya and Semichi (Makarova 1975: 41; Berkh 1974: 4-6; Coxe 1970: 25, 29-38). Continuing success in the gathering of furs further increased Russian interests, and many voyages were undertaken throughout the 1740s and 1750s, leading to the discovery of further islands along the Aleutian archipelago. The merchant Trapeznikov sailed to the Aleutians in the years 1749 through 1753, and Berkh (1974: 10) credits him with the discovery of the island of Atkha. Makarova indicates that a voyage under the command of Petr Bashmakov discovered eight islands east of the Near Islands in the years 1753-1754, though she does not give a name to any of these islands (1975: 47). Berkh suggests that the small islands encountered by Bashmakov were likely in the vicinity of Umnak Island (1974: 15). The names of 13 islands discovered on a second voyage by Bashmakov in 1756-1758 are similarly unknown (Makarov 1975: 51). Nevertheless, the bulk of the remaining Aleutian Islands were discovered during a period of increased Russian fur trade activity during the 1750s to 1770s. The islands of Umnak and Unalashka were discovered in the fall of 1759 by a crew under the command of Stepan Glotov (Makarova 1975: 53; Berkh 1974: 21),

---

2. The term "re-discovery" is used as this clearly does not represent the initial human discovery of the Aleutian Islands. All of the islands discussed in this section were in fact inhabited by Aleut peoples at the time of first Russian contact. However, for ease of discussion, the concept of discovery will be used throughout this discussion to represent the notion of the first non-Aleut contact.

who also discovered the island of Kad'iak on a second voyage in the 1763 (Makarova 1975: 61-62). In the years 1759 to 1763 two vessels, the Vladimir under the command of Dimitrii Pankov and the Gavriil under the command of Gavriil Pushkarev, visited a number of the more central Aleutian Islands, including Atkha, Amlia, Sigdak, Unimak, and Kyska as well as reaching the Aliaska Peninsula (Makarova 1975: 53-54; Berkh 1974: 23-24). Kyska Island was also visited by The Nikolai under the command of Luka Nasedkin during the same time period, and it is unclear which of these groups was the first to visit the island (Makarova 1975: 55). Makarova (1975: 60) credits the discovery of the Andreianov Islands to Andreian Tolstykh, who spent three years on the islands of Adakh, Tanaga, Chetkhina, Tagalak, Atkha and Amlia beginning in 1761 (cf. Berkh 1974: 29-30). An additional vessel, the Ioann Ustiuzhskii under the command of Aleksei Vorob'ev, visited the islands of Buldyr, Kyska, Avadak and Amchitka in the years 1761-1763 (Makarova 1975: 60-61). Thus, by the mid-1760s the majority of the island groups of the Aleutian Archipelago had been discovered by Russian voyagers. Russian fur trade activity continued in the region throughout the 1770s and 1780s, and Makarova indicates that "by the beginning of the 1780's all of the islands of the Aleutian chain had been discovered and exploited for fur gathering" (1975: 78). Coxe (1970) for example, writing in the 1780s, provides a reasonably good description of the names and positions of the major island groups in the Aleutian chain.

According to Makarova (1975) the 1780s and 1790s saw a shift in focus of the Russian fur trade to the North American coast and the islands just off that coast (cf. Crowell 1997). In addition, control of the fur trade became concentrated under fewer, more powerful companies. As a result of this concentration of power the United American Company, later renamed the Russian-American Company, was formed in 1797, and was put under the imperial protection of the Russian tsarist government as a means to hold its vast possessions in the North Pacific (Makarova 1975: 4; Crowell 1997). A desire to protect these Russian "possessions" arose from the increasing activity of other nations in the region of the North Pacific. Makarova (1975: 3) notes that the Aleutian Islands along with the coasts of Alaska and Kamchatka were visited by the English navigator James Cook in the late 1770's (cf. Collins 1945: 12). This raised the potential for competition as "Cook had shown his countrymen the way to places belonging, by right of prior discovery, to Russia" (Makarova 1975: 125). This potential competition was realised with the arrival of the English ship "Sea Otter" in 1785 under the command of James Hanna (1974: 87). Berkh also speaks of the merging of the Hudson Bay Company and the Northwest Company and their impending control of much of the Pacific Coast of Canada (1974: 85-86). The success of these early English ventures led to an increase in the activities of non-Russian

nations from Asia, Europe and the United States of America (Berkh 1974: 88-89; Dall 1885: 4).

This period of early Russian contact saw many dramatic changes for the Aleut people. Diseases were introduced which had devastating effects on the native populations of the Aleutian Islands (Golovin 1983: 133). Also, as the Aleut people were brought under Russian subjugation, they were very poorly treated by the Russian *promyshlenniks* (Golovin 1983: 107, 133; Veniaminov 1984: 250-256; Coxe 1970; Dumond 1987b: 17-18; Lantis 1970: 277-284; Laughlin 1980: 120-132; Turner 1976: 27; Veltre 1990; Crowell 1997).

3.3 Ethnography

Considerable ethnographic and historical information exists for the area of the Aleutian Islands (Jochelson 1966; Veniaminov 1984; Collins 1945; Black 1984; Lantis 1970). In addition, much information may be gathered from the accounts of early explorers and sailors in the area as described above (cf. Coxe 1970; Golovin 1983). Not surprisingly, the earliest ethnographic data for the Aleut come from the accounts of the early Russian explorers and fur traders, of which Makarova (1975) provides a summary. More recently, Lantis (1984) provides a good general discussion of Aleut ethnography and recent history, and this will form the basis for much of the discussions that follow, with other sources consulted when appropriate.

Aleut territory includes the westernmost section of the Alaska Peninsula and extends along the Aleutian archipelago to the last of the Near Islands, Attu, at the western end of the chain, also including the Shumagin Islands to the south of the Alaskan Peninsula (see Figure 3.1). The division between Eskimo and Aleut cultures on the Alaska peninsula is unclear (Lantis 1984: 161). Though the total Aleut population prior to contact was likely 12,000 to 16,000, smallpox epidemics and other problems associated with contact decimated the population as indicated above, much as they did elsewhere in the New World (Lantis 1984: 163; Lantis 1970; Veniaminov 1984; Laughlin 1975, 1980; Turner 1976; Veltre 1994). In contrast, population figures recorded from the late 18th century to the early 20th century vary from approximately 1500 to 3000 Aleuts (Lantis 1984: 163-164).

Although much of the knowledge of the pre-contact Aleut way of life was lost at contact, some aspects of the prehistoric Aleut ethnography have been reconstructed and recorded. The Aleut language is closely related to the Eskimo language, and Dumond (1965: 1231-1233; 1987b), in summarizing the work of several linguists who addressed the problem, argues that these two languages split from a common "Eskaleut" proto-language sometime between 3000 and 6000 years before present (cf. Lantis 1984: 161;

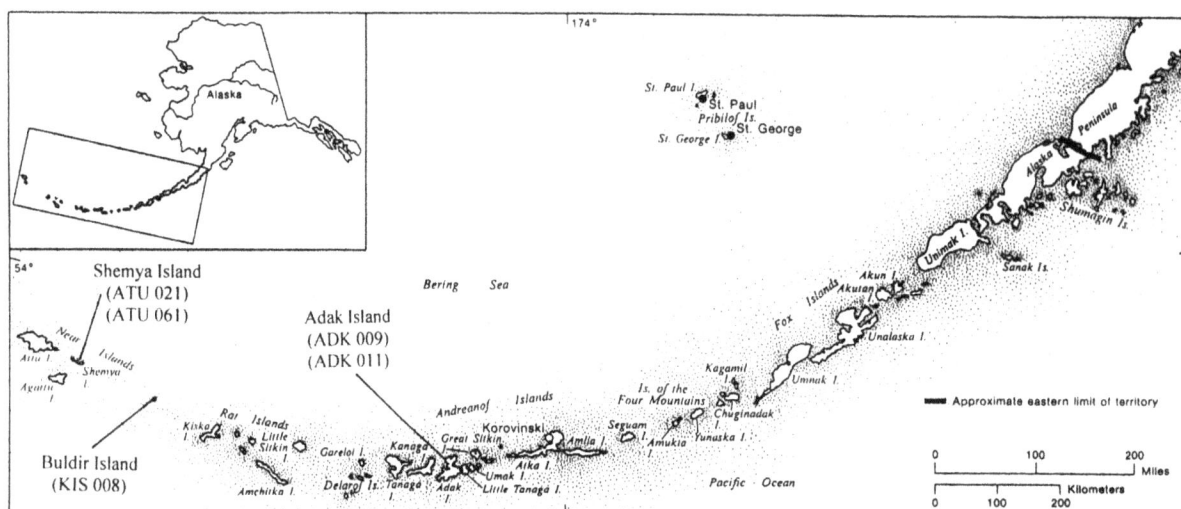

Figure 3.1 Map of study area showing location of study islands and sites (modified from Lantis 1984).

Collins 1945: 17; Woodbury 1984; Laughlin 1952). The Aleut language is often divided into Eastern and Western branches or dialects (Woodbury 1984: 49; Furuhelm 1877: 116; Collins 1945: 20; Dumond 1987a; Bergsland 1959; Lantis 1984: 161; Veniaminov 1984: 293-297; Dall 1870). The Western branch encompassed the inhabitants of the Near Islands, Rat Islands, and Andreanof Islands, and the Eastern branch was spoken in the Fox Islands, Shumagin Islands, Sanak Islands, Pribilof Islands, and on the Alaska Peninsula (Lantis 1984: 161). In contrast to the binary division of the Aleut language, Laughlin divides the Aleut language into Western, Central, and Eastern Dialects (1980: 109; 1952: 28; cf. Jochelson 1927: footnote 1; 1928: 419). This may reflect the fact that the Western dialect in the two dialect scheme has been divided into two major sub-dialects, Atkan and Attuan (Bergsland 1959; Woodbury 1984). A third sub-dialect, Qaxun, whose speakers occupied the Rat Islands, also existed in the Western Aleut branch prior to the 20th century (Bergsland 1959; Woodbury 1984). The self-designation in the Aleut language has been identified as *unanax* (Lantis 1984: 183) and *unung'un* (Dall 1877a: 22). The term *Aleut* "is thought to have come from the Koryak language or Chukchi language and to have been given by the early Russian visitors and the east Siberians who accompanied them to the Aleutian Islands" (Lantis 1984: 183; cf. Bergsland 1959: 11; Coxe 1970: 219; Veniaminov 1984: 157; Dall 1877a). Black and Liapunova, in contrast to this accepted origin of the term Aleut, suggest that "'Aleut' originally was a self-designation of the inhabitants of the Near Islands" (1988: 52). In addition to the close linguistic relationship between the Eskimos and Aleuts, Dumond (1987b) points out that the Aleuts and the Eskimos that occupied the

Pacific coastal area also shared many cultural traits.

Prior to the consolidation of the Aleut population following Russian contact, Aleut people occupied small, scattered settlements throughout the Aleutian Islands, with most households representing several nuclear families (Lantis 1984: 176). Families in a household were generally patrilineally related, with avuncular relationships also being particularly strong (Lantis 1984). According to Lantis (1970: 227) descent was matrilineal, though she indicates that many of the early sources on the Aleut are not clear on the form of descent (cf. Veltre 1994). Black (1984: 45-46) argues that Lantis failed to consider all the available sources, and concludes that descent was in fact patrilineal. Kinship terminology was recorded by Jochelson (1966: 69-71), and Lantis (1970: 240) describes it as bifurcate merging. Marriage was typically arranged through a period of bride service for one or two years, and cross-cousin marriages were preferred (Lantis 1984, 1970; Veniaminov 1984: 193). Also, Lantis indicates that "since both polyandry and polygyny were permitted, it is not surprising to find also that both simultaneous and successive levirate and sororate were acceptable marriages" (1984: 176; cf. Veniaminov 1984: 194-195; Coxe 1970: 217-218; Makarova 1975: 81-82). Matri-patrilocality was the most common form of residence, though this was not strictly enforced (Lantis 1984: 176; Veniaminov 1984: 193). Age seniority and status were important principles, with high status ascribed to those who were successful hunters (Lantis 1984: 176; Dall 1870: 388). This status often translated into somewhat of a leadership role, and Coxe states that "in each village there is a sort of chief," a position which "is not hereditary; but is generally conferred

12

on him who is most remarkable for his personal qualities; or who possesses a great influence by the number of his friends" (1970: 218-219; cf. Makarova 1975: 82; Lantis 1970). Feuding and warfare occurred in the period before European contact (Coxe 1970: 216; Collins 1945; Laughlin 1980: 54; Maschner and Reedy-Maschner 1998), and "warfare and the taking of slaves probably were the most important means of culture diffusion" (Lantis 1984: 177; cf. Makarova 1975: 83; Veniaminov 1984: 203-210; Moss and Erlandson 1992; Maschner and Reedy-Maschner 1998). Marsh (1954) outlines the pre-contact Eskimo-Aleut religion (cf. Jochelson 1966: 75-78; 1928: 416), and Lantis (1984) indicates that prior to the 19th century the influence of Christianity was small (cf. Veniaminov 1984: 217-239).

Lantis discusses variations in settlement patterns in different regions of the Aleutian archipelago, but indicates generally that "a typical village was located near a stream emptying into a bay and near a headland providing a handy lookout" (1984: 166; cf. Collins 1945: 21; Black and Liapunova 1988). Veniaminov adds that "a majority of villages are at present, and were formerly also, on the north side of the islands on the Bering Sea, as it is more abundant in fish, driftage [wood, etc.], and especially whales" (1984: 258, square brackets in original). Houses or *barabaras* (Aleut *ulax*) were large, rectangular, semisubterranean structures with "stall-like living spaces strung along the sides for...several nuclear families, with a long common space in the center under the large roof hole for entrance and light" (Lantis 1984: 166; cf. Coxe 1970: 214; Makarova 1975: 80-81; Veniaminov 1984: 262; Black and Liapunova 1988; Hoffman 1999). The size of these dwellings could be quite considerable, as Veniaminov indicates that "each hous[ed] from 10 to 40 families" (1984: 262; Collins 1945: 23; Laughlin 1980: 50-51; Dall 1870: 387). Aleut material culture is outlined in some detail by Lantis (1984: 169-173), who emphasises the quality of Aleut basketry and clothing (cf. Makarova 1975: 80; Veniaminov 1984: 266-270; Jochelson 1966: 59-62). The Aleut kayaks, called baidarkas since the period of Russian contact, were the major means of transportation, and when combined with harpoons, lances, bird darts, fish spears, and composite fish hooks provided the means of hunting and fishing (Lantis 1984: 171; Laughlin 1980: 27-28; Makarova 1975: 79; Veniaminov 1984: 270-275; Jochelson 1966: 55-56). Coxe indicates that the Aleut also constructed "large boats capable of holding forty men" (1970: 215; cf. Collins 1945: 27-28; Jochelson 1966: 56). The Aleut people also possessed bows and arrows, though Lantis (1984: 171) indicates that these were not useful in kayaks and were thus used primarily for warfare and for hunting land mammals in the easternmost areas of Aleut territory. The Aleuts' extensive knowledge of anatomy and medicine is emphasised by some authors (Marsh and Laughlin 1956; Veniaminov 1984: 290-293), a knowledge that was largely related to the practice of mummification of

the dead (Lantis 1984; Veniaminov 1984: 196; Laughlin 1980: 96-106; Jochelson 1928: 416-417; Hrdlicka 1941).

Of more specific relevance to the current study are data on the means of subsistence, particularly the harvesting and use of fish, in prehistoric times. The almost exclusively maritime base of prehistoric Aleut subsistence is emphasized in virtually all sources discussing Aleut ethnography or archaeology (Makarova 1975: 78-79; Veniaminov 1984: 276-279; Collins 1945: 2; Ransom 1946). Lantis is no exception, stating that:

> Most food came from the sea: all local whale species except the sperm whale and killer whale, sea lions, fur seals, sea otters, and occasionally walrus. *The fish were salmon, halibut, codfish, flounder, herring, sculpin*; of invertebrates, chiefly sea urchins but clams, limpets, and mussels also might be eaten...It is likely that the enjoyment of octopus meat is not only recent. Birds eaten were ducks and geese, occasionally cormorants and others. More often the eggs of other species were taken (1984: 174-175, emphasis added).

Coxe similarly indicates that "their principal nourishment is fish and whale fat" (1970: 213). Jochelson also provides a list of food resources, indicating that the most important fish species taken were halibut (*Hippoglossoides*), cod (*Gadus macrocephalus*), Hunchback, Red and Dog Salmon (*Oncorhynchus* sp.)[3], flounder (Pleuronectidae), herring (*Clupea harengus*), terpuck (*Hexagrammus asper*)[4], kisutch (*Oncorhynchus kisutch*), goletz (*Salmo malma*), and a shark (*Seminasus microcephalus*), the latter of which was not eaten, but rather used as a source of oil and skin (1966: 51). The Aleuts also relied heavily on oil as a food source, and Veniaminov states that "the main food of the Aleuts is fat [zhir–oil, blubber] of any [sea] animal except the sperm

---

3. The common names employed for salmon species employed by Jochelson (1966) have to some degree fallen out of use or are regional variations. Jochelson's "Hunchback" salmon is the pink salmon (*Oncorhynchus gorbuscha*), the "Red" salmon is the sockeye (*Oncorhynchus nerka*), and the "Dog" salmon is the chum salmon (*Oncorhynchus keta*) (Eschmeyer *et al.* 1983). In addition, Jochelson's kisutch is more commonly referred to as the coho or silver salmon (*Oncorhynchus kisutch*) (Eschmeyer *et al.* 1983).

4. The "terpuck" of Jochelson (1966), which he identifies as *Hexagrammus asper*, appears to correspond to Veniaminov's (1984) "terpug", which has been translated as the Atka mackerel. The Atka mackerel is in fact *Pleurogrammus monopterygius* (Witherell 1996). Turner (1886), however, distinguishes the "Terpóog," *Hexagrammus asper*, from *Pleurogrammus monopterygius*, which he variably calls "Spanish Mackerel," "Horse Mackerel," and "Alaskan Mackerel." Black states that the Atka mackerel is "called sometimes by the Russian term 'terpug'" (1998: 132).

whale" (1984: 277, square brackets in 1984 edition). Also, in contrast to the limited list of bird species provided above by Lantis (1984), Jochelson provides a large list of diverse species of birds that were of economic importance to the Aleut (1966: 53-54). The strong maritime dependence is clearly seen in these discussions, though the marine environment clearly provided a wide array of food resources. In addition to the maritime resources listed above, Aleuts who inhabited the western end of the Alaska Peninsula and Unimak Island also had limited access to terrestrial mammals such as caribou (Lantis 1984: 175). When hunting and fishing was unsuccessful or inhibited by poor weather in the winter, edible roots were dug or seaweed and shellfish collected on the beach (Lantis 1984: 175; Jochelson 1966: 11; Coxe 1970: 213; Makarova 1975: 80; Collins 1945). Lantis (1984: 176) provides a brief description of some of the plant species that were known to and harvested by the Aleuts.

Lantis (1984) has relatively little to say about the methods employed for hunting and fishing. Jochelson (1966) addresses this in some detail, however, though only his observations on fishing will be considered here. Small boats, baidarkas, are constructed by covering a frame of wood or bone with the skins of seals or sea-lions (Jocheslon 1966: 11), and these boats are then used for fishing and for hunting sea mammals. On the subject of fishing, Tolstykh, as translated in Jochelson, indicates that:

> In the summer they go to sea, sometimes sailing as far as two and a half versts (1.65 miles) from the shore, and catch halibut and cod, which are abundant; in winter they have to go as far as 20 versts (13.2 miles) or more from the shore. They catch the fish by hooks tied to lines about 150 fathoms long, made of seaweeds, which are as thick as an ordinary iron wire and twice more enduring than a hemp cord (Jochelson 1966: 11).

He also indicates that "during the summer, by means of small bags made of whale sinew and tied together like drag-nets, they catch different kinds of edible fish which enter the rivulets from the sea" (Tolstykh in Jochelson 1966: 11). Veniaminov provides a similar description, stating the following in reference to marine fish:

> The method of catching them is only one: by hook [na udu], that is, the [fishermen] go out to sea, how far from shore or how close to it depends upon the time of the year, and they let hooks down to the bottom. Therefore, success in catching sea fish depends very much

upon the winds (1984: 361).

Makarova also addresses the fishing techniques of the Aleuts, though in slightly less detail:

> The Aleuts...caught fish with the aid of darts and with bone hooks on lines. They fished the rivers with the first, and the sea (for cod and halibut) with the second (1975: 79).

Laughlin and Aigner add that Aleut marine fishing included both "deep-sea line fishing from boats and line fishing from the shore" (1975: 184-185). Turner (1886) provides accounts of Aleut fishing techniques for a number of specific fish species, including Halibut, Pacific cod, Greenling, Atka mackerel, and others. Ransom (1946) also provides descriptions of techniques applied to the catching and preparation of various fish and animals, though he largely focuses on the historic period. In terms of the relative contribution of the various sources to the Aleut diet, perhaps the best data are provided by Laughlin, who estimates that marine mammals and fish each contributed 30 percent, birds and eggs contributed 20 percent, invertebrates contributed 15 percent and plants contributed less than 5 percent (1980: 49, Table 4.2). He further states that "any of these categories could vary by 5 to 10 percent in successive years, in the same village and between villages, and in different parts of the chain" (Laughlin 1980: 45).

3.4 Culture History

Though knowledge of the prehistory of the Aleutian region is far from complete, relatively systematic archaeological work occurred in the region as early as the 1870s (Dall 1877b; Rau 1885). The first series of extensive excavations, however, were conducted by Jochelson during the years of 1909 and 1910 (Jochelson 1975). Jochelson (1975) and his crew excavated 57 pits at 13 village sites, as well as exploring 3 burial caves and 3 other cave sites. Other early work was conducted largely by avocational or amateur archaeologists (eg. Hurt 1950). Hrdlicka (1941) conducted archaeological excavations in the Aleutians in the years 1936 through 1938, though his explorations focussed on examination of burial caves, and was directed towards physical anthropological study rather than strictly archaeological work. Since the late 1930s, a series of more extensive archaeological explorations have contributed to understanding of Aleutian prehistory. In particular, Bank (1953, 1977), Laughlin (1951, 1952, 1963a, 1966, 1975, 1980; Laughlin and Marsh 1951, 1954; Laughlin et al. 1952; S. Laughlin et al. 1975; Black and Laughlin 1964), McCartney (1971, 1974, 1984), Aigner (1976, 1985; Aigner and Bieber 1976; Aigner et al. 1976), Turner (1970, 1972, 1976; Turner et al. 1974), Johnson (1988, 1992;

Johnson and Winslow 1991) and others (Nelson and Barnett 1955) conducted extensive archaeological work from the 1930s through the 1980s. More recently, members of the Western Aleutian Archaeological Project have conducted archaeological research in areas of the western Aleutians (Siegel-Causey *et al.* n.d.; Corbett *et al.* 1997a, 1997b; Lefevre *et al.* 1997; Bouchet *et al.* 1999, 2001), and other work has occurred in other regions of the Archipelago (Hoffman 1999; Hoffman *et al.* 2000).

Dumond (1987a, 1987b) and McCartney (1984) provide good, though slightly outdated, summaries of the prehistory or general culture history of the Aleutians. Though a number of early authors have suggested that the Aleuts were of direct Asiatic origin or were subject to largely Asian influences (Bank 1977), it is now generally accepted that they are closely related to the Eskimo peoples, and moved into the islands from the Alaska mainland (Collins 1945: 17; Laughlin 1963a, 1980; Laughlin and Marsh 1951; McCartney 1974; Woodbury 1984; Dall 1870, 1877b: 48; Spaulding 1953). Laughlin (1963a), however, calls attention to the fact that the core and blade industry found at the Anangula Blade site shows greater similarity to industries from Japan and Siberia than to those of mainland Alaska. Black also calls attention to the general disagreement between Soviet and American scholars about the nature of Aleut prehistory:

> American scholars, despite disagreements as to the exact nature, manner, and timing of Aleut settlement in specific segments of the archipelago, tend to view the Aleutian Islands as a cul-de-sac, where the ancestors or precursors of the modern Aleuts developed their technological kit long ago in virtually complete isolation from the rest of the world, adapting to an exclusively marine-mammal hunting and fishing mode of subsistence. Soviet scholars, in contrast, believe that the people of the Aleutian Islands at various times had significant contact with people in Asia, though they, too, argue among themselves about the exact nature and timing of such contacts (1984: 14; 1983).

In contrast to this, Jochelson, a Russian scholar, states that "the Aleut...had had no intercourse with Siberian natives before the islands were discovered by the Russians" (1975: 111; cf. Laughlin 1963b). Dumond further exemplifies this viewpoint, and he states that "it is clear that people directly ancestral to the modern Aleuts were occupying the Fox Island group as early as or not long after 2000 bc[5], the Rat Island group as early as 1000 bc and the Near Island group as early as 600 bc," and goes on to indicate that "there is no evidence of any kind to suggest that they or their immediate forebearers populated the Aleutian Islands from the west, directly from Asia, and many researchers now believe not only that Aleut colonization came from the east, but that it occurred over a period of time not much earlier than that represented by the dated occupations just mentioned" (1987b: 77).

The first model of prehistory proposed for the Aleutians was that of Dall (1877b), who argued for an essentially evolutionary scheme with three periods, the Littoral Period, the Fishing Period, and the Hunting Period (cf. Bank 1953; McCartney 1984; Jochelson 1975). Dall and his colleagues excavated shell midden sites on the islands of "Attu, Amchitka, Adakh, Atka, many localities in Unalashka, Amaknak Island, and the Shumagins, and made casual examinations or slight excavations in numerous other localities" (Dall 1877b: 47). Though the excavation methods employed by Dall (1877b: 47) were far from modern standards, these excavations nonetheless provided the basis for his three period scheme of Aleut culture history. The division into three periods was based primarily on the evidence of subsistence approaches both in the form of faunal remains and the technologies applied to gathering foods. The Littoral Period, represented by the Echinus layer, was dominated by the remains of sea urchins (echinoderms), though other shellfish were also present, and "bones of all vertebrates, except very rarely those of fish, seemed totally absent in this stratum" (Dall 1877b: 50-51). The Fishing Period, represented by the Fishbone layer, saw the introduction of fishing technology in the form of net-sinkers[6], and the presence of "a bed composed of fish-bones, intermixed with molluscan shells, and rarely the bones of birds" (Dall 1877b: 56-57). Though the Echinus and Fishbone layers were quite distinct, Dall indicates that the transition from the Fishing to the Hunting period was more gradual, with some mammal bone and hunting technology appearing in the upper part of the Fishbone layer (1877b). The Hunting period, represented by the Mammalian layer, saw the introduction of a wide range of hunting technology in the form of stone and bone points for arming darts or spears, and the presence of a wide range of sea mammal and bird remains in addition to

---

5. Dumond (1987) uses uncalibrated radiocarbon dates throughout his book, presenting these as uncalibrated calendrical dates from the pre-Christian era designated with a lowercase "bc". Dumond discusses this convention in the preface to his book (1987: 7-8), and Renfrew and Bahn provide a good summary of the conventions for the publication of radiocarbon dates (2000: 139).

6. Jochelson (1975: 107) indicates that "nets and seines became known to the Aleut only after the advent of the Russians and the stone sinkers found in [Dall's] excavations were used for fishing with line and hook."

fish and echini (Dall 1877b). This final period is further divided into three sub-layers, which Dall identifies as the Lower, Middle, and Upper Mammalian Layers based on the presence of increasing varieties of mammal and bird remains (1877b: 74-75). Dall also concluded that these three periods or cultural strata corresponded to major changes in the populations occupying the Aleutian Islands, and that the earliest occupants differed considerably from the Aleuts encountered by "the first civilized travelers" (1877b: 48-49).

Jochelson (1975) argued against the three stage model proposed by Dall, and criticises many of the conclusions and statements made by Dall (1877). He first argued that,

> Naming the first period "littoral" does not appear to be quite accurate, as it implies that the two following periods represent an inland and not a coastal culture. The third period would be more accurately described as a sea-mammalian culture, since under "mammals" land animals are usually understood (Jochelson 1975: 102).

Jochelson also indicates that the pattern of mammal bone layers above fish bone layers above echinus layers, while present at some sites that he excavated, was by no means the only pattern encountered, as "elsewhere heaps of echini and of mollusk shells were often found above the layers of mammal bones" (1975: 105-106). Jochelson is particularly critical of the fact that Dall equates each of his three periods with a stage in the mental and cultural development of the Aleut people. He states that "in the opinion of Doctor Dall, the Aleut who left behind them the Echinus layers did not possess even the embryonic beginnings of culture and did not have even the edged-stone implements of the so-called eolithic period" (Jochelson 1975: 103). Spaulding similarly criticises the conclusions of Dall, stating that:

> I presume that [Dall's] three stage interpretation was a naive reflection of the contemporary views of European archaeologists. Certainly no subsequent investigation has produced the slightest evidence to support Dall's conclusions (Spaulding 1953: 29).

Jochelson, conversely, argued for much greater continuity of culture than suggested by the simple tripartite division of Dall (Jochelson 1975: 104-110; Bank 1953; McCartney 1984: 120). This is particularly important, as this paradigm of cultural continuity formed the basis for most of the subsequent work on the Aleutians. Laughlin, however, argues that the relative homogeneity encountered by

Jochelson was a result of the chance selection of sites, and "[Jochelson] excavated sites which belonged wholly or predominantly to the later portions of the known sequence" (Laughlin 1952: 31). An exception to the strict continuity approach was the division of the human skeletal material from the Aleutians into two groups by Hrdlicka (1941), groups which he argued were representative of two successive migrations into the islands (cf. McCartney 1984: 120-121). These groups were referred to as the paleo-Aleut and neo-Aleut groups (Laughlin 1963a: 638). Bank (1953), however, comments that Hrdlicka failed "to find an accompanying abrupt change in culture upon the arrival of the later people" (1953: 40). The value of Hrdlicka's contribution to Aleut archaeology is in fact largely criticised by Laughlin and Marsh (1951) and by Spaulding (1953). The two-stage model was later supported, in a slightly altered form, by Laughlin and Marsh (1951; McCartney 1984: 121), though the physical anthropological evidence of Hrdlicka was shown to represent geographical, rather than temporal variation (Bank 1953; Black 1983). The relatively unique and old materials found at the Anangula site discussed below, were at one point argued by Laughlin (1951) to represent an occupation that precedes the paleo-Aleut occupation of the Aleutians.

Excavation at sites on Anangula (Ananiuliak) Island adjacent to Umnak Island (see Figure 3.1), which began in the early 1950s (Laughling and Marsh 1954; cf. Laughlin 1951, 1963a,b, 1966; Black and Laughlin 1964) and continued throughout the 1960s and 1970s (Laughlin 1975, 1980; S. Laughlin et al. 1975; Aigner 1985; Aigner and Bieber 1976), contributed much to the archaeology of the Aleutians, providing evidence of occupation as far back as 8000 years (McCartney 1984). The Anangula Blade site is located on the south-western tip of Anangula Island. Laughlin (1980) outlines a series of 33 radiocarbon dates that indicate an occupation at the Anangula Blade site spanning a period of about 1500 years between 7200 and 8700 uncalibrated radiocarbon years B.P. The Anangula Village site is half a kilometre from the Blade site, on the eastern shore of Anangula Island. A series of six radiocarbon dates from the Village site indicate a period of occupation between 4000 and 7000 years B.P. (Laughlin 1980: 72). The two sites on Anangula represent a continuity of occupation spaning a roughly 5000 year period from 9000 to 4000 years B.P. They also represent a transition from a unifacial lithic technology based on prismatic blades, represented at the Blade site and in the early levels of the Village site, to a bifacially based technology, represented at the Village site (Laughlin 1980: 72). The early occupations at Anangula have been argued to provide continuity with the later deposits at the site of Chaluka on nearby Umnak Island (Laughlin 1963a, 1966, 1975; Laughlin et al. 1952; Turner et al. 1974; McCartney 1984). Chaluka was occupied from approximately 4000 years B.P. until well into the contact period, being occupied even at the beginning of the 1900s when Jochelson was conducting archaeological work on Umnak Island (Laughlin 1980: 79). Excavations at Chaluka produced a wealth of artifactual material, including bone and ivory artifacts which had only been preserved in the most recent deposits at the Anangula village site (Laughlin 1963a). Together, the Blade and Village sites of Anangula and the site of Chaluka provide evidence of continuous human occupation of the area of Umnak Island for the past 9000 years[7], though this occupation is marked by a technological transition from the early deposits of the Blade site, through the Village site deposits into the recent deposits of Chaluka (Laughlin 1963a, 1975, 1980). In an earlier publication, Laughlin outlined a number of additional technological changes that occurred from the earliest deposits of Chaluka into the more recent materials (1952). The Sandy Beach Bay site on Umnak Island also provides some chronological continuity between the older deposits of the Anangula Blade site and the later deposits of Chaluka (Aigner *et al.* 1976). Though technological changes may have occurred, Laughlin and Aigner (1975) argue that the sites of Anangula, Sandy Beach Bay, and Chaluka provide "rich archaeological verification" of the continuity of the Aleut maritime adaptation.

When considering all but the most easterly of the Aleutian Islands, however, prehistoric occupation is marked by considerable continuity in occupations spanning the past 4000 years, which McCartney refers to as the midden period (1984: 121-122). This period is also characterized by relatively little change in artifacts over time or space (McCartney 1984: 122). Dumond (1987b) similarly identifies this as the "Aleutian Tradition," which he dates to the period after 2500 or 2000 bc (cf. McCartney 1984), and which is characterized as follows:

> Throughout the territory and time-period of the Aleutian tradition stone tool assemblages are dominated by chipped implements, many of which are stemmed points and knives of various forms, while polished slate appears only relatively late – at the end of the first millennium AD – and then is confined in many sites to the common transverse knife or ulu...the oil lamp appears throughout...and the bone-tool types are very similar to those in use by people of the Kodiak tradition...middens in the Aleutian zone contain large quantities of sea-mammal bones, which vary from site to site in the proportions in which they appear relative

to the other major components, such as the remains of invertebrates, especially of the sea urchin; of fish, especially marine fish such as cod, halibut, sculpin, and greenling; and of bird, both migratory and resident (Dumond 1987b: 67).

Dumond (1987b) further discusses the regional archaeological expressions of this tradition, indicating that it is represented by sites such as the Hot Springs site and Izembek Lagoon on the Alaska Peninsula, Chulka (see Turner 1972, 1976) and Chaluka (see Laughlin 1952, 1963a) in the Fox Islands, sites from Amchitka Island in the Rat Islands (see Turner 1970), and Krugloi Point in the Near Islands. Returning briefly to a consideration of slightly older material, Dumond (1987b) suggests that an earlier tradition, which he terms the Ocean Bay tradition, may also be present in the eastern Aleutian islands. This tradition is particularly characterized by elongated chipped stone implements, and may be evidenced in the Aleutians by materials from Anangula Island dating between 4000 and 2500 bc, and from the sites of Idaliuk Bay and Sandy Beach Bay (see Aigner *et al.* 1976) on Umnak Island, dating prior to 2000 bc (Dumond 1987b: 59). McCartney also proposes a tradition that predates the Aleutian tradition. His Anangula tradition dates back to about 6000 B.C., and "is known only from the Anangula site in the Fox Islands" (McCartney 1984: 124). The exception to the general similarity of materials dating to roughly the past 4000 years is the noticeable difference that occurs in the artifact assemblages from the Near Islands when compared to those from further east in the Aleutians (Corbett *et al.* 1997; McCartney 1971; Dumond 1987b: 75; Bank 1953). In contrast to the arguments for the general homogeneity of Aleutian materials, Bank states that "there was considerable cultural diversity throughout the Aleutians, and perhaps there are more local expressions of Aleutian culture, differing from the regional picture, than have generally been recognized" (1953: 45). Black, however, notes a lack of "published systematic comparison[s] of finds from different regions of the archipelago" (1983: 53).

As indicated above, members of the Western Aleutian Archaeological Project have recently been excavating materials from a number of sites in the central and western Aleutians. These include several sites from Shemya Island (sites ATU-003 and ATU-061) and Attu Island, both of which form part of the group referred to as the Near Islands, Buldir Island (site KIS-008), which is an isolated island located between the Near Islands to the west and the Rat Islands to the east, and Adak Island, in the Andreanof Islands. Of these sites, only material from Buldir Island (Corbett *et al.* 1997b; Lefevre *et al.* 1997; Bouchet *et al.* 1999) and from one site on Adak Island (Bouchet *et al.* 2001) have been published. Recent work has also been

<hr>

7. The absence of sites earlier than 9000 years BP and the shortage of early Holocene sites in general may relate to changing sea levels (Winslow 1991; Johnson and Winslow 1991).

conducted at the eastern end of the archipelago by Hoffman and colleagues (2000; Hoffman 1999).

3.5 Aleutian Faunal Record

Of more immediate interest than the general culture history of the Aleutians, are the faunal data that have been collected and the faunal analysis that has been done, particularly that relating to fish remains. In his early work at the end of the 19th century, Dall (1877b) used faunal remains in combination with hunting and fishing technologies to classify Aleut prehistory into three phases, as discussed above. His faunal analysis did not extend beyond a simple identification of remains, however, and even that was relatively limited. Specifically, Dall provides lists of species of molluscs, fish, and birds and mammals comprising his Echinus, Fish, and Mammalian layers (1877b: 50, 57, 74-75). Of the fish remains, he simply states that "they are chiefly the bones of the head and vertebrae of two kinds of salmon (hoikoh' of the Russians, and another, *Salmo* sp.), and similar parts of the cod (*Gadus macrocephalus*, Tilesius), the halibut (*Hippoglossus vulgaris*?, Cuvier), and several species of herring, sculpins, and flounders, which I cannot, at the date of this writing, specifically identify" (Dall 1877b: 57). Jochelson (1975) similarly provided a simple species list for faunal remains encountered during his excavations in 1909-1910. In terms of fish bone, he indicated that cod (*Gadus macrocephalus*) and halibut (*Hippoglossoides*) dominated the assemblages (Jochelson 1975: 107). Other early faunal work provided a similar lack of data, and was largely dominated by consideration of mammals to the exclusion of other fauna (Eyerdam 1936).

The early deposits of the Anangula Blade site were lacking in faunal remains, which presumably suffered the same fate as the organic artifacts which "have long since decomposed in [the] acidulous soil" (Laughlin 1980: 67). The Anangula village site was more productive, as it produced remains of birds, fish, and sea mammals in deposits rich in sea urchin shells (Laughlin 1980: 73), though Laughlin does not provide any more detail or analysis of these remains. In discussing the Chaluka faunal remains, Laughlin (1980: 89-91) provides somewhat better information, discussing in some detail the relative contributions of the various sea mammals and birds. Fish, however, are dealt with in a single line which reads "of the fish, halibut and cod last much better in the village deposits than do salmon and other smaller fish" (Laughlin 1980: 91). In an earlier publication, Laughlin (1963a) also outlines the Chaluka faunal remains, with some very basic quantification in the form of the percentage of bones in each level contributed by the five categories of Bird, Fish, Pinniped, Sea Otter, and Cetacean. Laughlin again emphasizes the dominance of cod and halibut among the fish, stating that "the cod constituted some 80 percent of all the fish remains" (1963a: 637).

Lippold's (1966, 1972) work on the faunal remains from the site of Chaluka provided slightly better data, as bone counts were included and relative proportions of various taxa calculated, though "fish" were not identified to any lower taxonomic level. This work was again largely dominated by mammalian remains, with fish remains discussed only briefly for comparative purposes (Lippold 1966, 1972).

Work elsewhere in the Aleutians provided a similar level of faunal analysis. In describing the faunal remains from work on Amchitka Island, Turner (1970) simply indicates that whale bones and chiton and mussel remains are rare relative to remains from Chaluka, and birds were far more common. He further indicates that fish, sea urchin and sea mammal remains are equally common in materials from Amchitka and Chaluka (Turner 1970: 121).

Clearly, much of the early faunal analysis that has been conducted in Aleutian material has failed to take advantage of the potential of more detailed quantitative approaches to faunal analysis (see Chapter 2). This is well stated by McCartney, who states that "quantification and analysis of faunal remains are rare for the Aleutians...and little is known of the importance of particular foods prehistorically" (1975: 293). An exception to this generalization is presented by Denniston (1974), in an analysis of faunal remains from Ashishik Point. Aside from simply identifying the faunal remains in her assemblage, Denniston attempted to determine the largest number of individuals represented in the sample, an estimate was made of the rough size of each animal, and a rough estimation of the nutritive contribution of each type of animal was made (1974). This then allowed Denniston to compare the relative dietary contributions of various sea mammals, and of several more general taxa, namely Mammals, Whales, Fish, Birds, and Invertebrates (1974: 145-148). Certainly this represents an improvement over earlier Aleutian faunal analyses in terms of the amount of data generated. The relative contributions of different species of fish, however, is not presented, not to mention birds or invertebrates. Denniston does, however, indicate that cod seems to have ranked second in overall importance to the occupants of Ashishik point behind sea lions (1974: 151).

More recently, considerably more faunal work has contributed to a better understanding of prehistoric Aleutian economies, though to a large extent the focus in this recent work has been on bird remains (Corbett *et al.* 1997a; Lefevre *et al.* 1997; Yesner and Aigner 1976). Material from the island of Buldir has been published, and shows a dominance of bird in terms of NISP, followed by sea mammal and finally fish (Lefevre *et al.* 1997). In terms of meat contribution, however, Steller sea lion (*Eumetopias jubata*) dominated (Lefevre *et al.* 1997: 121). Preliminary data from sites on Shemya, however, suggest that fish remains were largely under-represented at Buldir (Crockford n.d.; Orchard 1998). The Buldir site (KIS-008) has yielded dates far more recent than either of the sites from Shemya Island (Siegel-Causey *et al*. n.d.), and thus the assemblages may represent a change in subsistence adaptation (Orchard 1998). Very recently, Hoffman and colleagues (2000), published a detailed analysis of salmon remains from two sites on Unimak Island. Nevertheless, analyses of Aleutian Islands fish remains remain almost non-existent, and it is critical that detailed analyses be carried out on these relatively under-analysed remains.

CHAPTER 4. IDENTIFICATION OF THESIS PROBLEM

Despite the potential of statistical methods, such as linear regression, to contribute to the interpretation of faunal remains in terms of diet and subsistence, as discussed in Chapter 2, such approaches have been little used, in the Aleutians or generally. This is indicated by Desse and Desse-Berset, who state that though the potential of such approaches have been well known since the publication of Casteel's 1976 book, "osteometry has not been systematically applied (and is still under-employed!) to fish bones from archaeological sites" (1996a: 171). Hales and Reitz (1992) also indicate a need for further information on the use of fish populations in prehistoric diet. Lefèvre *et al.* (1997) echo this need for further work, indicating that, in particular, parts of the Aleutian Archipelago are lacking in such analysis. This was made evident in the outline of Aleutian faunal work provided above (pp. 53-56). For the most part, faunal analysis in the Aleutian Islands has focussed on the simple identification of remains, with methods of quantification rarely applied. Furthermore, even when methods of quantification have been employed the analyses that have been conducted have focussed primarily on mammal or bird remains, with scant attention given to the equally important fish remains.

As discussed briefly in Chapter 2, the work of Mitchell (1988) exemplifies the need to apply advanced techniques such as linear regression to the analysis of archaeological faunal assemblages. In comparing faunal assemblages between sites and between culture phases in the Queen Charlotte Strait area of British Columbia, Mitchell employs what he terms the "minimum live weight" of a species (1988: 254). This he calculates by multiplying the MNI by an average weight of an individual of a given species, which is equivalent to White's method (pp. 19-20). Although this may provide a rough estimate of the weight contribution of a given species, there is a large margin of error associated with such an approach. In my analysis of Pacific cod remains from Shemya Island using the regression approach, I demonstrated that the average size of a species in an archaeological assemblage may differ greatly from modern averages or averages generated from commercial fishing records (Orchard 1998). As the averages employed by Mitchell (1988) are based on such modern records, it is possible that the individuals encountered in the archaeological assemblage differed greatly in size from the modern averages used in weight estimates. Thus, to better estimate the weight contribution of a given species, the simple regression approach should be employed.

In another publication Mitchell (1990) brings up the problem that arises from a large portion of faunal assemblages often being unidentifiable to the species level. As a means of dealing with this problem, he suggests that larger taxonomic levels should be used when quantifying faunal data (Mitchell 1990). Though the use of genus or even family-level analysis is obviously possible when using quantification methods such as NISP, MNI, or simple meat-weight, the use of such taxonomic levels when using statistical regression for estimating fish size is not as clearly viable. Desse and Desse-Berset (1996b) have explored this possibility, however, and have demonstrated that regression analysis may be applied to at least the level of the sub-family. The ability to perform such general or familial analyses arises from the large degree of similarity that exists between many species which are related on the genus or even family level. More specifically, Desse and Desse-Berset (1996b) examined the regression relationships between various species of groupers (family Serranidae, sub-family Epinephelinae). They concluded that "whatever the specific identity or the geographic origin of each specimen, the relationship between its body measurements and its body size or weight appears on the same curve," and thus "all groupers, from the smallest species to the largest one, fit a similar set of regression equations" (Desse and Desse-Berset 1996b: 126). Similarly, Barrett (1994) conducted a regression analysis of various species representing various genera of the cod family (Gadidae) with highly significant results (ie. r^2=98.7). This is further reflected in a separate publication by Desse and Desse-Berset, where they state that when applying osteometry to fish "the relationship estimated between various bone measurements, or between bone measurements and fish length, is a general one for the species, often valid for the genus and, occasionally, for a whole family as well" (1996a: 176). Thus, by generating genus level regression formulae, the difficulty of identifying certain types of fish to the species level based on skeletal remains is avoided.

The osteometric analysis done on the archaeological specimens can also reveal information that may simplify the application of similar techniques in future studies. Previous work with Pacific cod (Orchard 1998), for example, revealed that certain skeletal elements provided better estimates of live size, certain skeletal elements were more often preserved in archaeological samples, and certain measurements of skeletal elements were more often available on archaeological specimens. Barrett (1997) also discusses the selection of certain elements as more suited to such analyses. Such results provide valuable data for future studies, and may provide a general idea of the skeletal elements one may expect to encounter in similar sites.

This study, then, seeks to address the problems or shortcomings of previous zooarchaeological approaches to the analysis of fish remains on the North Pacific Coast by developing and testing a more informative and revealing methodology. Through the collection of comparative data and the generation of regression formulae for a number of fish taxa commonly found in archaeological deposits in the region, this project will provide an easily applied tool that subsequent researchers may employ in similar analyses. In addition, the Aleutian Islands case study described below provides a means of testing this methodology while contributing to understanding of the relatively poorly known culture history and prehistoric ecology of the Aleutian region.

The Aleutian Islands case study involves the application of the simple linear regression method of estimating fish length to the analysis of remains from a number of archaeological sites in the Aleutian Islands. These include two sites from Shemya Island, sites 2 (ATU-021) and 7 (ATU-061), in the Near Islands at the western end of the Aleutian Archipelago (see Figure 3.1, p. 12). Material from Buldir Island (site KIS-008) will also be analysed. Buldir is an isolated island that is located between the Near Islands at the western end of the archipelago and the Rat Islands to the east. Finally, material will be analysed from two sites on the island of Adak (sites ADK-009 and ADK-011), which is one of the Andreanof Islands, located roughly in the middle of the Aleutian Chain. These sites provide an interesting case study as they represent materials from both the western and central Aleutians, which will allow for a geographical comparison of results. In addition, the extremely isolated Buldir Island may provide a slightly different environmental setting, while geographically representing a "stepping stone" between the western and central data (Corbett *et al.* 1997b). The choice of units and levels for analysis from each site, as described below, was based simply on the availability of material. This material was either present at the University of Victoria, as it had been recently analysed by Pacific IDentifications, or was provided by Debra Corbett of the US Fish and Wildlife Service, Alaska.

Of these islands, only material from Buldir has been published in any detail. In terms of the quantity of skeletal elements found, bird dominates the Buldir assemblage, followed by sea mammal and finally fish, though Steller sea lion (*Eumetopias jubata*) dominated in terms of meat weight (Lefèvre *et al.* 1997: 121). As indicated above, Buldir Island occupies an extremely isolated position between the Near and Rat islands. Lefèvre and colleagues indicate that "with an area of 20.2 km², [Buldir] is the only landfall between Shemya Island, 104 km to the west, and Kiska Island, 117 km to the east" (1997: 118; cf. Corbett *et al.* 1997b). The Buldir Midden Site, KIS-008, is located in the north facing bay at the northwest corner of the island (Corbett *et al.* 1997b; Lefèvre *et al.* 1997). KIS-008 has produced dates ranging from 220±60 to 1160+50 uncalibrated radiocarbon years BP (Corbett *et al.* 1997b; Corbett n.d.). The material analysed below is all derived from excavation pit 4, which consisted of sixteen 1m x 1m

units excavated in 1993 and 1997. Pit 4 is located in a shallow housepit depression on the south side of the Buldir midden (Corbett n.d.). All of the material analysed below is from cuts (levels) 4 and 5 of the 1997 excavations. Corbett (n.d.) indicates that preservation at the site was generally poor, with faunal materials present in small concentrations in pit features and pockets between and under cobbles. The house feature from which the pit 4 materials are derived represents a single occupation, with radiocarbon dates of 220±60, 250±70, and 390±80 uncalibrated radiocarbon years BP (1410 to 1700 AD) (Corbett n.d.).

The results of excavations at Shemya and Adak Islands have not been published, so relatively limited information is available. Shemya Island is the easternmost of the Near Islands, which are collectively the most westerly group of islands in the Aleutian Archipelago. Siegel-Causey *et al.* provide a brief description of the island, indicating that "with an area of 14.3 km² and a shoreline 22 km long...the island is low and flat on the south side but rises to nearly 80 m above sea level on the north" (n.d.: 3). Shemya Island is now the site of an Air Force base, and though construction since World War II has destroyed some sites, "the [continued] existence of seven prehistoric villages on Shemya is confirmed" (Siegel-Causey *et al.* n.d.: 4). Site 2 (ATU-021), located on the north coast near the western end of Shemya Island, is a relatively small village site (Corbett n.d.). The faunal material analysed below derives from levels 1 through 4 in excavation unit 3. Radiocarbon dates from this unit are 1700±70 and 1980±60 uncalibrated radiocarbon years BP (Corbett n.d.).

Site 7 (ATU-061) is located near the western end of the southern coast of Shemya Island, and has produced dates ranging from 2570±140 to 3540±60 uncalibrated radiocarbon years BP (Siegel-Causey *et al.* n.d.). Pit 1 was a 2m x 2m unit located in the northern portion of the site, and the faunal samples analysed below were all collected from the SE quadrant of the unit (Corbett n.d.). The SE quadrant forms a large prehistoric excavation feature, likely a semi-subterranean house pit. Levels 1 through 9 analysed below fall within this house feature, while level 10 is located stratigraphically below the feature. Despite this distinction, however, dates from within and below the house feature are all essentially contemporaneous. Radiocarbon dates from within the house feature are 2570±140 (IEMAE 1206) and 3080±110 (IEMAE 1205) uncalibrated radiocarbon years BP, and a single date from below the feature is 3096±155 (IEMAE 1175) uncalibrated radiocarbon years BP (Corbett n.d.).

Adak Island is a relatively large island located roughly in the middle of the Andreanof Islands, which themselves occupy a fairly central location in the Aleutian Archipelago. Site ADK-009 is located in Sweeper Cove on the northeast corner of Adak Island (Corbett n.d.). The faunal material analysed comes from levels 1-2 and A through N of excavation unit 1, which was excavated in 1999. Levels 1 and 2 lie stratigraphically above the lettered levels and represent a 1m x 2m unit. The lettered levels represent a 1m x 1m unit that continued below the numbered levels (Corbett n.d.). Four radiocarbon dates spanning the lettered levels are essentially contemporaneous, ranging from 1040±70 to 1240±90 uncalibrated radiocarbon years BP (calibrated at AD 1000 to AD 1460) (Corbett n.d.). A date from level 1, stratigraphically above the lettered levels, is 1710±70 uncalibrated radiocarbon years BP (calibrated to AD 740-1065), though this date was derived from a bone that may be intrusive from elsewhere (Corbett n.d.).

Site ADK-011 is located 1.75 kilometres north of Zeto Point on the north central coast of Adak Island (Corbett n.d.). The site is quite large, consisting of more than a hundred pit features stretching for approximately 200 metres along a sandy ridge (Corbett n.d.). Material analysed below derives from units excavated in two features in 1999. As the available faunal material was derived from three separate excavation units with varying radiocarbon dates, three separate units of aggregation have been defined for the purposes of this analysis. The first aggregation unit includes materials from levels 1 through 3 of excavation unit 1 in house feature 1. A single date from this unit comes from level 3, and gives an age of 440±40 uncalibrated radiocarbon years BP (Corbett n.d.). Excavation unit 2 of house feature 1 is a trench that was excavated off excavation unit 1. Material was analysed from levels 3 and 4 of this unit. No direct dates are available for these materials, though a date from level 5 of excavation unit 2 is 2490±50 uncalibrated radiocarbon years BP (Corbett n.d.). Finally, material was also analysed from levels 3 and 6 of excavation unit 2 in house feature 2. Dates from levels 3 and 5 of this unit were 220±50 and 180±60 uncalibrated radiocarbon years BP respectively (Corbett n.d.).

In summary, this thesis aims to exemplify the type of detailed faunal analysis that is possible in archaeological contexts in the region of the northern Pacific coast of North America. The value of statistical regression as a technique for estimating the original live size of archaeological faunal specimens will be demonstrated. Furthermore, the collection of comparative data for several fish taxa commonly found in the northeastern Pacific and the generation of regression formulae for these taxa comparing skeletal element size to live size, will facilitate the application of this technique by others in future projects. The testing of this methodology in the context of an Aleutian Islands case study, will contribute directly to the understanding of prehistoric subsistence and culture history of the Aleutian Islands. Specifically, the detailed analysis of materials from Shemya, Buldir, and Adak Islands will increase understanding of Aleutian prehistory and subsistence through a regionally and temporally diverse sample.

CHAPTER 5. METHODOLOGY

5.1 Overview

As outlined in Chapter 2, regression is a useful tool in faunal analyses for estimation of the size of animals from their archaeological remains. This thesis seeks to test this methodology and to produce a set of comparative data that will simplify the application of the regression approach by subsequent faunal analysts working in the region of the Northeastern Pacific. Specifically, regression is employed in the analysis of comparative specimens of a number of species and genera of fish that are known to have had prehistoric relevance to the Aleut people (see Chapter 3), and are present in Aleutian archaeological material analysed to date (Crockford n.d.). The taxa analysed include Pacific cod (*Gadus macrocephalus*), Walleye pollock (*Theragra chalcogramma*), Atka Mackerel (*Pleurogrammus monopterygius)*, Irish Lords (*Hemilepidotus* sp.), Rockfish (*Sebastes* sp.), and Greenling (*Hexagrammos* sp.). In addition to their ethnographic and archaeological use, the current commercial importance of several of these species, particularly Walleye pollock, Pacific cod, Atka Mackerel and some species of Rockfish, makes the inclusion of these taxa and the consideration of their biology particularly relevant (see Witherell 1996).

5.2 Regression Approach

As discussed in Chapter 2, and concluded by Casteel (1976, 1977b), regression provides the most accurate method for estimating the original live size of archaeological fish specimens. Simply stated, regression involves the determination of the relationship between two variables (Johnson and Bhattacharyya 1992). This is most commonly done through the least-squares regression method. If the two variables under consideration, X and Y, are plotted against each other, the least-squares approach determines the equation for the line that minimizes the sum of squares of the vertical distances from the data points to the regression line (Ricker 1973; Casteel 1976). This relationship may take a number of forms, but when comparing the live size of fish to the size of skeletal elements, linear and exponential relationships are most common (Casteel 1974a,c, 1976; Desse and Desse-Berset 1996a; Harvey *et al.* 1994; Owen and Merrick 1994a; Rojo 1986; Smith 1995)[8]. Both linear and exponential relationships may be expressed in terms of mathematical formulae which describe the relationship between the two variables being compared (Johnson and Bhattacharyya 1992). These formulae may then be applied to the estimation of one variable from the other.

Fish length and the dimensions of skeletal elements have been shown to be highly linearly correlated, and thus a direct linear regression is possible. This results in a regression formula of the form:

$$Y = \alpha + \beta X$$

where Y is the live length of the fish and X is the skeletal element dimension being compared, and α and β are constants that define the regression formula. The dimensions of skeletal elements and weight of fish, however, are related exponentially, not linearly, and thus a logarithmic transformation is used to generate regression formulae comparing weight to the skeletal element measurements. The regression equation thus takes on the form:

$$\log Y = \log \alpha + \beta(\log X)$$

This can then be converted to a non-logarithmic form as follows:

$$Y = \alpha X^{\beta}$$

where Y is the live weight of the fish and X is the skeletal element dimension (see Casteel 1974a, 1976: 28, 84-85; Reitz *et al.* 1987; Rojo 1986). An alternate method that has been employed for the estimation of weight involves a second regression comparing the length and weight of fish. Due to the high correlation encountered in these regressions, Desse and Desse-Berset have found that such a double regression approach provides very similar results to a direct regression of fish weight from skeletal element size (1996a: 175-176). However, as Casteel (1976) argues, the direct estimation of weight from skeletal element size is more parsimonious, and thus only the single regression approach is employed here. The degree of correlation between measurements and length, weight, and age data is measured using the coefficient of determination, r-squared. Casteel describes the r^2 value as being a measure of the variance in the original data that is accounted for by the calculated line of regression (1976: 96).

The statistical analyses employed in this thesis were all carried out using the student edition of MINITAB® for windows. Aside from allowing for the easy calculation of regression formulae comparing two variables, MINITAB® also automatically calculates a number of other useful descriptive statistics (McKenzie *et al.* 1995), including r^2. MINITAB® also automatically generates the following for each regression analysis: p-values for t-tests on the significance of the prediction variables, the standard error of the estimate, an ANOVA table which includes a p-value for an F-ratio test of the hypothesis that all of the predictor coefficients are zero, and a list of unusual observations (McKenzie *et al.* 1995: T-203 - T-204). The MINITAB® outputs of the regression analyses reported

---

8. Leach *et al.* (1996) discuss a number of other relationships that may also be applied to the comparison of live size of fish to the size of their skeletal elements.

below for this project are available from the author.

5.3 Comparative Data

As mentioned above, six fish taxa were selected for analysis using the regression approach. Of these taxa, Pacific cod, Walleye pollock, and Atka Mackerel were analysed at the species level, while the other three, Irish Lords, Rockfish, and Greenling, were subjected to genus level analyses. The applicability of regression analysis at the level of the genus was discussed in some detail in Chapter 4. The genus level analyses were performed in order to account for archaeological specimens which could not be identified to the species level. These six taxa account for a large proportion of the archaeological fish remains recovered from Aleutian sites (see Table 5.1).

Table 5.1 Relative proportions of fish taxa in a sample of the Aleutian sites analysed to date. For each site, both the NISP value and the percentage of the total NISP for identified fish remains are given. Data are from Crockford (n.d.).

Species	Buldir Pit 4		Shemya 6 Pit 6/A/1		Shemya 6 Pit 6/A/2		Shemya 7	
	NISP	%	NISP	%	NISP	%	NISP	%
Pacific cod	57	5.22	115	3.25	122	5.05	173	5.67
Walleye pollock			39	1.10	19	0.79	7	0.23
Unid. Gadid			1237	35.00	604	24.98	978	32.03
Atka Mackerel	931	85.33	271	7.67	183	7.57	172	5.63
Irish Lords	7	0.64	456	12.90	596	24.65	1061	34.75
Rockfish	86	7.88	567	16.04	401	16.58	117	3.83
Other Greenling	7	0.64	449	12.71	272	11.25	294	9.63
Other Sculpins	1	0.09	58	1.64	27	1.12	84	2.75
Flatfish	2	0.18	236	6.68	154	6.37	164	5.37
Other			106	3.00	40	1.65	3	0.10
Total	1091	100	3534	100	2418	100	3053	100
First Seven		99.73		88.68		90.86		91.78

For the generation of regression formulae, comparative specimens of known length and weight were used. These included specimens available from the faunal collections of the Department of Anthropology at the University of Victoria and the National Marine Mammal Lab (NMML) in Seattle. Though no sources have been found which provide clear indications of the minimum sample size required for such analysis, Owen and Merrick (1994a) suggest that a minimum sample of 30 to 40 is generally desirable. Reitz *et al.* indicate that "statistically it is generally agreed that accurate formulae can be generated from small samples" (1987: 308). Good results have been obtained with sample sizes of 31 (Desse and Desse-Berset 1996a), 20 (Smith 1995), and 13 (Orchard 1998). Comparative specimens analysed included 31 Pacific cod specimens, 50 Walleye pollock specimens, 96 Atka Mackerel specimens, 8 Irish Lord specimens[9] (genus *Hemilepidotus*), 35 Rockfish specimens (genus *Sebastes*), and 22 Greenling specimens (genus *Hexagrammos*).

A number of skeletal elements for each species or genera were selected for osteometric analysis based on ease of identification to species or genus level and prevalence in previous archaeological and biological studies. In the interests of standardization, the guidelines outlined by Barrett (1997, 1994) and the selection of elements in earlier projects (Orchard 1998) were also taken into consideration when choosing skeletal elements for analysis. Such standardization is critical if results from various projects are to be comparable, as emphasized by Driver (1993) and Barrett (1997). The following elements were analysed for all six taxa (see Figures 5.1-5.6, pp. 27-38): vomer, dentary, angular, premaxilla, quadrate, epihyal, interhyal, hypobranchial #3, pharyngobranchial #2, vertebra #1 (atlas). In addition, several other elements were analysed for a selection of the six taxa as follows: epibranchials 3 and 4, and vertebra #9 for Pacific cod and Walleye pollock; primary otoliths for Walleye pollock, Atka mackerel, Greenling, Rockfish, and Irish Lords; the articular, hyomandibular, hypohyal #2, inferior pharyngeal, and penultimate vertebra for Atka Mackerel, Greenling, Rockfish, and Irish Lords; the basihyal for Atka Mackerel, Greenling, and Rockfish. Rojo (1991), Cannon (1987), Mujib (1967), and Leach (1997) provide good general descriptions of the various skeletal elements chosen for

---

9. The "Irish Lord" category includes both true Irish Lords and the Butterfly Sculpin, as they both represent the same genus (*Hemilepidotus*).

24

analysis. For the most part these sources agree on the naming and identification of the elements listed above, but the naming of the angular and articular is variable in many sources. For the purposes of this thesis, the distinction between the angular and articular presented by Casteel (1976) and Gregory (1959) will be employed.

A suite of osteometric measurements was then defined for each of the selected elements, using, where possible, measurements defined by Orchard (1998) and Sternberg (1992). Measurements on specific elements were diagrammed following the format of Cannon (1987) and Orchard (1998) to facilitate easy reproduction of measurements by future researchers, as illustrated in Figures 5.1-5.6 (pp. 27-38). The measurements used may also be described in textual form as follows[10]:

Vomer
    1-Maximum width of toothed surface.
    2-Maximum antero-posterior diameter of toothed surface.
Dentary
    1-Maximum antero-posterior diameter of the body (superior margin).
    2-Maximum height of the symphysis.
    3-Minimum antero-posterior diameter from the symphysis to the external posterior incision.
Angular
    1-Maximum antero-posterior diameter.
    2-Maximum height perpendicular to the ventral margin.
Articular
    1-Maximum antero-posterior diameter of the body.
    2-Length between the post-articular process and the ventral anterior angle.
    3-Maximum antero-posterior diameter of the articular (quadrate) facet.
    4-Maximum width of the articular (quadrate) facet.
Premaxilla
    1-Maximum antero-posterior diameter of the body.
    2- Maximum height of the ascending process.
    3- Maximum height of the articular process.
Quadrate[11]
    3-Maximum length of the articulation.
    4-Maximum length from the articulation to the posterior end of the ventral margin.

Hyomandibular
    1-Maximum antero-posterior diameter.
    2-Maximum height.
    3-Maximum length of the largest facet on the dorsal margin.
Hypohyal #2
    1-Maximum length perpendicular to the anterior margin.
Epihyal
    1-Maximum length of the ventral margin.
    2-Height of the posterior process.
    3-Maximum height perpendicular to the ventral margin.
Interhyal
    1-Maximum dorso-ventral diameter.
Basihyal
    1-Maximum antero-posterior diameter.
    2-Maximum width of the anterior process.
Epibranchial #3
    1-Maximum dimension between the plane created by the dental plate and the dorsal (pharyngobranchial) articulation and the tip of the opposite process.
Epibranchial #4
    1-Maximum length.
Hypobranchial #3
    1-Maximum length.
Pharyngobranchial #2
    1-Maximum diameter perpendicular to the plane created by the posterior portion of the lateral (epibranchial) articulation.
    2-Length between the most posterior tooth sockets and the anterior end of the lateral (epibranchial) articulation.
Inferior Pharyngeal
    1-Maximum dorso-ventral diameter.
    2-Maximum width across the centre of the body.
    3-Maximum width of toothed surface.
    4-Maximum length of the ventral (hypobranchial) articulation.
Vertebra #1 (atlas), Vertebra #9, Penultimate Vertebra
    1-Maximum height of the centrum.
    2-Maximum width of the centrum.
    3-Maximum antero-posterior diameter of the centrum.
Primary Otoliths
    1-Maximum antero-posterior diameter.
    2-Maximum height.

---

10. The measurement descriptions listed are taken, where possible, from Sternberg (1992), and also draw on the morphological terminology described by Rojo (1991).

11. Measurements 1 and 2 for the quadrate are defined by Sternberg (1992), but were not included in this analysis.

The defined measurements were then taken from the comparative specimens discussed above using electronic slide calipers precise to one hundredth of a millimetre. With paired elements, the bone from the right side of the body was measured whenever possible, as is standard practice when dealing with osteological material. These data were then used to generate regression formulae, using the single regression technique outlined above, which compare the length and weight data to each of the osteological measurements taken. Regression analyses were carried out using MINITAB® for Windows.

5.4 Archaeological Application

Once the comparative formulae were generated through the above methodology, these formulae were applied to the study of the dietary use of these fish species and genera by prehistoric populations in the Aleutian Islands. As discussed in Chapter 4 (pp. 20-21), archaeological material was available for 5 sites in the central and western Aleutian archipelago. This provided a sample that allowed for a comparison of the varying use of the six fish taxa as dietary sources over limited geographic and temporal scales. Such a multi-site analysis allows for a more regional perspective, and the use of regional studies rather than simple local studies is often favoured in reconstructions of prehistoric diet and nutrition (Yesner 1980; Yesner and Aigner 1976).

Analysis of archaeological materials for the purposes of dietary reconstruction involved, first, the identification of skeletal remains to the lowest taxonomic level possible. Identification of fish remains from the Aleutian sites under study was largely carried out under contract by Susan Crockford of Pacific IDentifications. Material from the site of Shemya 7 was identified by myself. Only elements that were identifiable to a taxonomic level relevant for size estimation were included in this analysis. This resulted in a relatively large sample, with the sample sizes varying for different sites. Specifically, excavation unit 1 at site 009 on Adak Island produced 1418 measurable archaeological specimens; excavation units 1 and 2 at site 011 on Adak Island produced 743 measurable archaeological specimens; pit 4 at site KIS 008 on Buldir Island produced 148 measurable archaeological specimens; excavation unit 3 at site ATU-021 on Shemya Island produced 388 measurable archaeological sxpecimens; and pit 1 at site ATU-061 on Shemya Island produced 1089 measurable archaeological specimens.

The archaeological specimens were then subjected to the same osteometric measurements that were applied to comparative specimens, again using electronic slide calipers accurate to one hundredth of a millimetre. When archaeological specimens were complete, all possible measurements were taken. Where specimens were nearly complete, or fragmentary specimens were deemed interesting due to an apparently unusual size[12], minimal or approximate measurements were taken, and the uncertainty recorded using one of the following categories:

"(>)" -indicates specimens that may have been complete, but the completeness was uncertain.

">" -indicates slightly incomplete specimens, where the true dimension should be slightly larger than that recorded.

">>" -indicates very incomplete specimens that were deemed important to measure due to unusual size. True dimension would be considerably larger than that recorded.

"~" -approximate measurements. True dimension was approximated, as in the case where one half of a symmetrical element such as the vomer was present.

The size data gathered for archaeological specimens was then used to estimate the original live length and weight of these archaeological specimens using the regression formulae generated from comparative specimens discussed above. For each archaeological specimen only a single length and weight estimate was generated. Where multiple dimensions had been recorded for a single specimen, the most complete measurement on the dimension that represented the regression formula with the highest r-squared value, as indicated by the comparative data, was used.

The estimated lengths and weights were then applied to the analysis and interpretation of the subsistence of the occupants of each site and where possible to the reconstruction of aspects of the biology and population structure of the fish taxa under consideration. In order to facilitate comparison of the relative contributions of the various taxa to the assemblages from each site, and by extension to the diet of the occupants of each site, it was necessary to quantify the archaeological remains as outlined in Chapter 2. As varying numbers of skeletal elements have been analysed for each taxon, NISP values for each taxon and each site are not comparable. As such, MNI was used as the method of quantification. As the purpose of this quantification is simply to provide a basis for comparing the *relative* proportions of the various taxa, advanced forms of MNI that seek to reconstruct actual or original numbers (see Chapter 2) are not necessary. Thus, White's (1953b) approach, which simply takes the greatest number of either right or left elements from the most common element, formed the basis for the calculation employed here. This approach is modified somewhat to take advantage of the detailed size estimations that have

---

12. This has the potential to introduce a bias into the analysis, though in practice MNI determinations and subsequent analyses used virtually all complete specimens. Only in a very few situations were slightly

incomplete specimens included, and it was never necessary to include very incomplete specimens or specimens where measurements needed to be approximated.

been generated and to include Casteel's (1976) suggestion that such size estimations be used to better determine MNI values. Specifically, the estimated sizes and the number of identical elements of each estimated size will be considered, and the total MNI increased to accommodate specimens that can not be accounted for by the initial MNI determined through White's method. For the purposes of size comparison, specimens whose estimated sizes do not overlap at the 95% confidence level are considered to represent unique individuals. The sum of the estimated weights of the individual specimens used to calculate the MNI value were then used as an indication of the relative contribution of each taxon to the subsistence of the site occupants responsible for the deposits. The range and mean of the estimated lengths and weights were also determined, as these have implications for the population biology of the taxa and the technologies used to harvest them.

The results of these various analyses and quantifications are represented in graphical and tabular form in the next chapter, and the implications of these results discussed in Chapter 7.

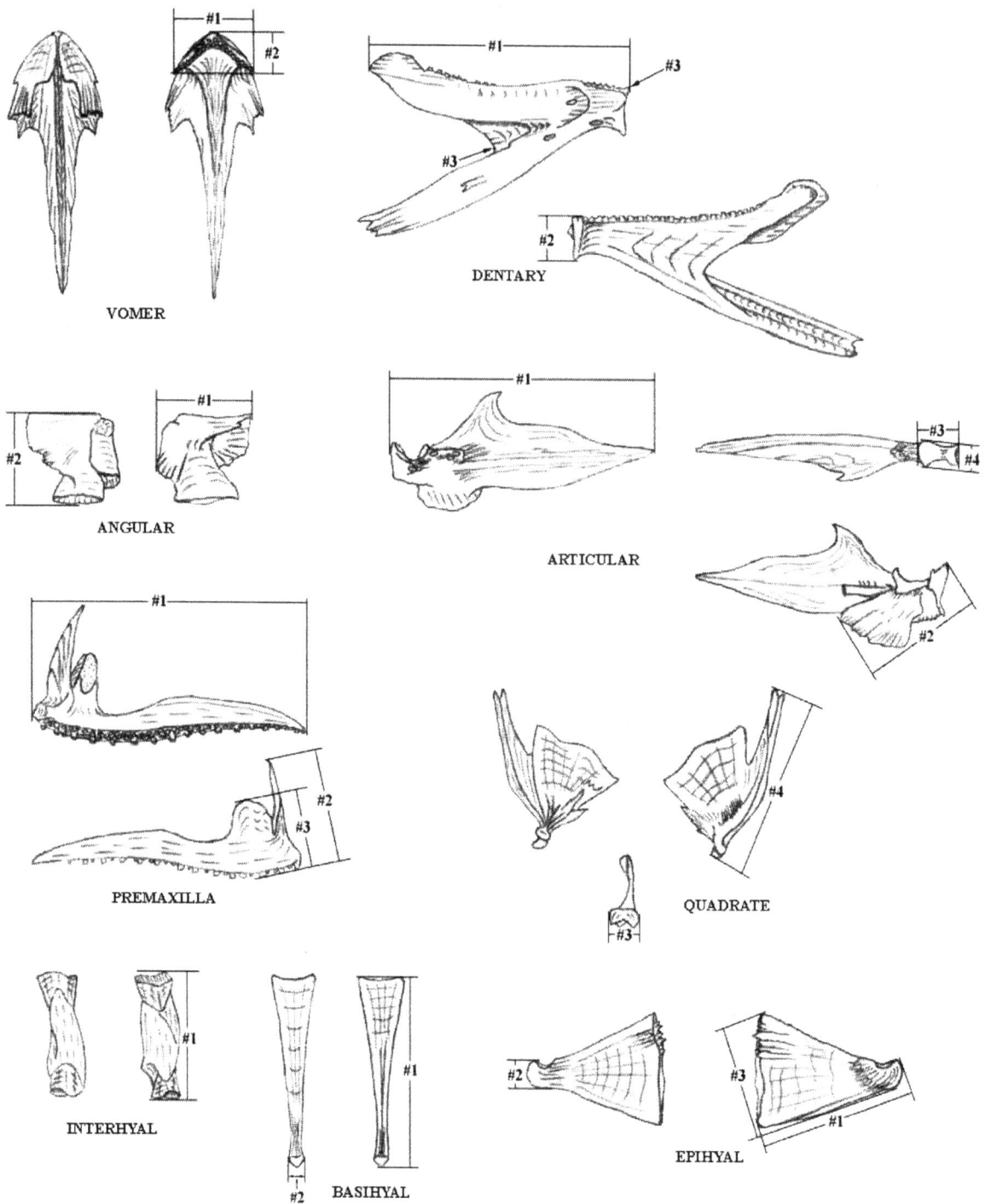

VOMER

DENTARY

ANGULAR

ARTICULAR

PREMAXILLA

QUADRATE

INTERHYAL

BASIHYAL

EPIHYAL

Figure 5.1 Atka Mackerel bone diagrams. For Paired elements, the element from the right side of the body is diagrammed, with the exception of the quadrate, which is from the left side.

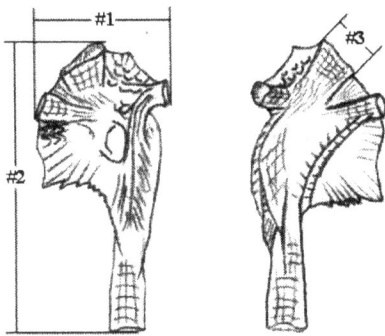

HYOMANDIBULAR

HYPOHYAL #2

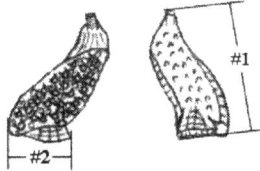

PHARYNGOBRANCHIAL #2

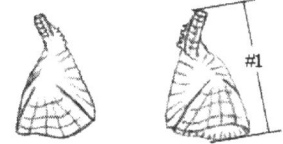

HYPOBRANCHIAL #3

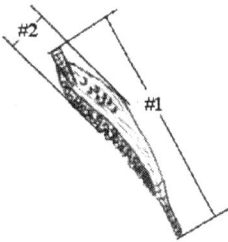

INFERIOR
PHARYNGEAL

ANTERIOR   POSTERIOR

VERTEBRA #1

OTOLITH

PENULTIMATE
VERTEBRA

ANTERIOR

Figure 5.1 (cont.) Atka Mackerel bone diagrams. For paired elements, the element from the right side of the body is diagrammed.

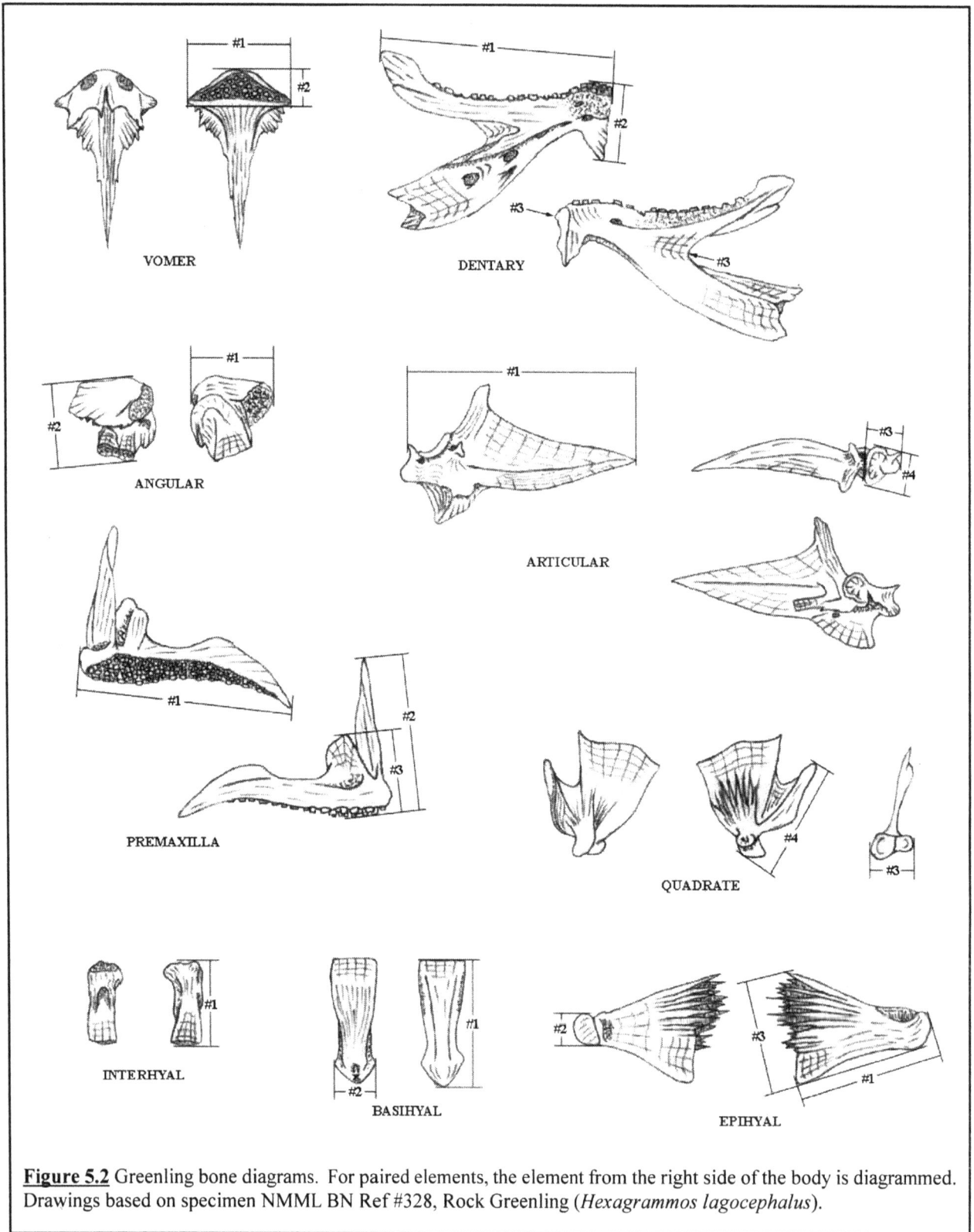

Figure 5.2 Greenling bone diagrams. For paired elements, the element from the right side of the body is diagrammed. Drawings based on specimen NMML BN Ref #328, Rock Greenling (*Hexagrammos lagocephalus*).

VOMER

DENTARY

ANGULAR

ARTICULAR

PREMAXILLA

QUADRATE

INTERHYAL

BASIHYAL

EPIHYAL

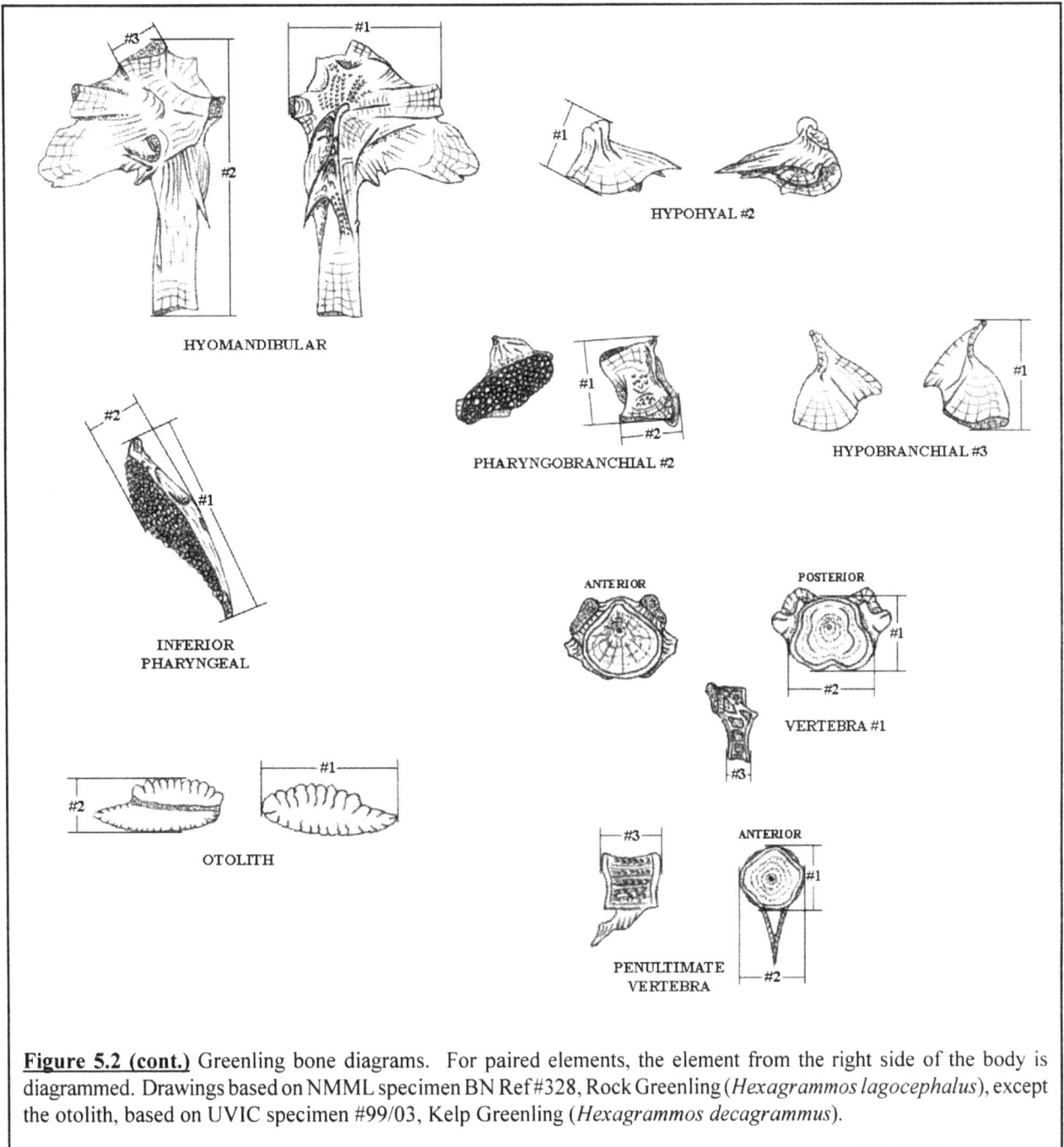

HYOMANDIBULAR

HYPOHYAL #2

PHARYNGOBRANCHIAL #2

HYPOBRANCHIAL #3

INFERIOR
PHARYNGEAL

ANTERIOR

POSTERIOR

VERTEBRA #1

OTOLITH

PENULTIMATE
VERTEBRA

ANTERIOR

Figure 5.2 (cont.) Greenling bone diagrams. For paired elements, the element from the right side of the body is diagrammed. Drawings based on NMML specimen BN Ref #328, Rock Greenling (*Hexagrammos lagocephalus*), except the otolith, based on UVIC specimen #99/03, Kelp Greenling (*Hexagrammos decagrammus*).

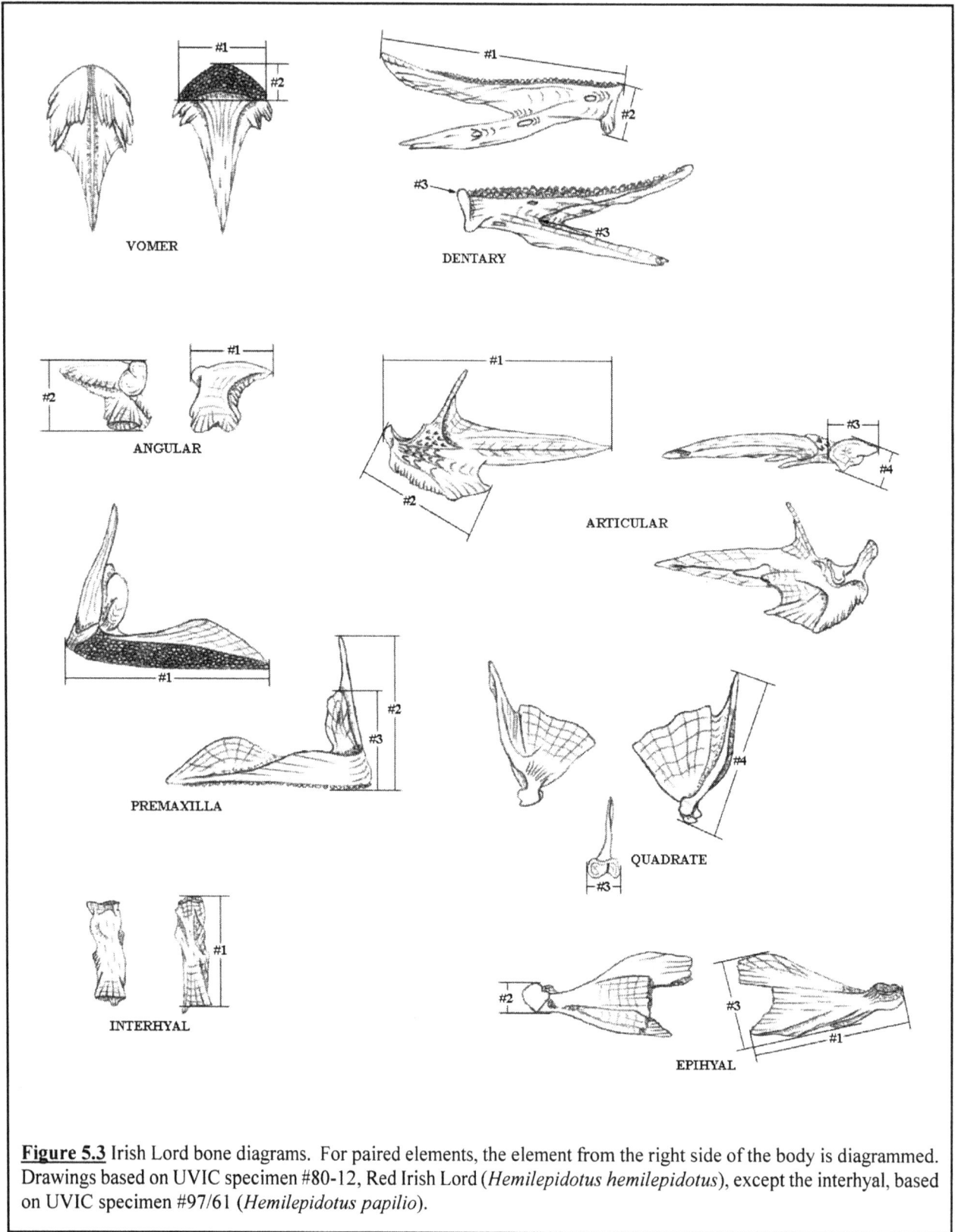

VOMER

DENTARY

ANGULAR

ARTICULAR

PREMAXILLA

QUADRATE

INTERHYAL

EPIHYAL

Figure 5.3 Irish Lord bone diagrams. For paired elements, the element from the right side of the body is diagrammed. Drawings based on UVIC specimen #80-12, Red Irish Lord (*Hemilepidotus hemilepidotus*), except the interhyal, based on UVIC specimen #97/61 (*Hemilepidotus papilio*).

32

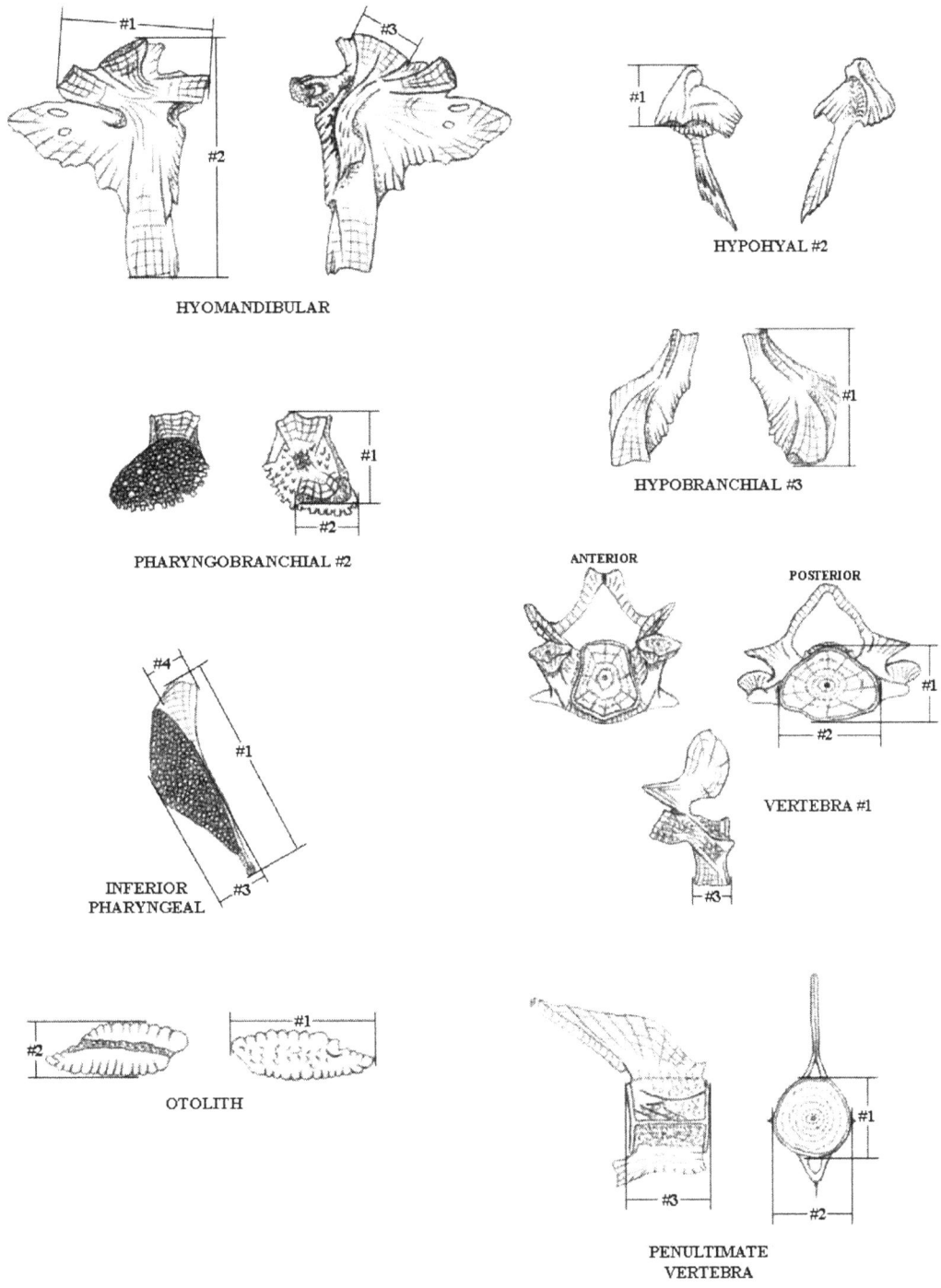

HYPOHYAL #2

HYOMANDIBULAR

HYPOBRANCHIAL #3

PHARYNGOBRANCHIAL #2

ANTERIOR

POSTERIOR

VERTEBRA #1

INFERIOR
PHARYNGEAL

OTOLITH

PENULTIMATE
VERTEBRA

Figure 5.3 (cont.) Irish Lord bone diagrams. For paired elements, the element from the right side of the body is diagrammed. Drawings based on UVIC specimen #80-12, Red Irish Lord (*Hemilepidotus hemilepidotus*), except the penultimate vertebra, based on UVIC specimen #94/26, Yellow Irish Lord (*Hemilepidotus jordani*).

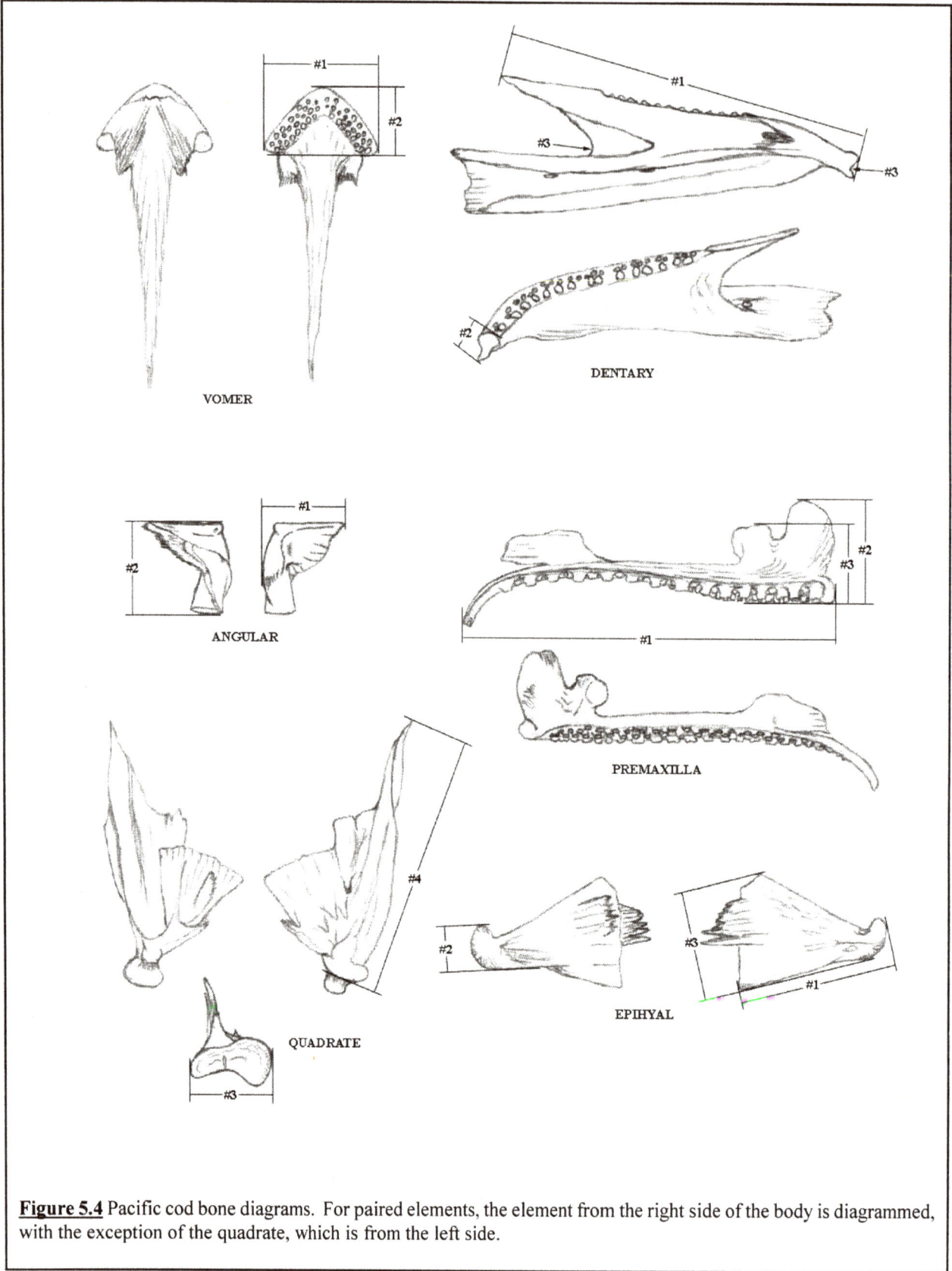

VOMER

DENTARY

ANGULAR

PREMAXILLA

QUADRATE

EPIHYAL

Figure 5.4 Pacific cod bone diagrams. For paired elements, the element from the right side of the body is diagrammed, with the exception of the quadrate, which is from the left side.

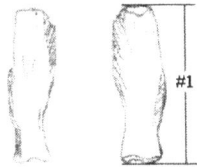
INTERHYAL

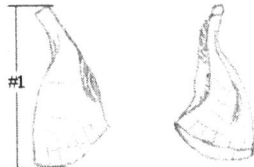
HYPOBRANCHIAL #3

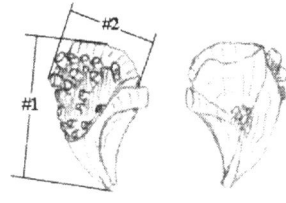
PHARYNGOBRANCHIAL #2

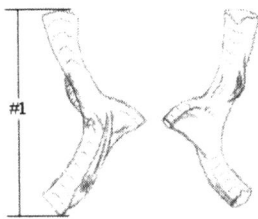
EPIBRANCHIAL #4

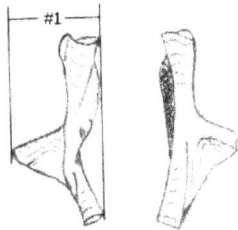
EPIBRANCHIAL #3

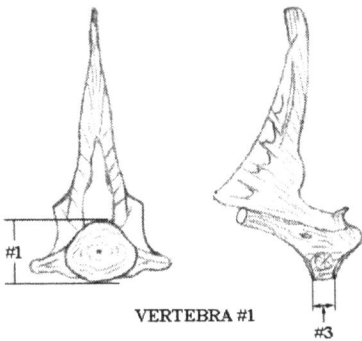
VERTEBRA #1

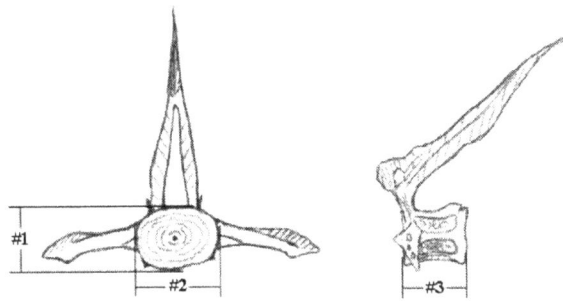
VERTEBRA #9

Figure 5.4 (cont.) Pacific cod bone diagrams. For paired elements, the element from the right side of the body is diagrammed.

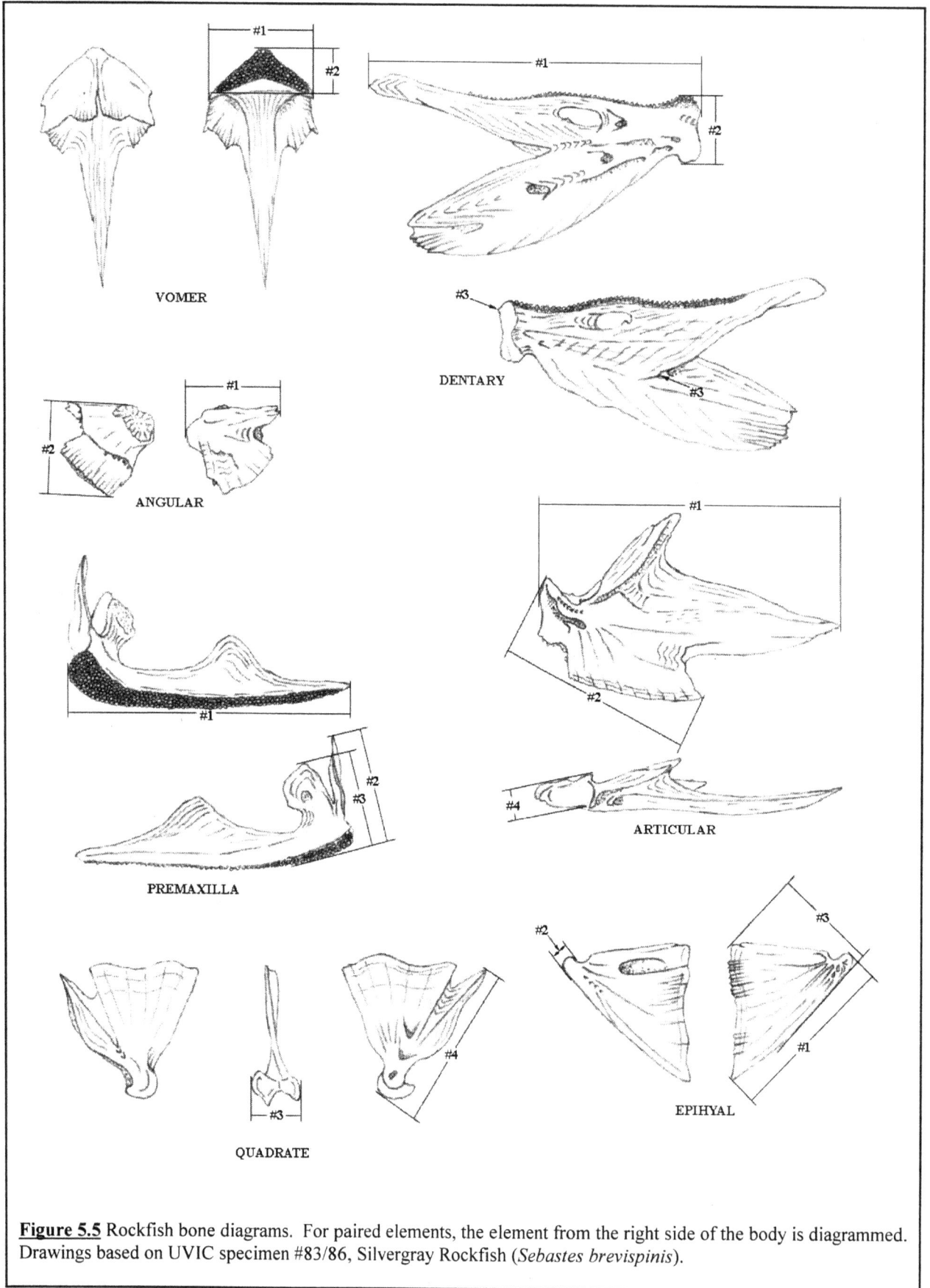

VOMER

DENTARY

ANGULAR

PREMAXILLA

ARTICULAR

QUADRATE

EPIHYAL

Figure 5.5 Rockfish bone diagrams. For paired elements, the element from the right side of the body is diagrammed. Drawings based on UVIC specimen #83/86, Silvergray Rockfish (*Sebastes brevispinis*).

36

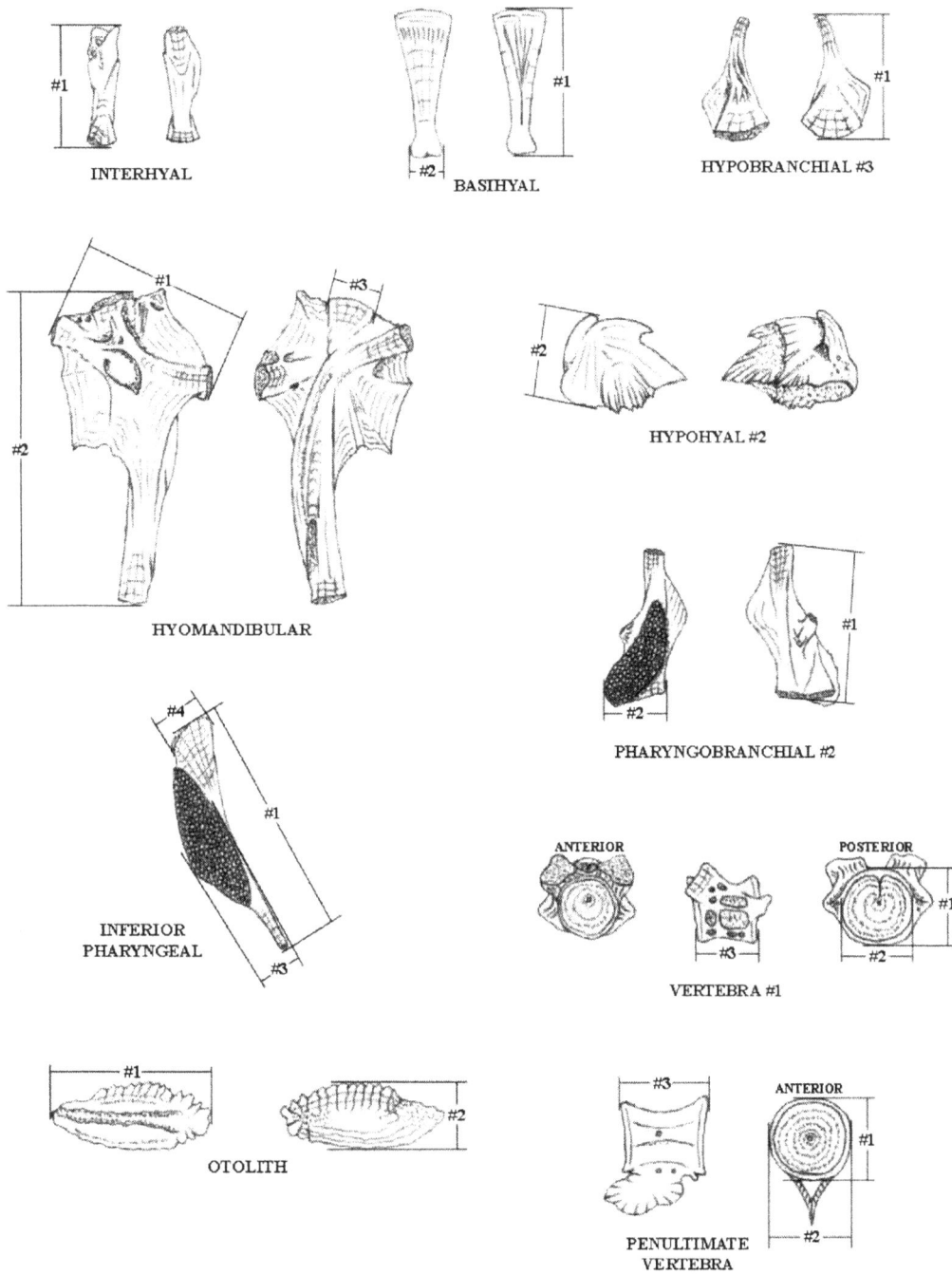

INTERHYAL

BASIHYAL

HYPOBRANCHIAL #3

HYOMANDIBULAR

HYPOHYAL #2

INFERIOR PHARYNGEAL

PHARYNGOBRANCHIAL #2

ANTERIOR   POSTERIOR

VERTEBRA #1

OTOLITH

PENULTIMATE VERTEBRA

ANTERIOR

Figure 5.5 (cont.) Rockfish bone diagrams. For paired elements, the element from the right side of the body is diagrammed. Drawings based on UVIC specimen #83/86, Silvergray Rockfish *(Sebastes brevispinis)*.

37

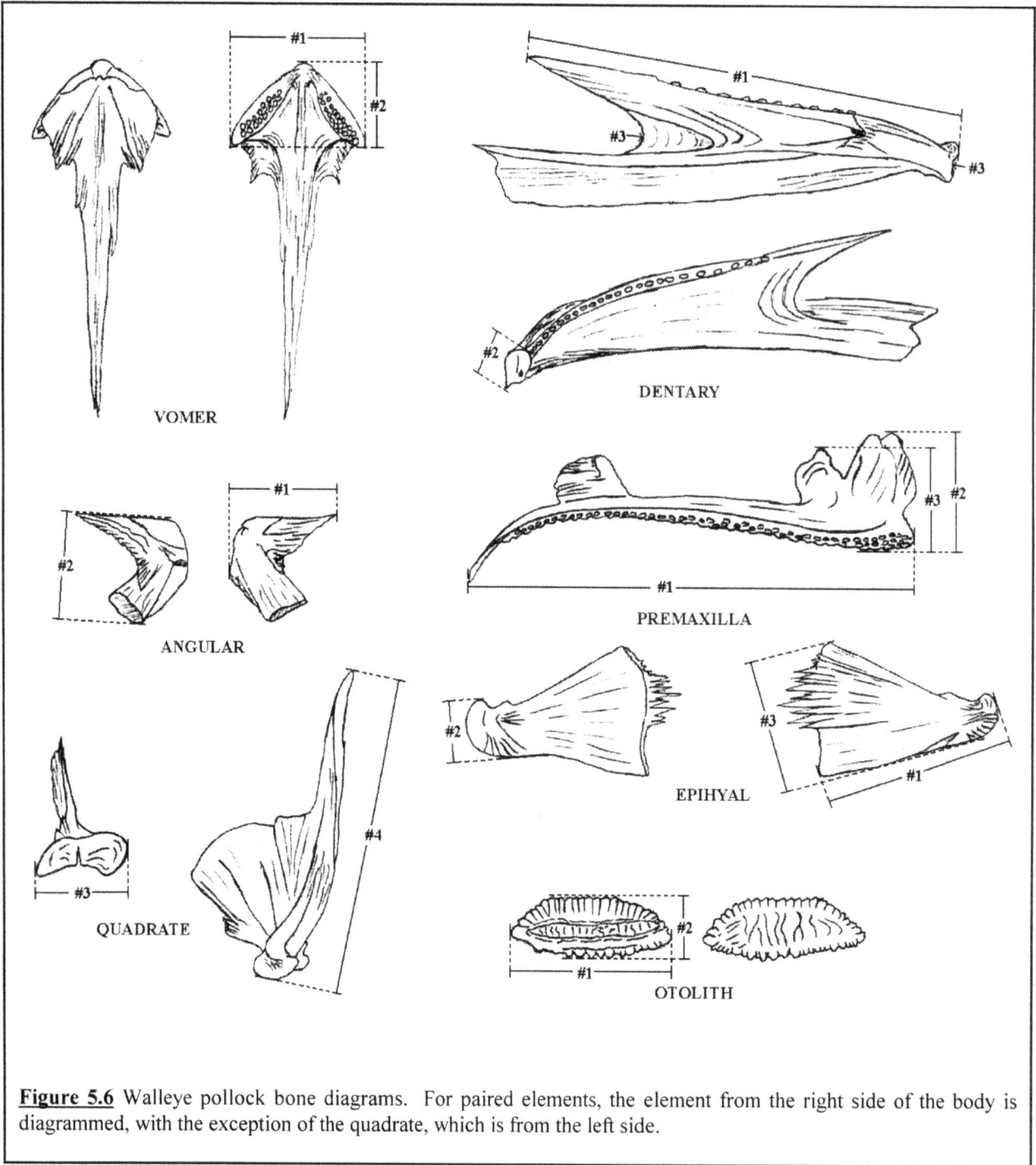

Figure 5.6 Walleye pollock bone diagrams. For paired elements, the element from the right side of the body is diagrammed, with the exception of the quadrate, which is from the left side.

VOMER

DENTARY

ANGULAR

PREMAXILLA

QUADRATE

EPIHYAL

OTOLITH

INTERHYAL

HYPOBRANCHIAL #3

PHARYNGOBRANCHIAL #2

EPIBRANCHIAL #4

EPIBRANCHIAL #3

VERTEBRA #1

VERTEBRA #9

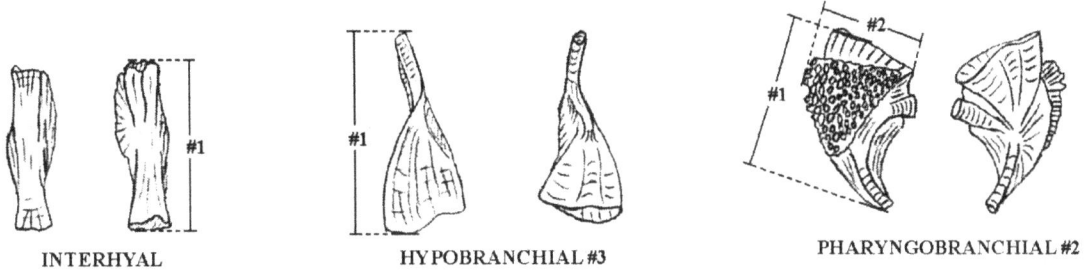

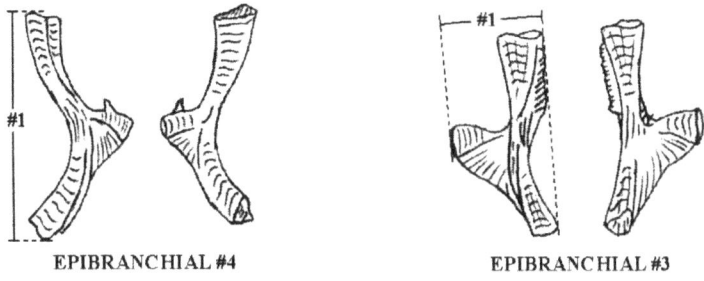

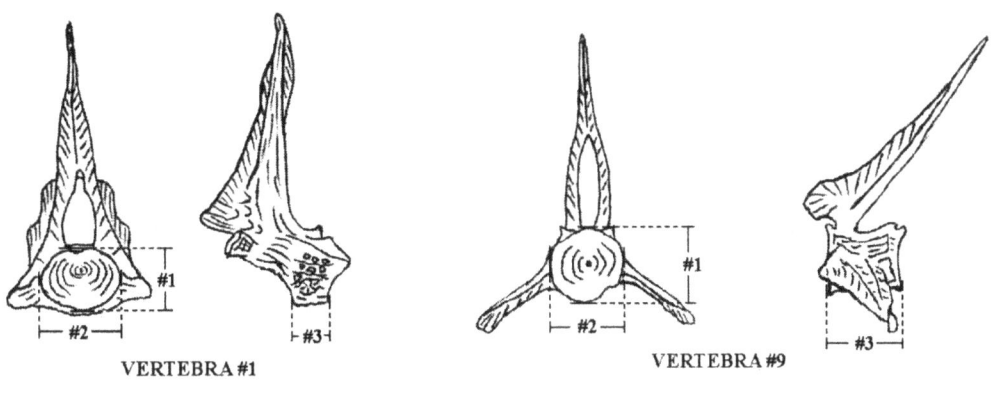

Figure 5.6 (cont.) Walleye pollock bone diagrams. For paired elements, the element from the right side of the body is diagrammed.

CHAPTER 6. RESULTS

The following chapter outlines the results of the analysis described in Chapter 5. The chapter is divided into two sections, reflecting the two major components of this thesis. The first section (6.1) outlines the results of regression analysis conducted on comparative data from the six fish taxa under consideration. The following section (6.2) documents the results of the application of the comparative regression formulae to archaeological material from the five Aleutian Islands sites that are being analysed. A discussion of these results is presented in Chapter 7, including a consideration of problematic cases and potential sources of error, as well as a discussion of the implications of the results and their potential to contribute to an understanding of the methodology, Aleut culture history, and Aleutian Islands biology and ecology.

6.1 Comparative Data/Regression[13]

All of the comparative specimens used in this analysis were relatively complete. Some of the specimens, however, were missing skeletal elements. As a result, regression analysis of some measurements was not done with the full complement of comparative specimens for each taxon. The actual number of comparative specimens contributing to any given regression calculation are listed in Tables 6.1 through 6.12 (pp. 44-55) for length and weight regressions. Sample sizes for Atka Mackerel and Walleye pollock were large, with ranges of 89 to 96 and 44 to 58 respectively (Tables 6.1, 6.2, 6.11, and 6.12). Sample sizes for Greenling, Pacific cod, and Rockfish were intermediate in size. Between 10 and 22 specimens contributed to all Greenling regressions, with the majority of regressions utilizing sample sizes of between 19 and 22 (Tables 6.3 and 6.4). Sample size was 25 for all Pacific cod fork length regressions, with weight regressions derived from sample sizes of 29 or 30 (Tables 6.7 and 6.8). Rockfish sample sizes were more variable, with a range of 8 to 34. The majority of Rockfish regressions, however, were derived from sample sizes of greater than 25 specimens (Tables 6.9 and 6.10). Particularly low sample sizes of 8 and 9 occurred only for the basihyal, as this element was not available for many of the comparative specimens. Irish Lord sample sizes were much more problematic, due to a lack of available comparative specimens from the genus *Hemilepidotus*. Sample sizes for Irish Lord regressions ranged from 5 to 7 specimens (Tables 6.5 and 6.6). All of the measurement data for comparative specimens is summarized in Appendix 1[14].

Tables 6.1 through 6.12 (pp. 44-55) also summarize the results of regression analysis conducted on data from comparative specimens. The form of length measurement used for each taxon varies due to the varying techniques applied to the recording of comparative specimens. In all cases, either fork length (FL) or total length (TL) was used. Fork length represents the maximum length of a fish from the tip of the snout to the fork of the tail, while total length represents the maximum length from the tip of the snout to the maximum extended tip of the spines of the tail (see Casteel 1976: 50). As is seen in Tables 6.1 through 6.12, most measurements were found to be very highly correlated with length and weight[15]. Atka Mackerel regressions demonstrated particularly good results, with r-squared values ranging from 0.565 to 0.969 with an average of 0.914 for fork length regression, and from 0.576 to 0.965 with an average of 0.913 for weight regression (Tables 6.1 and 6.2). Greenling regressions showed even stronger results, with r-squared values ranging from 0.839 to 0.997 with an average of 0.962 for total length regression, and from 0.916 to 0.996 with an average of 0.984 for weight regression (Tables 6.3 and 6.4). Irish Lord regressions were somewhat weaker, though the majority of the r-squared values were fairly strong. R-squared values for Irish Lord regressions ranged from 0.251 to 0.988 with an average of 0.909 for total length regression, and from 0.285 to 0.995 with an average of 0.937 for weight regression (Tables 6.5 and 6.6). Pacific cod regressions produced very strong results, with r-squared values ranging from 0.853 to 0.987 with an average of 0.968 for fork length regression, and from 0.915 to 0.993 with an average of 0.977 for weight regression (Tables 6.7 and 6.8). Results of Rockfish regressions were the weakest of the six taxa analysed. R-squared values for Rockfish ranged from 0.550 to 0.923 with an average of 0.823 for total length regression, and from 0.765 to 0.996 with an average of 0.917 for weight regression (Tables 6.9 and 6.10). Finally, Walleye pollock regression results were also very strong, with r-squared values ranging from 0.902 to 0.977 with an average of 0.941 for fork length regression, and from 0.944 to 0.992 with an average of 0.987 for weight regression (Tables 6.11 and 6.12).

The results of applying the generated regression formulae to the archaeological sample are outlined in section 6.2 below. However, a particular issue arising from this application is more appropriately discussed in the context of the comparative data. This issue relates to the range of sizes of the comparative specimens of each taxon and the relationship of these ranges to the archaeological

---

13. Much of the analysis of comparative specimens for Atka Mackerel, Pacific cod, and Walleye pollock was carried out by the author under contract to the U.S. National Marine Fisheries Service.

14. Comparative data are available from the author in electronic format.

---

15. The few relatively isolated cases with poor correlations and low r-squared values are discussed in more detail in Chapter 7.

specimens. Specifically, some of the archaeological specimens are larger than the size range encompassed by the comparative specimens. Table 6.13 (pp. 56-57) summarize the NISP (number of identified specimens present) values for each taxon for each archaeological site under consideration, broken down by skeletal element. This table also summarizes the number of each element for each taxon that exceeds the size range of the comparative specimens. This was determined simply by comparing the measured dimensions of archaeological specimens to the measurements taken from comparative specimens. None of the archaeological specimens are smaller than the smallest comparative specimens for any of the six taxa. All of the archaeological specimens of Atka Mackerel fall within the size range of the comparative specimens. Similarly, the comparative size ranges for Greenling, Rockfish, and Walleye pollock encompass virtually all of the archaeological specimens, with only a very small number of specimens exceeding these size ranges. Pacific cod and Irish Lords are more problematic. The majority of Pacific cod specimens fall within the size range of comparative specimens, but a significant number (17.3%) exceed this size range (Table 6.14, p. 57). The case of Irish Lords is even more extreme, with the majority of archaeological specimens (72.0%) exceeding the comparative range (Table 6.14, p. 57).

The fact that some of the archaeological specimens exceed the size ranges encompassed by the comparative material is problematic because the relationship described by statistical regression does not necessarily hold true beyond the range of the comparative material from which the regression formulae were generated. In this analysis, two solutions were employed to deal with this problem. For Pacific cod, a relatively small proportion of the archaeological specimens exceed the comparative size range. Furthermore, a relatively large sample size of comparative specimens was available and the regression relationships were very strong as described by the r-squared values reported above. In addition, examination of regression plots for the relevant elements and measurements suggests that the linear relationships described by the regression formulae still hold at the extremes of the comparative range (Figures 6.1 through 6.26, pp. 60-63). As such, the regression formulae summarized in Tables 6.7 and 6.8 as described above were felt to be applicable to the entire archaeological sample of Pacific cod for the purposes of this analysis.

Unfortunately, more significant problems exist in the case of the Irish Lord data. The sample size of comparative specimens of Irish Lords is very small, ranging from 5 to 7 specimens as described above. In addition, the majority of the archaeological specimens of Irish Lord that were measured exceed the size range of this small sample of comparative specimens. As a result of these two major problems, it was felt to be unreasonable to apply the

generated regression formulae to the archaeological specimens of Irish Lord, and thus the Irish Lord taxon was excluded from further stages of the analysis. The Irish Lord taxon, then, is only quantified as far as the level of NISP.

6.2 Archaeological Application

The first stage in the analysis of the archaeological material involved the sorting and measuring of archaeological specimens of the six taxa under analysis. Archaeological material was available from 5 sites in the central and western Aleutian Archipelago (see Chapters 4 and 5). Identification of faunal remains was done by comparison to comparative specimens held in the collection of the Department of Anthropology, University of Victoria. As indicated above, NISP values for each site are summarized by taxon and element in Table 6.13 (pp. 56-57). These are further summarized in Table 6.15 (p. 58), which simply presents the total NISP values by taxon for each site. These values do not represent the true total NISP values, however, as these NISP values are based solely on the skeletal elements that were chosen for regression analysis for each taxon. The values do, however, provide a very rough indication of the relative abundance of the various taxa. The two sites from Adak Island (ADK 009 and ADK 011) show similar NISP results, with Greenling contributing the greatest abundance and Pacific cod representing a close second. Irish Lords contribute a smaller but significant proportion of skeletal remains, with Atka Mackerel, Rockfish, and Walleye pollock representing relatively insignificant amounts of material. The Buldir Island site (KIS 008) presents a relatively unique picture amongst the 5 sites, with Atka Mackerel dominating the assemblage. This is followed by Rockfish, Pacific cod, and very small amounts of Greenling and Irish Lord. The Shemya Island sites also show some general differences from the sites on the other two islands, though they also show a degree of intra-island variation. Pacific cod is the most common taxon at both the Shemya 2 and Shemya 7 sites. At Shemya 2, Pacific cod is followed by Rockfish and Irish Lords, which in turn are followed by Atka Mackerel and Greenling, with only a small amount of Walleye pollock. At Shemya 7, Pacific cod is followed closely by Irish Lords, which is followed by Greenling, Atka Mackerel, Rockfish, and again only a very small amount of Walleye pollock. In fact, it is perhaps of interest to highlight the relative absence of Walleye pollock at all of the sites.

As indicated above, Table 6.13 also summarizes the number of each element for each taxon that contributes to the total NISP. It is evident from these tables that certain elements are far more prevalent in the archaeological materials analysed. In particular, three elements, namely dentary, quadrate, and premaxilla, are dominant throughout the deposits for all of the taxa under consideration. In addition, the articular is relatively common amongst Atka Mackerel and Greenling, and the epihyal is relatively common amongst Irish Lords and Pacific cod.

Following the methodology outlined in Chapter 5, all of the skeletal elements listed in Table 6.13 were measured, using as many of the defined dimensions as possible[16]. As described in Chapter 4 above, all but one of the sites considered are represented by deposits which seem to represent a single occupation and which date to a relatively narrow period of time. As such, all of these sites are analysed as single units of aggregation. The exception is site ADK 011 on Adak Island, which is separated into three units of aggregation based on excavation units and radiocarbon dates. These measurement data were then used to generate estimates of the original lengths (fork or total) of the fish from which each skeletal element was derived. The ranges of estimated lengths for each taxon in each site are summarised in Table 6.16 (p. 58). Pacific cod are the largest fish based on these length estimates, though they overlap with the other taxa at the lower end of the length range. The other taxa are all fairly similar to each other in terms of the range of lengths represented.

The estimated lengths were then used to assist in the determination of MNI (minimum number of individuals) values following the methodology outlined in Chapter 5 (p. 26-27). Table 6.17 (p. 59) summarizes the MNI values by taxon for each site. Aside from the exclusion of Irish Lords in MNI calculations, the relative MNI values for each site provide a similar picture to that provided by NISP results, as described above. The Adak 009 site is still dominated by Greenling, with Pacific cod a close second, followed distantly by Atka Mackerel and Walleye pollock. MNI results from the Adak 011 site vary somewhat from NISP results, as the site has been divided into three separate units of aggregation for the purposes of MNI calculation. Remains from excavation unit one of house pit one at the Adak 011 site show slightly different results than those of NISP, as Pacific cod contributes the majority of individuals, followed by Greenling and a small number of Rockfish. Excavation unit two of house pit one and house pit two both show a pattern similar to that of NISP, with Greenling dominating the MNI, followed by Pacific cod, Atka Mackerel, and Rockfish. The Buldir Island site (KIS 008) is again dominated by Atka Mackerel, followed by smaller numbers of Pacific cod, Rockfish, and Greenling. Pacific cod accounts for the largest number of individuals from the Shemya 2 site, followed by Rockfish, Atka Mackerel, Greenling, and Walleye pollock. Finally, Shemya 7 material is also dominated by Pacific cod, followed by Atka Mackerel, Greenling, Rockfish, and Walleye pollock.

Following the determination of MNI for each site, regression formulae were used to generate weight estimates for each of the individuals from each taxon for each site. These weight estimates are summarized in Table 6.18 (p. 59). In terms of weight, Pacific cod represents the largest average taxon in all of the archaeological sites under consideration, with an average estimated weight that falls above 5000 grams in all cases. The average weight of Pacific cod is slightly variable, with the Buldir 008 and Shemya 2 sites representing larger fish, on average, than those found at other sites. The Rockfish taxon is also represented by fairly large average weights in several cases. The average weight of Rockfish, however, is even more variable, ranging from a low of only 784 grams at the Shemya 7 site to a high of 3380 grams at the Shemya 2 site. Walleye pollock are somewhat more consistent in terms of average estimated weight, though the small MNI for pollock at all of the sites decreases the significance of these data somewhat. Greenling and Atka Mackerel weights also vary significantly, though not to the same extent as do those of Rockfish, and these two taxa almost invariably represent the smallest fish of the five taxa included in this study. Mean estimated weights for Greenling range from a low of 494 grams at the Shemya 7 site to a high of 1470 grams at the Buldir 008 site, while those of Atka Mackerel range from a low of 421 grams from house pit 2 at the Adak 011 site to a high of 1026 grams at the Adak 009 site.

The relative proportions of the five taxa in the various archaeological sites and units of analysis were compared on the basis of the total estimated weights of each taxon. The total estimated weight was calculated by summing the estimated weights for each of the individual specimens that contributed to the MNI determined above. Table 6.19 (p. 60) summarizes the total estimated weights for each taxon by site. This table also summarizes the relative proportions of each taxon in each site in the form of the percentage of the total estimated weight for all taxa in the site. In contrast to the picture presented by the NISP and MNI figures presented above, Pacific cod dominates all of the archaeological assemblages by estimated weight. Considering the other taxa, however, some inter-site differences are evident. Greenling is the only other taxon to make a significant contribution to the Adak Island assemblages in terms of weight, with only very small amounts of Atka Mackerel, Rockfish and Walleye pollock. Atka Mackerel makes a substantial contribution to the total estimated weight of the Buldir 008 assemblage, with Greenling and Rockfish also present in significant proportions, each contributing roughly 8 percent of the total estimated weight. The Shemya Island sites show the greatest diversity of taxa, being the only two sites to contain all five of the analyzed taxa. Both of the Shemya sites contain roughly equivalent proportions of Atka Mackerel, Greenling, and Walleye pollock by weight, though these three taxa are all present in only small amounts. The only

16. The measurement data for all archaeological specimens analyzed in this thesis are available from the author.

difference between the two sites is seen in a comparison of the quantities of Pacific cod and Rockfish. Though Pacific cod dominates both sites in terms of weight, the percentage of the total weight contributed by Pacific cod at the Shemya 2 site (70.00%) is lower than that of the Shemya 7 site (88.81%). This difference is accounted for by the significantly greater contribution of Rockfish to the total estimated weight of the Shemya 2 site.

Table 6.1 Results of fork length (FL) regression for Atka mackerel (*Pleurogrammus monopterygius*) comparative specimens. Regression formulae take the following form: FL = α + βX, where X represents the skeletal measurement in question. FL and X are in millimetres.

Bone	Mea. #	α	β	r-squared	n
Vomer	1	74.73	40.28	0.933	91
Vomer	2	70.01	79.07	0.873	91
Dentary	1	60.33	12.13	0.959	91
Dentary	2	121.57	48.77	0.886	91
Dentary	3	47.55	24.29	0.959	91
Angular	1	71.84	58.73	0.912	91
Angular	2	87.33	72.18	0.931	91
Articular	1	29.83	11.65	0.965	91
Articular	2	47.09	28.94	0.945	91
Articular	3	58.35	70.07	0.922	91
Articular	4	108.37	75.98	0.936	91
Premaxilla	1	82.03	11.89	0.944	91
Premaxilla	2	50.80	26.48	0.947	91
Premaxilla	3	36.65	43.32	0.947	91
Quadrate	3	113.56	65.31	0.931	91
Quadrate	4	41.33	19.11	0.957	91
Interhyal	1	90.03	58.41	0.873	91
Epihyal	1	72.60	22.75	0.961	91
Epihyal	2	127.82	103.66	0.686	91
Epihyal	3	51.18	32.17	0.953	91
Basihyal	1	45.17	25.45	0.957	91
Basihyal	2	175.32	99.28	0.565	91
Hyomandibular	1	56.11	24.56	0.956	91
Hyomandibular	2	48.69	11.86	0.963	91
Hyomandibular	3	-22.27	77.37	0.892	91
Hypohyal 2	1	62.69	60.27	0.948	91
Inferior Pharyngeal	1	46.45	16.50	0.955	90
Inferior Pharyngeal	2	98.95	85.76	0.910	90
Pharyngobranchial 2	1	68.49	34.18	0.952	91
Pharyngobranchial 2	2	66.83	82.24	0.917	91
Hypobranchial 3	1	78.56	38.81	0.955	91
Vertebra 1	1	65.89	61.13	0.969	91
Vertebra 1	2	43.68	54.22	0.968	91
Vertebra 1	3	22.83	146.53	0.734	91
Penultimate Vertebra	1	6.52	87.53	0.959	91
Penultimate Vertebra	2	34.65	76.82	0.959	91
Penultimate Vertebra	3	-5.02	107.97	0.937	89
Otolith	1	5.68	65.92	0.878	90
Otolith	2	-110.31	202.64	0.846	91

Table 6.2 Results of weight (Wt) regression for Atka mackerel (*Pleurogrammus monopterygius*) comparative specimens. Regression formulae take the following form: $Wt = \alpha X^{\beta}$, where X represents the skeletal measurement in question. X is in millimetres, and Wt. is in grams.

Bone	Mea. #	α	β	r-squared	n
Vomer	1	2.12	2.89	0.931	96
Vomer	2	13.88	2.91	0.874	96
Dentary	1	0.05	2.96	0.950	96
Dentary	2	12.78	2.45	0.905	96
Dentary	3	0.24	3.07	0.948	96
Angular	1	6.55	2.85	0.906	96
Angular	2	17.54	2.67	0.924	96
Articular	1	0.01	3.25	0.943	96
Articular	2	0.36	3.11	0.924	96
Articular	3	7.16	3.04	0.902	96
Articular	4	31.75	2.48	0.942	96
Premaxilla	1	0.10	2.77	0.942	96
Premaxilla	2	0.29	3.11	0.938	96
Premaxilla	3	0.81	3.29	0.950	96
Quadrate	3	23.68	2.46	0.935	96
Quadrate	4	0.08	3.19	0.948	96
Interhyal	1	9.52	2.72	0.903	96
Epihyal	1	0.48	2.82	0.947	96
Epihyal	2	77.07	2.55	0.758	96
Epihyal	3	0.58	3.07	0.943	96
Basihyal	1	0.23	3.12	0.938	96
Basihyal	2	174.57	2.01	0.576	96
Hyomandibular	1	0.29	3.04	0.932	96
Hyomandibular	2	0.02	3.12	0.948	96
Hyomandibular	3	1.07	3.94	0.896	96
Hypohyal 2	1	5.78	2.91	0.933	96
Inferior Pharyngeal	1	0.07	3.09	0.947	95
Inferior Pharyngeal	2	35.85	2.55	0.925	95
Pharyngobranchial 2	1	1.23	2.90	0.939	96
Pharyngobranchial 2	2	13.63	2.99	0.921	96
Hypobranchial 3	1	2.69	2.74	0.931	96
Vertebra 1	1	6.92	2.85	0.955	96
Vertebra 1	2	2.60	3.09	0.956	96
Vertebra 1	3	27.44	3.69	0.793	96
Penultimate Vertebra	1	4.00	3.58	0.955	96
Penultimate Vertebra	2	5.69	3.23	0.965	96
Penultimate Vertebra	3	5.95	3.77	0.923	94
Otolith	1	1.15	3.72	0.897	94
Otolith	2	8.34	5.04	0.857	95

Table 6.3 Results of total length (TL) regression for Greenling (*Hexagrammos* sp.) comparative specimens. Regression formulae take the following form: $TL = \alpha + \beta X$, where X represents the skeletal measurement in question. TL and X are in millimetres.

Bone	Mea. #	α	β	r-squared	n
Vomer	1	40.88	30.94	0.959	20
Vomer	2	5.51	86.74	0.981	20
Dentary	1	25.41	14.48	0.962	20
Dentary	2	51.82	46.20	0.879	20
Dentary	3	19.19	27.07	0.978	20
Angular	1	15.80	56.11	0.982	16
Angular	2	44.37	60.65	0.965	16
Articular	1	9.55	14.66	0.974	20
Articular	3	25.68	72.60	0.952	20
Articular	4	51.42	65.52	0.921	20
Premaxilla	1	41.03	15.06	0.953	21
Premaxilla	2	10.02	20.82	0.987	20
Premaxilla	3	20.35	36.03	0.984	21
Quadrate	3	35.69	71.84	0.940	21
Quadrate	4	0.83	25.92	0.989	21
Interhyal	1	49.91	61.36	0.971	13
Epihyal	1	31.23	25.84	0.979	20
Epihyal	2	17.07	96.20	0.961	20
Epihyal	3	9.10	38.54	0.980	20
Basihyal	1	5.89	33.93	0.988	16
Basihyal	2	41.23	110.15	0.839	16
Hyomandibular	1	28.42	24.32	0.980	20
Hyomandibular	2	12.20	14.07	0.972	20
Hyomandibular	3	7.45	71.14	0.962	20
Hypohyal 2	1	40.28	56.11	0.965	20
Inferior Pharyngeal	1	23.30	19.73	0.978	15
Inferior Pharyngeal	2	53.68	85.66	0.901	15
Pharyngobranchial 2	1	-3.29	53.13	0.997	15
Pharyngobranchial 2	2	28.89	75.16	0.971	15
Hypobranchial 3	1	39.14	42.37	0.979	10
Vertebra 1	1	41.71	55.18	0.950	20
Vertebra 1	2	6.20	63.67	0.978	20
Vertebra 1	3	-13.51	150.95	0.922	20
Penultimate Vertebra	1	5.70	81.59	0.987	19
Penultimate Vertebra	2	21.12	76.44	0.968	19
Penultimate Vertebra	3	6.46	99.83	0.982	19
Otolith	1	-47.42	75.13	0.968	16
Otolith	2	-63.53	175.38	0.981	16

Table 6.4 Results of weight (Wt) regression for Greenling (*Hexagrammos* sp.) comparative specimens. Regression formulae take the following form: $Wt = \alpha X^{\beta}$, where X represents the skeletal measurement in question. X is in millimetres, and Wt. is in grams.

Bone	Mea. #	α	β	r-squared	n
Vomer	1	1.30	2.79	0.992	21
Vomer	2	9.45	2.98	0.979	21
Dentary	1	0.06	3.04	0.993	21
Dentary	2	4.27	2.89	0.976	21
Dentary	3	0.38	3.00	0.992	21
Angular	1	3.79	2.84	0.983	17
Angular	2	8.96	2.75	0.994	17
Articular	1	0.03	3.25	0.995	21
Articular	3	7.75	3.07	0.987	21
Articular	4	14.18	2.68	0.986	21
Premaxilla	1	0.19	2.76	0.989	22
Premaxilla	2	0.12	3.10	0.993	21
Premaxilla	3	1.02	2.93	0.993	22
Quadrate	3	10.90	2.89	0.989	22
Quadrate	4	0.15	3.21	0.995	22
Interhyal	1	10.38	2.63	0.986	14
Epihyal	1	0.69	2.74	0.994	21
Epihyal	2	15.44	3.11	0.971	21
Epihyal	3	0.67	3.18	0.996	21
Basihyal	1	0.50	3.06	0.988	16
Basihyal	2	40.12	2.87	0.916	16
Hyomandibular	1	0.46	2.83	0.992	21
Hyomandibular	2	0.02	3.29	0.994	21
Hyomandibular	3	3.77	3.38	0.985	21
Hypohyal 2	1	6.72	2.74	0.994	21
Inferior Pharyngeal	1	0.16	2.99	0.994	16
Inferior Pharyngeal	2	32.17	2.70	0.973	16
Pharyngobranchial 2	1	1.37	3.15	0.987	16
Pharyngobranchial 2	2	10.82	2.92	0.978	16
Hypobranchial 3	1	2.48	2.85	0.988	10
Vertebra 1	1	5.85	2.85	0.988	20
Vertebra 1	2	2.78	3.27	0.982	20
Vertebra 1	3	32.01	3.26	0.944	20
Penultimate Vertebra	1	6.95	3.20	0.980	20
Penultimate Vertebra	2	10.06	2.87	0.984	20
Penultimate Vertebra	3	15.03	3.02	0.986	20
Otolith	1	0.68	4.08	0.963	16
Otolith	2	14.30	4.46	0.979	16

Table 6.5 Results of total length (TL) regression for Irish Lord (*Hemilepidotus* sp.) comparative specimens. Regression formulae take the following form: $TL = \alpha + \beta X$, where X represents the skeletal measurement in question. TL and X are in millimetres.

Bone	Mea. #	α	β	r-squared	n
Vomer	1	-21.46	37.90	0.956	7
Vomer	2	-11.89	82.29	0.971	7
Dentary	1	3.88	9.35	0.975	7
Dentary	2	28.78	50.70	0.938	7
Dentary	3	9.63	21.67	0.965	7
Angular	1	-76.70	70.88	0.691	7
Angular	2	35.75	50.32	0.943	6
Articular	1	-14.51	11.68	0.979	7
Articular	2	-6.22	21.31	0.976	7
Articular	3	-29.01	67.62	0.922	7
Articular	4	19.29	60.78	0.887	7
Premaxilla	1	50.11	11.07	0.968	7
Premaxilla	2	-138.86	31.02	0.917	7
Premaxilla	3	-59.63	40.24	0.920	7
Quadrate	3	39.27	67.52	0.968	7
Quadrate	4	5.67	17.41	0.988	7
Interhyal	1	-66.06	53.91	0.979	6
Epihyal	1	57.18	13.41	0.940	6
Epihyal	2	-26.28	152.17	0.919	6
Epihyal	3	11.51	28.56	0.848	6
Hyomandibular	1	-19.13	24.59	0.971	6
Hyomandibular	2	36.15	12.04	0.952	6
Hyomandibular	3	-40.30	90.44	0.251	6
Hypohyal 2	1	-12.62	82.94	0.986	7
Inferior Pharyngeal	1	-4.53	19.05	0.901	6
Inferior Pharyngeal	3	14.09	67.90	0.935	7
Inferior Pharyngeal	4	87.10	54.33	0.743	7
Pharyngobranchial 2	1	6.17	39.06	0.957	6
Pharyngobranchial 2	2	11.48	50.32	0.942	6
Hypobranchial 3	1	123.15	13.69	0.973	5
Vertebra 1	1	-42.83	82.38	0.936	7
Vertebra 1	2	25.71	55.49	0.867	7
Vertebra 1	3	1.32	103.19	0.847	7
Penultimate Vertebra	1	31.42	75.55	0.857	7
Penultimate Vertebra	2	-2.90	74.85	0.903	7
Penultimate Vertebra	3	-172.95	158.53	0.937	7
Otolith	1	-136.79	64.95	0.941	6
Otolith	2	-71.19	111.32	0.976	6

Table 6.6 Results of weight (Wt) regression for Irish Lord (*Hemilepidotus* sp.) comparative specimens. Regression formulae take the following form: $Wt = \alpha X^{\beta}$, where X represents the skeletal measurement in question. X is in millimetres, and Wt. is in grams.

Bone	Mea. #	α	β	r-squared	n
Vomer	1	0.44	3.11	0.982	7
Vomer	2	7.20	2.88	0.983	7
Dentary	1	0.02	2.76	0.981	7
Dentary	2	4.44	2.59	0.973	7
Dentary	3	0.34	2.66	0.980	7
Angular	1	0.28	4.21	0.797	7
Angular	2	6.18	2.42	0.958	6
Articular	1	0.02	2.97	0.986	7
Articular	2	0.21	2.78	0.983	7
Articular	3	2.07	3.21	0.962	7
Articular	4	6.23	2.61	0.926	7
Premaxilla	1	0.31	2.25	0.976	7
Premaxilla	2	0.00	4.31	0.941	7
Premaxilla	3	0.16	3.48	0.951	7
Quadrate	3	13.28	2.41	0.985	7
Quadrate	4	0.14	2.76	0.994	7
Interhyal	1	0.28	3.67	0.989	6
Epihyal	1	0.48	2.27	0.972	6
Epihyal	2	29.68	3.16	0.952	6
Epihyal	3	0.55	2.77	0.891	6
Hyomandibular	1	0.15	3.00	0.984	6
Hyomandibular	2	0.16	2.47	0.981	6
Hyomandibular	3	2.51	3.64	0.285	6
Hypohyal 2	1	6.67	2.95	0.995	7
Inferior Pharyngeal	1	0.08	2.99	0.950	6
Inferior Pharyngeal	3	6.03	2.80	0.965	7
Inferior Pharyngeal	4	24.85	1.92	0.801	7
Pharyngobranchial 2	1	0.80	2.98	0.977	6
Pharyngobranchial 2	2	1.95	2.94	0.958	6
Hypobranchial 3	1	3.10	1.83	0.991	5
Vertebra 1	1	2.72	3.37	0.963	7
Vertebra 1	2	4.10	2.76	0.916	7
Vertebra 1	3	12.90	3.06	0.892	7
Penultimate Vertebra	1	10.72	2.73	0.923	7
Penultimate Vertebra	2	5.62	2.92	0.943	7
Penultimate Vertebra	3	2.02	4.63	0.948	7
Otolith	1	0.09	4.27	0.965	6
Otolith	2	4.53	3.58	0.991	6

Table 6.7 Results of fork length (FL) regression for Pacific cod (*Gadus macrocephalus*) comparative specimens. Regression formulae take the following form: $FL = \alpha + \beta X$, where X represents the skeletal measurement in question. FL and X are in millimetres.

Bone	Mea. #	α	β	r-squared	n
Vomer	1	28.30	28.41	0.968	25
Vomer	2	-14.97	60.41	0.961	25
Dentary	1	20.85	10.43	0.981	25
Dentary	2	91.23	87.29	0.972	25
Dentary	3	4.38	16.54	0.975	25
Angular	1	96.36	47.19	0.941	25
Angular	2	96.32	50.27	0.987	25
Premaxilla	1	9.40	13.71	0.969	25
Premaxilla	2	28.60	41.39	0.986	25
Premaxilla	3	16.58	53.17	0.984	25
Quadrate	3	105.19	56.88	0.956	25
Quadrate	4	35.25	17.92	0.963	25
Interhyal	1	74.01	33.86	0.964	25
Epihyal	1	72.44	25.66	0.974	25
Epihyal	2	101.37	84.99	0.966	25
Epihyal	3	43.99	35.66	0.977	25
Pharyngobranchial 2	1	48.39	38.33	0.957	25
Pharyngobranchial 2	2	73.13	56.08	0.853	25
Hypobranchial 3	1	51.44	36.11	0.963	25
Epibranchial 3	1	92.52	54.17	0.973	25
Epibranchial 4	1	53.71	23.64	0.984	25
Vertebra 1	1	76.35	55.58	0.985	25
Vertebra 1	3	74.54	100.63	0.958	25
Vertebra 9	1	121.66	43.91	0.986	25
Vertebra 9	2	98.62	46.01	0.986	25
Vertebra 9	3	61.35	61.72	0.986	25

Table 6.8 Results of weight (Wt) regression for Pacific cod (*Gadus macrocephalus*) comparative specimens. Regression formulae take the following form: $Wt = \alpha X^{\beta}$, where X represents the skeletal measurement in question. X is in millimetres, and Wt. is in grams.

Bone	Mea. #	α	β	r-squared	n
Vomer	1	0.26	3.09	0.976	30
Vomer	2	1.33	3.28	0.974	30
Dentary	1	0.01	3.11	0.986	30
Dentary	2	19.73	2.81	0.976	30
Dentary	3	0.02	3.24	0.985	30
Angular	1	4.74	2.70	0.957	29
Angular	2	7.01	2.60	0.989	29
Premaxilla	1	0.02	3.10	0.982	30
Premaxilla	2	0.78	3.11	0.982	30
Premaxilla	3	1.46	3.15	0.985	30
Quadrate	3	6.57	2.81	0.973	30
Quadrate	4	0.07	3.07	0.974	30
Interhyal	1	1.47	2.75	0.977	29
Epihyal	1	0.47	2.87	0.985	30
Epihyal	2	28.78	2.59	0.970	30
Epihyal	3	0.82	2.96	0.985	30
Pharyngobranchial 2	1	0.89	3.01	0.978	30
Pharyngobranchial 2	2	2.74	3.08	0.915	30
Hypobranchial 3	1	0.99	2.92	0.980	29
Epibranchial 3	1	7.03	2.67	0.976	29
Epibranchial 4	1	0.30	2.91	0.991	29
Vertebra 1	1	5.73	2.76	0.986	30
Vertebra 1	3	25.97	2.82	0.961	30
Vertebra 9	1	7.74	2.48	0.993	30
Vertebra 9	2	5.80	2.59	0.986	30
Vertebra 9	3	4.73	2.94	0.987	30

Table 6.9 Results of total length (TL) regression for Rockfish (*Sebastes* sp.) comparative specimens. Regression formulae take the following form: TL = α + βX, where X represents the skeletal measurement in question. TL and X are in millimetres.

Bone	Mea. #	α	β	r-squared	n
Vomer	1	44.98	28.50	0.823	34
Vomer	2	20.87	63.22	0.815	34
Dentary	1	86.49	6.01	0.895	31
Dentary	2	73.34	35.77	0.863	33
Dentary	3	40.91	14.54	0.898	31
Angular	1	69.10	39.75	0.873	27
Angular	2	56.67	42.07	0.761	27
Articular	1	99.98	6.35	0.879	33
Articular	2	75.14	10.72	0.908	33
Articular	4	96.03	61.25	0.824	33
Premaxilla	1	54.12	8.87	0.874	34
Premaxilla	2	27.98	20.24	0.621	32
Premaxilla	3	-3.80	29.53	0.769	34
Quadrate	3	73.78	50.92	0.854	32
Quadrate	4	28.99	15.78	0.882	32
Interhyal	1	55.30	25.42	0.765	23
Epihyal	1	55.53	12.91	0.867	33
Epihyal	2	150.21	73.77	0.814	34
Epihyal	3	39.02	20.95	0.869	34
Basihyal	1	107.32	15.85	0.923	9
Basihyal	2	65.41	102.50	0.875	9
Hyomandibular	1	44.98	17.18	0.891	33
Hyomandibular	2	32.99	9.94	0.846	34
Hyomandibular	3	56.17	53.75	0.853	34
Hypohyal 2	1	85.49	34.97	0.857	28
Inferior Pharyngeal	1	52.62	12.59	0.838	25
Inferior Pharyngeal	3	63.62	61.96	0.775	26
Inferior Pharyngeal	4	89.47	48.45	0.634	25
Pharyngobranchial 2	1	83.24	20.93	0.845	20
Pharyngobranchial 2	2	78.90	48.04	0.730	20
Hypobranchial 3	1	59.81	26.29	0.866	14
Vertebra 1	1	59.94	43.71	0.867	31
Vertebra 1	2	59.45	41.91	0.911	31
Vertebra 1	3	74.53	59.51	0.796	31
Penultimate Vertebra	1	35.89	58.97	0.880	32
Penultimate Vertebra	2	88.84	48.28	0.865	32
Penultimate Vertebra	3	64.36	48.58	0.865	32
Otolith	1	-8.52	26.94	0.588	32
Otolith	2	-36.69	59.13	0.550	32

Table 6.10 Results of weight (Wt) regression for Rockfish (*Sebastes* sp.) comparative specimens. Regression formulae take the following form: Wt = αX^{β}, where X represents the skeletal measurement in question. X is in millimetres, and Wt. is in grams.

Bone	Mea. #	α	β	r-squared	n
Vomer	1	0.80	2.87	0.938	33
Vomer	2	6.63	2.83	0.897	33
Dentary	1	0.03	2.65	0.933	29
Dentary	2	5.03	2.44	0.925	31
Dentary	3	0.11	2.89	0.931	29
Angular	1	4.98	2.55	0.902	25
Angular	2	5.78	2.47	0.887	25
Articular	1	0.07	2.55	0.918	31
Articular	2	0.16	2.60	0.930	31
Articular	4	26.16	2.35	0.896	31
Premaxilla	1	0.04	2.78	0.926	32
Premaxilla	2	0.12	3.13	0.822	30
Premaxilla	3	0.31	3.11	0.878	32
Quadrate	3	10.67	2.50	0.911	31
Quadrate	4	0.11	2.92	0.924	31
Interhyal	1	1.03	2.69	0.933	21
Epihyal	1	0.15	2.71	0.937	31
Epihyal	2	109.42	1.94	0.812	32
Epihyal	3	0.40	2.78	0.930	32
Basihyal	1	1.66	2.21	0.953	8
Basihyal	2	65.20	2.39	0.996	8
Hyomandibular	1	0.34	2.66	0.933	31
Hyomandibular	2	0.04	2.82	0.934	32
Hyomandibular	3	8.83	2.59	0.905	32
Hypohyal 2	1	3.99	2.59	0.960	26
Inferior Pharyngeal	1	0.21	2.57	0.921	24
Inferior Pharyngeal	3	13.61	2.59	0.907	25
Inferior Pharyngeal	4	16.49	2.24	0.797	24
Pharyngobranchial 2	1	2.09	2.33	0.974	20
Pharyngobranchial 2	2	9.99	2.50	0.938	20
Hypobranchial 3	1	1.15	2.65	0.986	13
Vertebra 1	1	5.92	2.55	0.975	29
Vertebra 1	2	4.67	2.62	0.980	29
Vertebra 1	3	13.03	2.62	0.932	29
Penultimate Vertebra	1	6.78	2.80	0.951	30
Penultimate Vertebra	2	12.86	2.43	0.971	30
Penultimate Vertebra	3	6.43	2.69	0.906	30
Otolith	1	0.05	3.65	0.865	30
Otolith	2	0.56	3.76	0.765	30

Table 6.11 Results of fork length (FL) regression for Walleye pollock (*Theragra chalcogramma*) comparative specimens. Regression formulae take the following form: FL = α + βX, where X represents the skeletal measurement in question. FL and X are in millimetres.

Bone	Mea. #	α	β	r-squared	n
Vomer	1	24.05	32.15	0.941	54
Vomer	2	11.40	61.31	0.966	54
Dentary	1	13.60	10.50	0.953	57
Dentary	2	31.74	89.14	0.917	59
Dentary	3	10.39	15.44	0.952	57
Angular	1	36.08	58.58	0.927	49
Angular	2	42.18	73.30	0.923	48
Premaxilla	1	3.91	14.73	0.967	58
Premaxilla	2	7.34	57.68	0.956	58
Premaxilla	3	9.78	62.34	0.951	58
Quadrate	3	37.58	73.15	0.922	58
Quadrate	4	0.49	19.02	0.950	58
Interhyal	1	37.70	41.45	0.921	49
Epihyal	1	30.26	27.34	0.938	57
Epihyal	2	19.89	97.09	0.912	57
Epihyal	3	17.75	41.25	0.974	57
Pharyngobranchial 2	1	39.11	45.77	0.940	51
Pharyngobranchial 2	2	48.55	67.49	0.902	51
Hypobranchial 3	1	32.99	38.68	0.958	49
Epibranchial 3	1	46.77	64.72	0.932	52
Epibranchial 4	1	33.93	28.93	0.945	54
Vertebra 1	1	41.08	68.09	0.943	57
Vertebra 1	2	48.21	58.52	0.909	56
Vertebra 1	3	33.24	125.79	0.934	58
Vertebra 9	1	54.92	55.32	0.920	52
Vertebra 9	2	55.45	54.63	0.912	52
Vertebra 9	3	22.18	61.97	0.977	52
Otolith	1	-15.08	23.90	0.960	45
Otolith	2	-23.10	62.63	0.974	52

Table 6.12 Results of weight (Wt) regression for Walleye pollock (*Theragra chalcogramma*) comparative specimens. Regression formulae take the following form: $Wt = \alpha X^{\beta}$, where X represents the skeletal measurement in question. X is in millimetres, and Wt. is in grams.

Bone	Mea. #	α	β	r-squared	n
Vomer	1	0.26	3.13	0.984	53
Vomer	2	1.65	3.11	0.982	53
Dentary	1	0.01	3.18	0.983	56
Dentary	2	7.53	3.14	0.970	58
Dentary	3	0.02	3.19	0.982	56
Angular	1	2.90	2.89	0.976	48
Angular	2	6.38	2.83	0.974	47
Premaxilla	1	0.01	3.32	0.984	57
Premaxilla	2	1.08	3.26	0.984	57
Premaxilla	3	1.50	3.23	0.982	57
Quadrate	3	5.57	2.93	0.981	57
Quadrate	4	0.02	3.33	0.980	57
Interhyal	1	0.94	2.97	0.977	48
Epihyal	1	0.24	3.00	0.980	56
Epihyal	2	8.49	3.04	0.953	56
Epihyal	3	0.59	3.07	0.988	56
Pharyngobranchial 2	1	1.46	2.90	0.964	50
Pharyngobranchial 2	2	5.06	2.92	0.944	50
Hypobranchial 3	1	0.74	2.96	0.976	48
Epibranchial 3	1	5.71	2.70	0.979	51
Epibranchial 4	1	0.35	2.92	0.980	53
Vertebra 1	1	5.17	2.87	0.982	56
Vertebra 1	2	3.65	2.92	0.969	55
Vertebra 1	3	26.06	2.85	0.983	57
Vertebra 9	1	3.96	2.76	0.980	51
Vertebra 9	2	3.86	2.76	0.979	51
Vertebra 9	3	2.42	3.00	0.992	51
Otolith	1	0.05	3.24	0.975	44
Otolith	2	0.63	3.51	0.988	51

Table 6.13 Summary of NISP values by element for each taxa for each archaeological site. The number of archaeological specimens that exceed the size range of the comparative data are also recorded "(>)".

		Adak 009		Adak 011		Buldir 008		Shemya 2		Shemya 7	
		NISP	(>)	NISP	(>)	NISP	(>)	NISP	(>)	NISP	(>)
Atka Mackerel	Articular	3	0	3	0	13	0	9	0	4	0
	Basihyal					2	0				
	Dentary	2	0	3	0	25	0	17	0	17	0
	Epihyal	3	0	2	0	9	0	2	0	11	0
	Hyomandibular	1	0			6	0			7	0
	Penultimate Vert.			2	0	12	0				
	Premaxilla	1	0	2	0	9	0	4	0	10	0
	Quadrate			3	0	14	0	2	0	24	0
	Vertebra #1					15	0	1	0	9	0
	Vomer			3	0					2	0
	Total:	**10**	**0**	**18**	**0**	**105**	**0**	**35**	**0**	**84**	**0**
Greenling	Angular	9	0	1	0						
	Articular	125	0	57	0			10	0	12	0
	Basihyal			3	0						
	Dentary	151	0	49	0	1	0	9	1	18	0
	Epihyal	65	0	35	1	2	1	3	0	11	0
	Hyomandibular	128	0	2	0					15	0
	Hypohyal #2									1	0
	Penultimate Vert.			32	0					4	0
	Premaxilla	148	0	67	0			5	0	16	0
	Quadrate	143	1	51	0	2	0	2	0	20	0
	Vertebra #1	47	0	30	2			1	0	7	0
	Vomer	50	1	29	0			3	0	9	0
	Total:	**866**	**2**	**356**	**3**	**5**	**1**	**33**	**1**	**113**	**0**
Irish Lord	Angular			1	1			1	1	1	1
	Articular	13	3	9	6			8	4	19	15
	Dentary	20	11	24	14			15	10	62	51
	Epihyal	10	10	10	5			7	5	46	33
	Hyomandibular	9	4	1	1	1	1			26	14
	Hypohyal #2									4	4
	Inf. Pharyngeal									3	2
	Interhyal			1	1					9	9
	Penultimate Vert.									9	9
	Pharyngobr. #2									2	2
	Premaxilla	11	11	19	17			12	11	41	36
	Quadrate	18	13	15	9			17	15	67	48
	Vertebra #1	7	5	7	3	1	1	3	3	29	18
	Vomer	3	3	5	1			1	1	25	14
	Total:	**91**	**60**	**92**	**58**	**2**	**2**	**64**	**50**	**343**	**256**

Table 6.13 (cont.) Summary of NISP values by element for each taxa for each archaeological site. The number of archaeological specimens that exceed the size range of the comparative data are also recorded "(>)".

		Adak 009		Adak 011		Buldir 008		Shemya 2		Shemya 7	
		NISP	(>)	NISP	(>)	NISP	(>)	NISP	(>)	NISP	(>)
Pacific cod	Angular	59	6	21	2			5	4	48	9
	Dentary	74	12	44	5			38	10	68	11
	Epibranchial #3			14	1	4	1	1	1	11	1
	Epibranchial #4			11	1	1	0	13	1	41	6
	Epihyal	39	2	37	6			20	6	44	8
	Hypobranchial #3			15	1					7	0
	Interhyal	55	14	18	4			14	8	38	12
	Pharyngobr. #2			6	0	2	0			19	4
	Premaxilla	107	16	43	5	1	1	44	4	96	17
	Quadrate	91	13	38	2	1	1	23	4	73	10
	Vertebra #1			10	1					15	3
	Vertebra #9									5	1
	Vomer	24	9	15	3	2	2	11	6	31	7
	Total:	**449**	**72**	**272**	**31**	**11**	**5**	**169**	**44**	**496**	**89**
Rockfish	Angular					2	0				
	Articular					2	0	5	0	5	0
	Dentary			2	0	5	1	20	1	7	0
	Epihyal					3	0	9	0	6	0
	Hyomandibular			1	0	2	0			9	0
	Hypohyal #2					1	0			1	0
	Premaxilla					6	0	24	7	6	0
	Quadrate			1	0	2	0	12	0	11	0
	Vertebra #1					1	0	1	1		
	Vomer			1	0			3	0	1	0
	Total:	**0**	**0**	**5**	**0**	**24**	**1**	**74**	**9**	**46**	**0**
Walleye pollock	Dentary							6	0	2	0
	Premaxilla	1	1					1	0	2	0
	Quadrate							1	0	1	0
	Vomer									2	0
	Total:	**1**	**1**	**0**	**0**	**0**	**0**	**8**	**0**	**7**	**0**

Table 6.14 Summary of archaeological specimens from all sites that exceed the size ranges of comparative specimens. The total number of archaeological specimens that exceed the comparative size range is recorded "Total >", as well as their percentage of the total NISP for each taxon "Percent >".

	Total NISP	Total >	Percent >
Atka Mackerel	252	0	0.00
Greenling	1373	7	0.51
Irish Lords	592	426	71.96
Pacific cod	1397	241	17.25
Rockfish	149	10	6.71
Walleye pollock	16	1	6.25

Table 6.15 Summary of NISP values for each taxon by site.

	Adak 009	Adak 011	Buldir 008	Shemya 2	Shemya 7
Atka Mackerel	10	18	105	35	84
Greenling	866	356	5	33	113
Irish Lord	91	92	2	64	343
Pacific cod	449	272	11	169	496
Rockfish	0	5	24	74	46
Walleye pollock	1	0	0	8	7

Table 6.16 Summary of length estimations by taxon for each archaeological site under consideration. Lengths are shown with an uncertainty of two standard deviations, or a 95% confidence interval. Note: EU represents Excavation Unit, and HP represents House Pit.

Site	Unit of Aggregation	Taxon	Minimum Length (mm)	Maximum Length (mm)
Adak 009 (ADK 009)	EU1	Atka Mackerel	376 ± 3	441 ± 15
		Greenling	194 ± 8	595 ± 49
		Pacific cod	436 ± 18	1122 ± 33
		Walleye pollock	604 ± 24	
Adak 011 (ADK 011)	HP1 - EU1	Greenling	272 ± 10	423 ± 15
		Pacific cod	518 ± 13	914 ± 22
		Rockfish	291 ± 19	451 ± 18
	HP1 - EU2	Atka Mackerel	314 ± 4	376 ± 6
		Greenling	217 ± 8	571 ± 28
		Pacific cod	470 ± 14	967 ± 24
	HP2	Atka Mackerel	307 ± 4	340 ± 4
		Greenling	270 ± 8	492 ± 19
		Pacific cod	356 ± 13	1048 ± 57
		Rockfish	445 ± 18	588 ± 34
Buldir 008 (KIS 008)	Pit 4	Atka Mackerel	269 ± 5	451 ± 7
		Greenling	287 ± 10	626 ± 31
		Pacific cod	542 ± 13	1073 ± 29
		Rockfish	302 ± 25	593 ± 37
Shemya 2 (ATU 021)	EU3	Atka Mackerel	326 ± 3	453 ± 5
		Greenling	302 ± 17	547 ± 27
		Pacific cod	380 ± 12	1198 ± 49
		Rockfish	268 ± 29	988 ± 73
		Walleye pollock	391 ± 17	570 ± 30
Shemya 7 (ATU 061)	Pit 1 - SE	Atka Mackerel	297 ± 7	476 ± 19
		Greenling	208 ± 9	446 ± 16
		Pacific cod	351 ± 13	1250 ± 66
		Rockfish	288 ± 19	461 ± 22
		Walleye pollock	448 ± 16	558 ± 19

Table 6.17 MNI values for each taxon by site/aggregation unit.

	Adak 009	Adak 011			Buldir 008	Shemya 2	Shemya 7
		HP1-EU1	HP1-EU2	HP2			
Atka Mackerel	5	0	6	2	24	15	23
Greenling	92	10	28	32	5	9	21
Pacific cod	65	20	15	16	7	32	60
Rockfish	0	3	0	2	6	20	10
Walleye	1	0	0	0	0	5	5

Table 6.18 Summary of weight estimations by taxon for each archaeological site under consideration.

Site/Unit	Taxon	Mean Weight (g)	Minimum Weight (g)	Maximum Weight (g)
Adak 009 (ADK 009)	Atka Mackerel	1026	696	1284
	Greenling	598	134	4070
	Pacific cod	5775	922	21174
	Walleye pollock	2184	2184	2184
Adak 011 (ADK 011) HP1 - EU1	Greenling	624	308	1137
	Pacific cod	5150	1740	9380
	Rockfish	938	414	1500
Adak 011 (ADK 011) HP1 - EU2	Atka Mackerel	541	371	712
	Greenling	590	163	1767
	Pacific cod	5047	1092	12173
Adak 011 (ADK 011) HP2	Atka Mackerel	421	338	504
	Greenling	707	264	2265
	Pacific cod	5623	496	15556
	Rockfish	2648	1627	3669
Buldir 008 (KIS 008)	Atka Mackerel	737	209	1343
	Greenling	1470	358	4562
	Pacific cod	8281	2006	18285
	Rockfish	1214	437	3459
Shemya 2 (ATU 021)	Atka Mackerel	863	493	1342
	Greenling	974	469	2805
	Pacific cod	6898	728	24843
	Rockfish	3380	302	15588
	Walleye pollock	1055	600	2140
Shemya 7 (ATU 061)	Atka Mackerel	827	284	1685
	Greenling	494	126	1399
	Pacific cod	5747	464	30012
	Rockfish	784	387	1694
	Walleye pollock	1246	799	1979

Table 6.19 Total estimated weight by taxon per site, and relative proportions of taxa per site. All total weights are given in grams. Relative proportions for each taxon are represented by percentage of total weight of all taxa per site.

	Adak 009	Adak 011			Buldir 008	Shemya 2	Shemya 7
		HP1 - EU1	HP1 - EU2	HP2			
Atka Mackerel	5130g	0g	3243g	842g	17690g	12947g	19027g
	1.17%	0.00%	3.40%	0.71%	19.59%	4.11%	4.90%
Greenling	54995g	6236g	16522g	22628g	7348g	8768g	10371g
	12.57%	5.57%	17.30%	19.06%	8.14%	2.78%	2.67%
Pacific cod	375366g	102999g	75704g	89964g	57965g	220738g	344828g
	85.76%	91.92%	79.30%	75.77%	64.20%	70.00%	88.81%
Rockfish	0g	2814g	0g	5295g	7286g	67592g	7838g
	0.00%	2.51%	0.00%	4.46%	8.07%	21.44%	2.02%
Walleye pollock	2184g	0g	0g	0g	0g	5275g	6232g
	0.50%	0.00%	0.00%	0.00%	0.00%	1.67%	1.60%

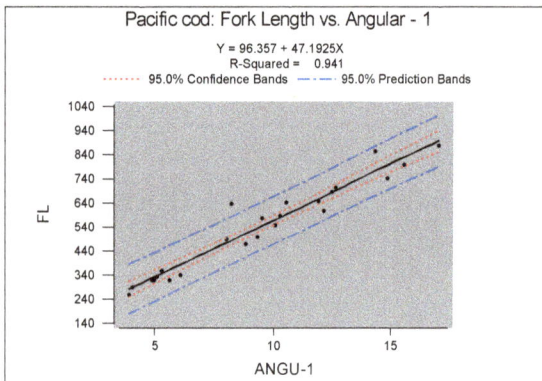

Pacific cod: Fork Length vs. Angular - 1
$Y = 96.357 + 47.1925X$
R-Squared = 0.941
95.0% Confidence Bands   95.0% Prediction Bands

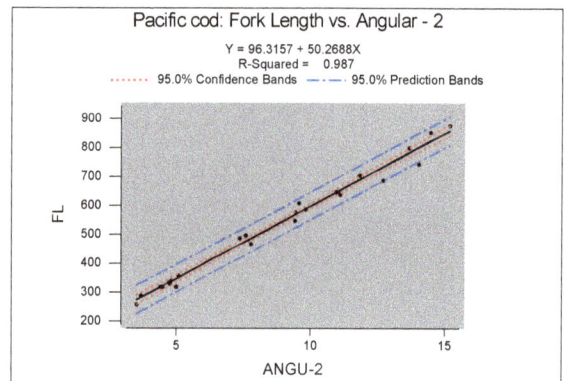

Pacific cod: Fork Length vs. Angular - 2
$Y = 96.3157 + 50.2688X$
R-Squared = 0.987
95.0% Confidence Bands   95.0% Prediction Bands

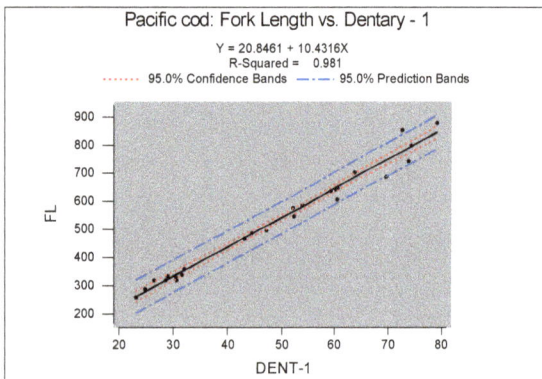

Pacific cod: Fork Length vs. Dentary - 1
$Y = 20.8461 + 10.4316X$
R-Squared = 0.981
95.0% Confidence Bands   95.0% Prediction Bands

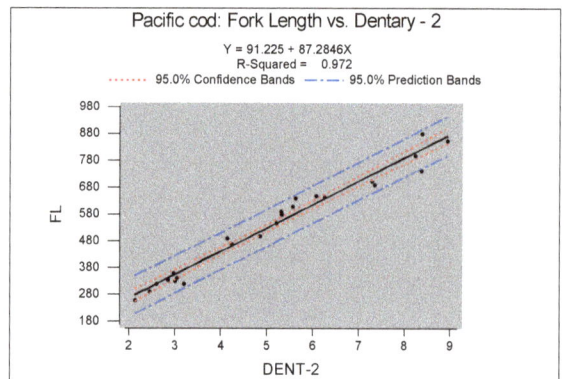

Pacific cod: Fork Length vs. Dentary - 2
$Y = 91.225 + 87.2846X$
R-Squared = 0.972
95.0% Confidence Bands   95.0% Prediction Bands

Figures 6.1 to 6.4 Regression plots for relevant Pacific cod elements.

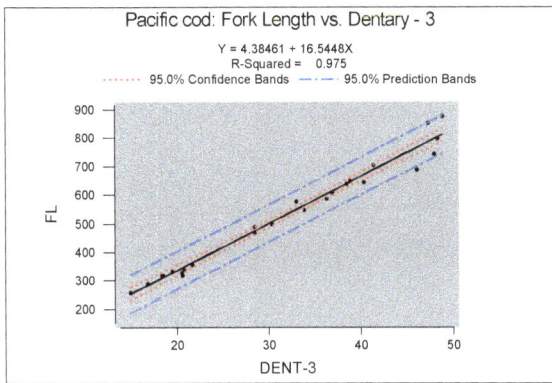

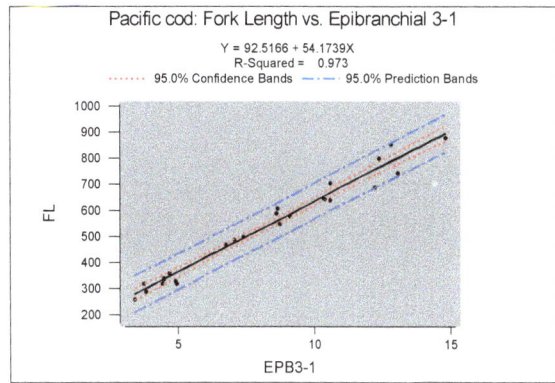

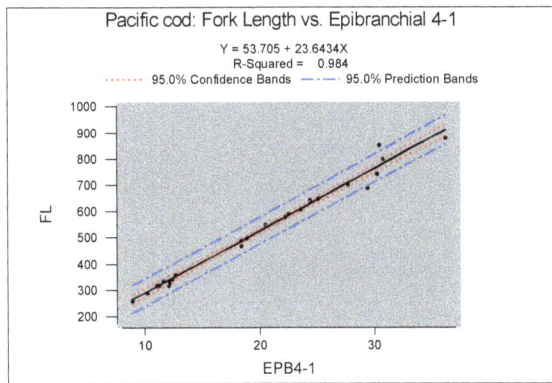

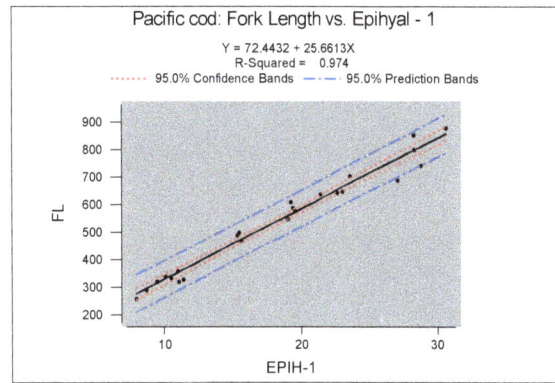

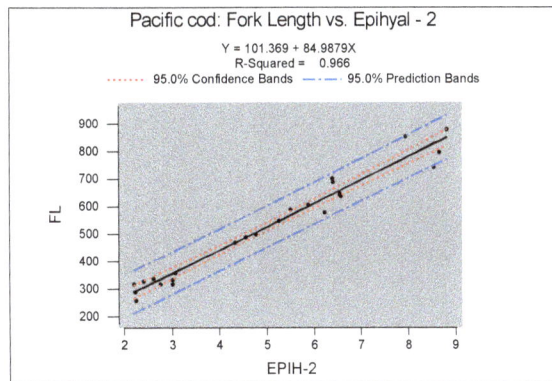

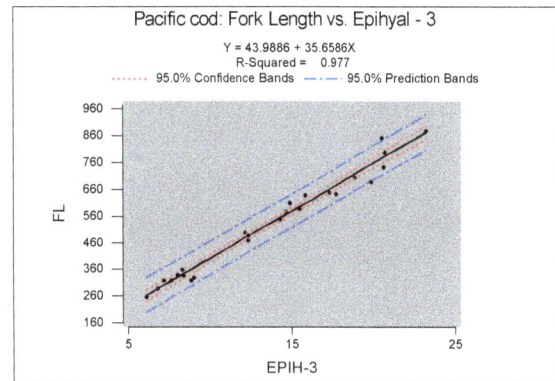

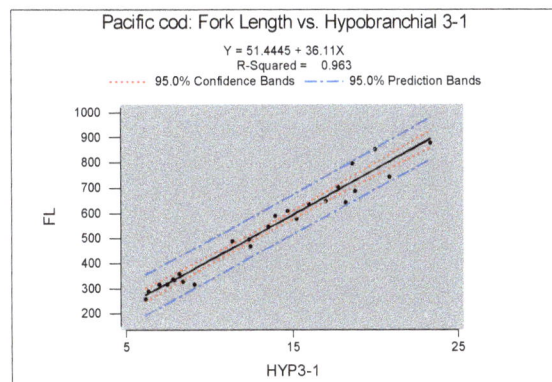

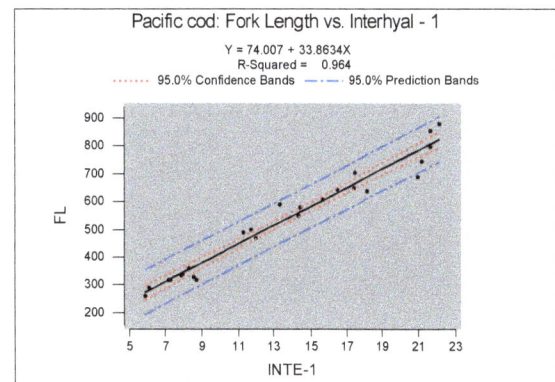

Figures 6.5 to 6.12 Regression plots for relevant Pacific cod elements.

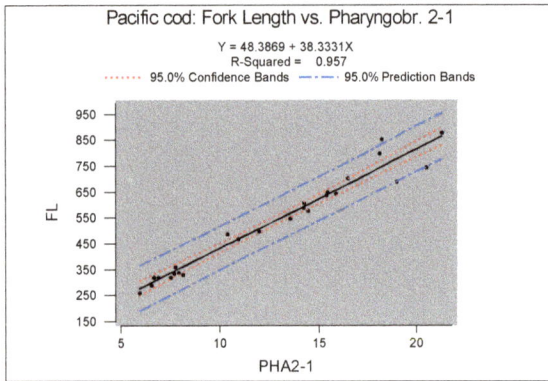

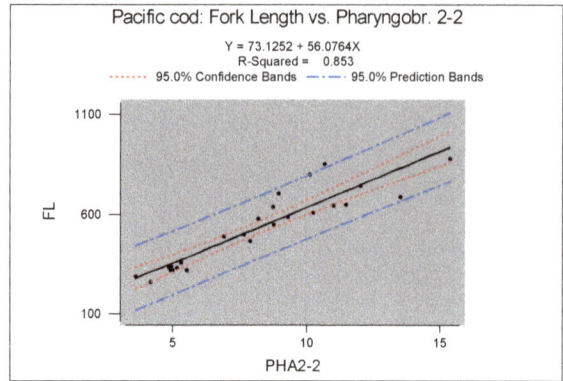

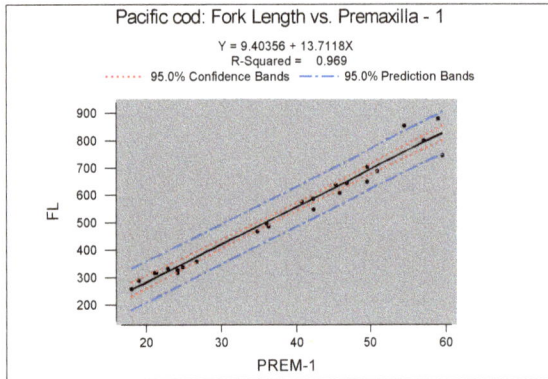

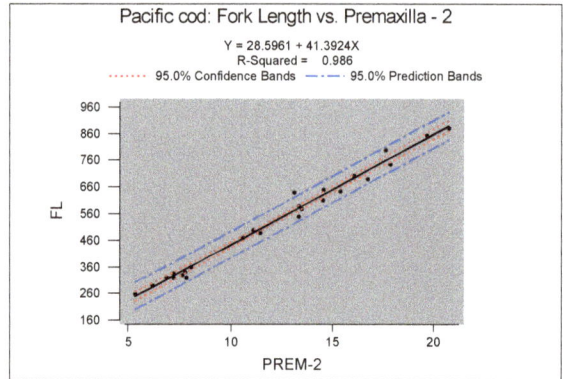

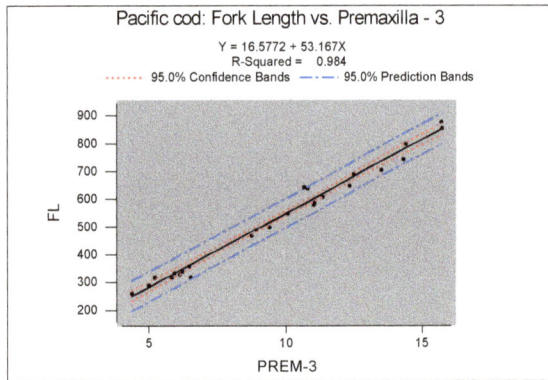

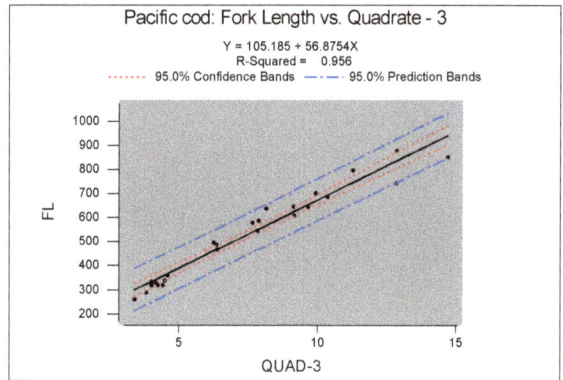

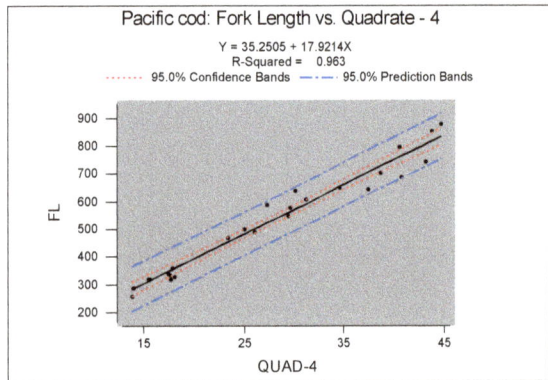

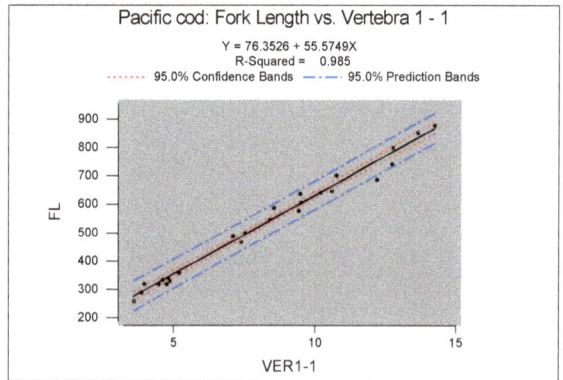

Figures 6.13 to 6.20 Regression plots for relevant Pacific cod elements.

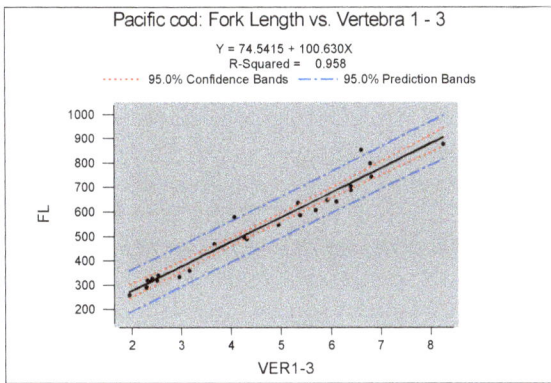

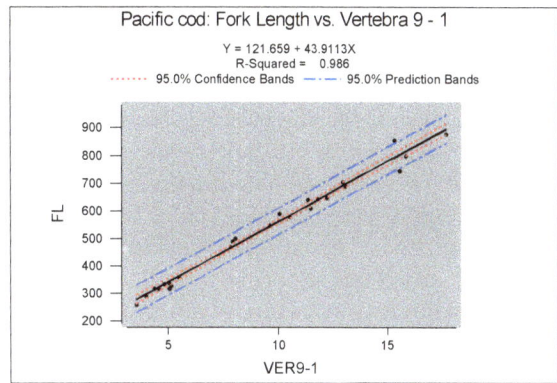

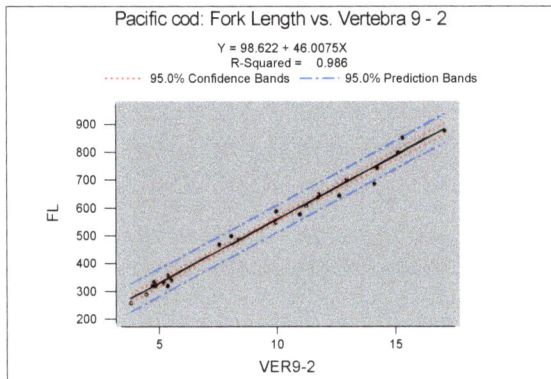

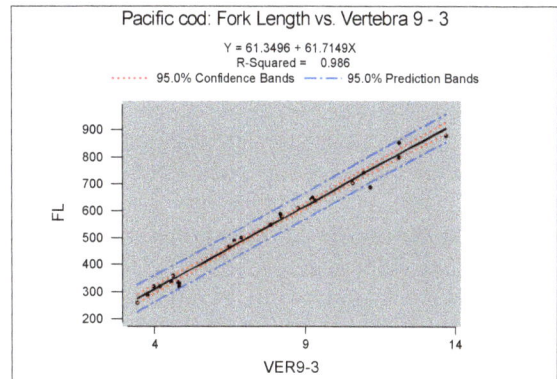

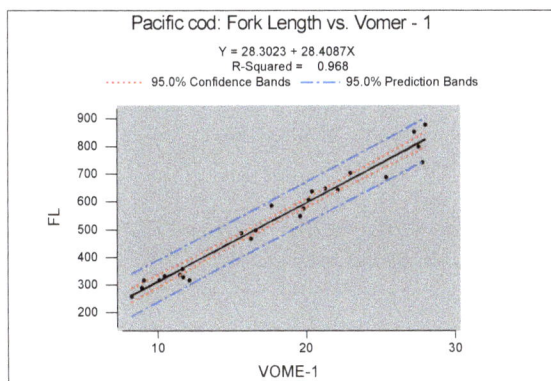

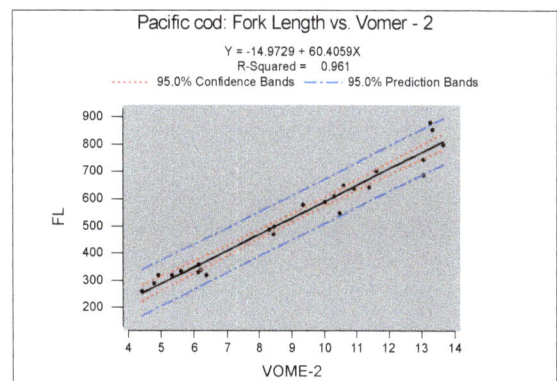

Figures 6.21 to 6.26 Regression plots for relevant Pacific cod elements.

CHAPTER 7. DISCUSSION

The results presented in the previous chapter give rise to several interesting topics for discussion[17]. These topics can be divided into three broad categories which parallel the major themes or goals of this thesis, namely the methodology itself, the implications of the results for Aleut culture history, and the potential of the results for increasing our understanding of the biology of the taxa under consideration and the ecology of the Aleutian Islands region. Accordingly, the chapter is divided into three sections reflecting these broad categories. The implications of the results for increasing our knowledge of Aleut culture history are outlined in section 7.2. This section includes an assessment of the use of the various fish taxa under consideration by Aleut people prehistorically, a discussion of regional and temporal variations in this use, and a consideration of the technologies and strategies that were likely employed in the harvesting of these resources. The final section, section 7.3, addresses the biological implications of the results, particularly the large size of many of the archaeological Pacific cod specimens. Before considering the biological or culture historical aspects, however, it is necessary to discuss the methodological considerations. Section 7.1 includes a general discussion of the results, an assessment of the utility of the methodology and a comparison to more traditional methods, and a discussion of limitations of the methodology and potential sources of error.

7.1 Methodological Considerations

The comparative skeletal specimens employed in this analysis were generally quite complete. Several reasons account for those cases where it was not possible to include all comparative specimens in the regression analysis for a given skeletal element or dimension. Firstly, for some comparative specimens original length or weight information was not available. Five of the Atka Mackerel comparative specimens, for example, were lacking associated fork length data, and thus only 91 specimens contributed to most of the fork length regression analyses. In other cases, specific elements were absent from comparative specimens or measurements were unattainable due to damage to comparative specimens. Small and delicate elements are occasionally lost or damaged during processing of skeletal material from whole fish. In addition, many of the specimens from the comparative collection of the Department of Anthropology at the University of Victoria have been in use for close to twenty years, and attrition due to the use of these comparative specimens has resulted in the loss or damage of some

elements.

The only additional situation in which measurements were unattainable arose from a skeletal anomaly which occurred on penultimate vertebrae from two Atka Mackerel comparative specimens (99/83 and 99/118). In these specimens the penultimate vertebrae appear to be formed through the fusion of two adjacent vertebrae. Following the classification system for vertebral anomalies presented by McHugh (1942) these appear to be Type 1 anomalies. McHugh describes Type 1 anomalies as a situation "in which two adjoining centra are fused to some extent and exhibit bilateral asymmetry" (1942: 348). The presence of such anomalies was felt to make measurement 3 unusable on these penultimate vertebrae, while measurements 1 and 2 remained unaffected (see Figure 5.1, pp. 28-29).

The generally high correlation seen in the regression analyses was expected due to the high levels of correlation reported between fish length or weight and skeletal size in previous studies (see p. 7). Nevertheless, there were some elements and measurements which showed considerably lower degrees of correlation as measured by r-squared values, and these situations should be considered when applying the generated regression formulae in future projects. In practice, measurements that yield poor levels of correlation should be avoided whenever possible in favour of measurements that yielded higher levels of correlation. Specific problematic cases for each taxon are discussed briefly below.

For Atka Mackerel (see Figure 5.1, p. 28-29), measurement 2 of the epihyal and measurement 2 of the basihyal both show relatively poor correlation, with r-squared values of 0.686 and 0.565 for fork length regression and 0.758 and 0.576 for weight regression respectively (Tables 6.1 and 6.2, pp. 44-45). These are both measurements on small, highly variable aspects of the bones, making the poor correlation unsurprising. Also, particularly for epihyal measurement 2, the dimension is more difficult to define than others, likely resulting in a larger degree of measurement error. In addition, measurement 3 of vertebra 1 shows a relatively poor correlation for Atka Mackerel, with an r-squared value of 0.734 for fork length and 0.793 for weight.

Irish Lord regressions were subject to a problem of small sample size as discussed below. Despite the lack of comparative specimens, however, Irish Lord regressions were generally very strong. The most obvious exception involves measurement 3 of the hyomandibular (see Figure 5.3, p. 33), which produced very low levels of correlation, with r-squared values of 0.251 for total length and 0.285 for weight (Tables 6.5 and 6.6, pp. 48-49). This poor

17. Some aspects of this chapter draw on discussions and conclusions previously presented as Orchard 1998.

64

correlation may be lessened with the inclusion of a larger sample of comparative specimens, though the current results suggests that hyomandibular measurement 3 should be excluded from future analyses of Irish Lords. In addition, measurement 1 of the angular and measurement 4 of the inferior pharyngeal show relatively low levels of correlation, with r-squared values of 0.691 and 0.743 for total length and 0.797 and 0.801 for weight respectively.

Rockfish regression results were generally poorer than those produced for other taxa. In particular, total length regressions showed relatively low levels of correlation, with angular measurement 2, premaxilla measurements 2 and 3, interhyal measurement 1, inferior pharyngeal measurements 3 and 4, pharyngobranchial 2 measurement 2, and otolith measurements 1 and 2 showing the lowest r-squared values (see Table 6.9, p. 52; Figure 5.5, p. 36-37). Results for weight regression were considerably better, with only two dimensions showing r-squared values less than 0.8, namely inferior pharyngeal measurement 4 and otolith measurement 2 (Table 6.10, p. 53). The generally low levels of correlation derived for Rockfish may result from the nature of the genus itself. *Sebastes* is a very diverse genus, with a large degree of variation in size and general morphology existing between the large number of species that occur in the north-eastern Pacific Ocean (Hart 1973). Comparative specimens from 16 different species were used to generate the regression formulae presented here, much more diversity than was present in either of the other genus-level regression sets.

The final three taxa, Greenling, Pacific cod, and Walleye pollock, all show very high levels of correlation in all of the regressions, with very few r-squared values falling below 0.9. For Greenling (Figure 5.2, pp. 30-31), dentary measurement 2 and basihyal measurement 2 produced r-squared values of 0.879 and 0.839 respectively for total length (Table 6.3, p. 46). For Pacific cod (Figure 5.4, p. 35), pharyngobranchial 2 measurement 2 produced an r-squared value of 0.853 for fork length.

One potential source of error that exists in the regression analyses in general involves sexual dimorphism within the taxa that are being considered. Brown and Wilderbuer, for example, state that "analysis of Pacific cod length-weight data indicate that female body weight increased at a higher rate in relation to length than did males" (1984: 212). Such a difference suggests that sex-specific regressions would be more accurate, particularly for weight. When dealing with archaeological remains, however, it is not possible to determine the sex of the skeletal material, and thus a general regression is more appropriate[18].

The size ranges of the comparative specimens relative to the size of the archaeological specimens for each taxa was discussed in some detail above (pp. 40-41). For four of the six taxa analyzed, the vast majority of the archaeological specimens were encompassed within the size range of the comparative specimens (Table 6.14, p. 57). This is to be expected as the comparative specimens are selected whenever possible to represent the range of sizes that are commonly encountered in the present. Pacific cod and Irish Lords were somewhat problematic, however, for a variety of reasons.

As indicated above, though the majority of the archaeological specimens of Pacific cod fall within the size range of the comparative material, 17.3% of the archaeological specimens exceed the comparative size range. The cultural and biological implications of the large size of many of the Pacific cod specimens will be discussed in sections 7.2 and 7.3 below. It is of interest here to discuss the methodological implications, and in particular the reasons for the lack of representativeness of the comparative specimens. The majority of the comparative specimens for Pacific cod are derived from modern fisheries sources. Clearly this source is constrained both by the size distributions of modern populations of Pacific cod and by the subset of this range that is targeted by modern commercial fisheries. In terms of the size of modern Pacific cod populations, Hart suggests that Pacific cod range in size up to one meter in length (1973: 223), while Vinnikov talks of cod up to 118cm in length with "modal groups...usually represented by fish of 30-60cm length" (1996: 188). Bakkala indicates that "lengths of Pacific cod in the eastern Bering sea observed during research vessel surveys have ranged from 7 to 110cm" (1984: 168). Foucher (1987) presents a summary of the length distribution of Canadian commercial catches of Pacific cod during the years 1974 to 1985. From these data, commercial catches of Pacific cod range from 27cm to 97cm, in no case exceeding 1m in length and only rarely exceeding 90cm in length (Foucher 1987). From this information, it is not surprising that the largest comparative specimen available for this analysis had a fork length of only 88cm (specimen GM-013). Based on MNI, 27 archaeological Pacific cod exceed 90cm in length and of those, 14 exceed 100cm in length, from a total MNI of 215 for Pacific cod. Despite the large size of many of the archaeological specimens of Pacific cod, very large modern specimens (ie. greater than 90 or 100cm) are not easily available for the purposes of comparative skeletal material. As discussed above in Chapter 6, however, regression results for Pacific cod show high levels of correlation (Tables 6.7 and 6.8, pp. 50-51), and regression plots indicate that the relationships between skeletal element dimensions and original size appear to hold at the extremes of the comparative range (Figures 6.1 to 6.26, pp. 60-63). As such, regression formulae generated from the limited

18. Though sex has not been included in the analysis presented here, sex information is available for a number of the comparative specimens used.

comparative range available were thought to be applicable to the relatively small percentage of archaeological specimens that exceeded the size range of the comparative data.

The case of Irish Lord specimens was somewhat different, as argued above in Chapter 6. The Irish Lord taxon was plagued by problems of both very small comparative sample size, and poor size representation. Only eight comparative specimens of the genus *Hemilepidotus* were available, including four true Irish Lords (*H. hemilepidotus* and *H. jordani*) and four Butterfly Sculpins (*H. papilio*). Irish Lords are not a commercially harvested species, nor are they commonly harvested by sport fisheries. As such, comparative specimens of the genus *Hemilepidotus* are not commonly available. In addition, the majority (72.0%) of the archaeological specimens analyzed exceeded the size range of the comparative specimens available for this project. For these reasons, regression formulae were not applied to the estimation of the length or weight of archaeological Irish Lord specimens. Unfortunately, based on NISP values (Table 6.15, p. 58) Irish Lords made significant contributions to most of the archaeological assemblages analyzed. These problems could be easily alleviated through the acquisition of additional comparative specimens for the genus *Hemilepidotus*, and to that end, the comparative data for the *Hemilepidotus* specimens analyzed here are included in Appendix 1.

The identification and measurement of the archaeological specimens from Aleutian Islands sites, aside from providing valuable insight into Aleut culture history and the biology of the Aleutian region as discussed below, provides useful information about the methodology employed in this project and about the future application of that methodology. In particular, it is interesting to consider the relative importance of the various skeletal elements, or the relative contribution that specific elements made to the total assemblage of each taxon from each site. This is discussed briefly above (p. 41), and summarized in Table 6.13 (pp. 56-57). It is apparent from these summary tables that different skeletal elements occurred in very different quantities in the archaeological assemblages analyzed. Three elements in particular, the dentary, quadrate, and premaxilla, were dominant amongst all taxa, though other elements also made significant contributions, such as the articular amongst the Atka Mackerel and Greenling, and the epihyal amongst the Irish Lords and Pacific cod.

A number of factors may account for the variation in abundance of the various skeletal elements considered, including biases in the analysis and collection of archaeological remains. Differential identification of remains, for example, may result in an overemphasis on bones that are particularly easy to identify to the genus or species level. One of the criteria used to select the elements

that were included in this analysis, however, was the ease of identifiability of these elements, and thus it seems unlikely that a systematic bias would have occurred during the identification of these remains. It is also possible that a bias occurred in the collection of faunal remains during excavation or post-excavation sorting. Information on the techniques employed are limited, so it is difficult to assess this potential source of bias. The five elements listed above as being most common in the archaeological assemblages, however, are all relatively large elements. Particularly small elements such as the branchials, hyopohyal #2, basihyal, and interhyal are scarce or absent in most of the archaeological material. This suggests that factors such as screen size may have played a role in biasing the samples somewhat. The cultural practices of the Aleut people responsible for these assemblages may also contribute to some of the bias that is seen in element frequencies. Virtually all of the most abundant elements in the archaeological assemblages are from the cranial region of the fish. This is somewhat biased, however, by the fact that the predominantly cranial elements were selected for this analysis. The post-cranial region is represented only by vertebrae, which are also relatively common in many of the archaeological assemblages. The only systematic bias that is apparent involves again the almost complete absence of branchial bones in most of the deposits. These are bones that comprise the gill structure in fish, a structure that is easily removed and discarded during the butchery and processing of harvested fish. Turner, in discussing the harvesting and preparation of Pacific cod by the Aleut, indicates that the gills are in fact removed from fish that are dried for winter use (1886: 90). Unfortunately, this bias may also be a result of the small size of these bones as discussed above. A final potential source of bias in the relative abundance of different skeletal elements involves taphonomic processes, or the differential preservation of the various skeletal elements. As has been indicated, the most abundant elements in the archaeological assemblages analyzed are all large, robust bones, whereas those which are less abundant are fairly small, and in many cases more fragile.

Regardless of the specific reasons that account for the differential abundance of skeletal elements in the material analyzed, this result suggests that certain skeletal elements are more useful for this type of analysis. Based on the results of this analysis, dentaries, quadrates, and premaxillae are likely to be particularly common elements in such studies elsewhere. In addition, other elements including the articular, epihyal, hyomandibular, penultimate vertebra and vertebra #1 are also likely to be relatively common. This provides a guideline for the elements that are likely to be of importance in future studies, and should thus be used for comparative analyses. Furthermore, measurements on these elements generally have strong correlations with live length and weight, the exceptions being epihyal measurement 2, hyomandibular measurement 3, and vertebra 1 measurement 3 for some taxa.

A variety of methods or levels of quantification were employed and presented in Chapter 6, including number of identified specimens present (NISP), minimum numbers of individuals (MNI), and estimated weight. Again, the implications of these various results for Aleut culture history and for the regional biology of the various taxa will be discussed in more detail below in sections 7.2 and 7.3. The methodological aspects of these various quantification methods will be discussed here. The general problems and limitations of NISP and MNI are discussed in some detail in Chapter 2. One of the first problems with using NISP as a method of quantification involved the presence of varying numbers of skeletal elements in different species. The selection of a specific set of skeletal elements for the purposes of this analysis alleviates this problem to some degree, as these elements occur in the same numbers in each species or taxon under consideration. However, the set of skeletal elements used varies somewhat from taxon to taxon, and thus there is still a slight problem in terms of different numbers of skeletal elements for each taxon. This is also an important issue, however, as the NISP values presented here represent only the number of specimens of each taxon for the elements selected for consideration. This differs from standard NISP values, which represent all of the identifiable specimens for each taxon from each assemblage. Thus, the NISP values presented in Tables 6.13 to 6.15 (pp. 56-58) are not comparable with NISP values from other sources. Other problems with NISP discussed in Chapter 2, such as the effects of differential butchery practices and the potential interdependence of specimens, are also potentially problematic in the NISP values presented. However, NISP is used here simply as a summary of the archaeological assemblages that were analyzed, and not as a basis for drawing conclusions or interpretations from the material. Unfortunately, due to the sample size and size range problems discussed above for the Irish Lord taxon, NISP provides the only available source of quantification for Irish Lords. It is necessary, therefore, to exclude Irish Lords from much of the discussion that follows regarding Aleut culture history and Aleutians biology. Nevertheless, it is apparent from Table 6.15 (p. 58) that Irish Lords are a significant taxon in the sites under consideration, particularly in the Shemya 7 site.

The problems that arise from NISP are largely accounted for through the calculation of MNI values for each taxon from each site. As discussed in Chapter 2, however, MNI is subject to a number of its own problems. One of the major arguments leveled against simple MNI calculations involves the highly conservative nature of the statistic, and the fact that these calculations tend to greatly underestimate the actual or original numbers of individuals represented by an assemblage. For the purposes of this analysis, MNI is calculated simply as a means of comparing the relative abundance of the various taxa, and to provide a basis for the determination of estimated weights for each taxon. Neither actual nor original numbers of individuals are necessary for these purposes. However, following the suggestion of Casteel (1976), lengths estimated using the regression formulae discussed above were employed to better determine the true MNI. The use of estimated lengths allowed for the inclusion in the total MNI of individuals represented in the archaeological assemblage that were not accounted for by the MNI simply determined from the most common skeletal element. This approach had a significant effect on final MNI figures, as in virtually every situation the final MNI was increased from the base MNI determined using White's method (see Chapter 2).

In terms of this project, the generation of weight estimates using the regression approach represents the most important of the forms of quantification applied, particularly for the consideration of Aleut subsistence and culture history. One of the most important conclusions of this thesis arises from a comparison of the results that were obtained in the project through the regression approach to the results that would have been obtained using a more traditional meat weight approach. In Chapter 2, the work of Mitchell (1988) was used as an example of the traditional meat weight approach. Mitchell calculated meat weight by employing a standard average weight for each taxa and simply multiplying that weight by the calculated MNI values (Mitchell 1988). The standard average weights that Mitchell employed were derived from Wigen (1980), who also employs the traditional meat weight approach using these standard average sizes. Wigen provides average weights for four of the taxa considered here: 2268.0g for Pacific cod (*Gadus macrocephalus*), 919.0g for Walleye pollock (*Theragra chalcogramma*), 1337.7g for Rockfish (*Sebastes* sp.), and 485.0g for Greenling (*Hexagrammos* sp.) (Wigen 1980: Table 2, pages 68-72). These averages are in many cases based on very few comparative specimens. Atka Mackerel and Irish Lords are not listed by Wigen (1980), as neither of these taxa were present in the archaeological material that she analyzed. Comparing the four taxa for which average weights are available, however, provides interesting insight into the variability between the traditional meat weight approach and the regression approach employed here. Table 6.18 (p. 59) summarizes the mean estimated weights for each taxon for each of the five Aleutian Islands site that were considered in this thesis. Before comparing these results to the standard average sizes presented by Wigen (1980), it is already apparent that the use of such standard average weights would provide very different results for total weight, as the average weight for each taxon varies considerably from site to site based on the regression approach. The variation between the two approaches is further emphasized when the actual mean or average weight figures are considered, as summarized in

Table 7.1 (p. 68). Beginning with a consideration of Pacific cod, mean estimated weights for Pacific cod based on regression results range from 5150g to 8281g, with a total mean of 5896g (Table 7.1). Regression generated mean weights range from 2.27 to 3.65 times larger than the average weight of 2268.0 g presented by Wigen (1980). Mean weights for Walleye pollock generated through the regression approach range from 1055g to 2184g, with a total mean of 1245g (Table 7.1), 1.15 to 2.38 times larger than the average of 919.0g of Wigen (1980).

Table 7.1 Comparison of Standard Mean Weights (from Wigen 1980) to Regression Estimated Mean Weights. For regression estimated weights, the minimum and maximum mean weights from the various archaeological assemblages are listed along with the mean estimated weight for the archaeological specimens as a whole (Total Mean Weight). All weights are given in grams.

Taxon	Standard Mean Weight (Wigen 1980)	Regression Estimated Weight		
		Total Mean Weight	Minimum Mean Weight	Maximum Mean Weight
Pacific cod	2268.00	5896	5150	8281
Walleye pollock	919.00	1245	1055	2184
Greenling	485.00	644	494	1470
Rockfish	1337.70	2215	784	3380

Greenling range from a mean size of 494g to 1470g, with a total mean of 644g, based on regression (Table 7.1), 1.02 to 3.03 times larger than Wigen's (1980) average of 485.0 g. For these three taxa, then, total weights would have been greatly underestimated in virtually all cases. Rockfish are perhaps the most variable taxon in terms of regression generated mean weights, and the range of 784g to 3380g (Table 7.1) spans the average of 1337.7 g provided by Wigen (1980). In no case, however, does the regression generated mean weight for Rockfish match the average provided by Wigen, nor does Wigen's average match the total regression estimated mean weight of 2215g, and thus the total weight would have been underestimated or overestimated in all cases using the traditional meat weight approach.

Based on this simple comparison, it is clear that the regression approach provides a much more fine grained method for calculating meat weight. The large degree of variability of mean weights from site to site in the Aleutian Islands data is particularly telling. Even if more accurate average weights were generated for each taxon, no single average weight would provide accurate results for all sites using the traditional meat weight approach. The regression approach, then, provides several major advantages over the traditional meat weight approach. First, it allows for an individual by individual comparison of the size of specimens represented in the archaeological sample, allowing for a comparison of the range of sizes represented rather than just the average or total weight represented by an assemblage. Secondly, by extension of this individual-level approach, the regression approach avoids the assumption that "average" sized fish were harvested by all people across different regions and times. As demonstrated by the large variation in mean sizes from the Aleutian Island sites analyzed above, such an assumption is clearly not well founded.

Though the use of regression for estimating the original live size of archaeological fish specimens can address some of these problems encountered in previous approaches, the methodology outlined here is not without its problems. It is important to consider these limitations and potential sources of error before turning to a discussion of the implications of the results for Aleut culture history. Firstly, though fish were very important in Aleut subsistence prehistorically, a number of other resources were also heavily used. The relative importance of fish, sea mammals, birds, invertebrates and plants likely varied considerably from site to site and region to region. Laughlin, however, estimates that fish generally contributed roughly 30 percent of the total Aleut diet (1980: Table 4.2, 49). In only considering fish remains, this project is only analyzing a particular subset of the total subsistence of the Aleut who occupied the sites under consideration. A further limitation of the analysis presented here is that only a selected subset of the total number of fish taxa that are present in the sites has been analyzed. These taxa were selected, however, largely because they represent the most common taxa amongst recently analyzed Aleutian Islands sites, generally comprising in the vicinity of 90 percent or more of the fish remains by NISP (see Table 5.1, p. 24). A further limitation involves the previously discussed problems surrounding the Irish Lord taxon. Despite the relative abundance of Irish Lords in several of the assemblages under consideration based on NISP (Table 6.15, p. 58), the small and unrepresentative sample of comparative specimens for this taxon made further analysis of Irish Lord material impossible.

Another potential source of error in interpretations about Aleut subsistence based on the analysis described above involves the assumption that all of the fish bones that comprise the analyzed assemblages were deposited in the site as a direct result of human subsistence activity. This assumption may not be well founded, as it is likely that some of the remains may have been transported into the sites as stomach contents of directly harvested food items. Pacific cod feed on Walleye pollock, Rockfish, Atka Mackerel and other smaller taxa (Clausen 1981; Bakkala 1984; Kasahara 1961; Yang 1999), and thus could account for the transport of specimens of some of these taxa into the sites being analyzed. Based on stomach content analysis, Bakkala (1984) concludes that pollock represent the most common prey item for Pacific cod in the eastern Bering Sea (cf. Clausen 1981). This was well exemplified by the stomach contents of two Pacific cod that were processed for use as comparative skeletal specimens for this project. Specimen 00/79 had a fork length of 80.0 cm and a weight of 7200 g. Though this specimen is considerably smaller than many of the archaeological specimens, its stomach contained a Walleye pollock with a fork length of 44.5 cm and a weight of 588 g. This cod specimen also contained two small Rockfish with total lengths of 25.0 cm and 20.5 cm, and weights of 188.0 g and 102.8 g respectively. In addition, the stomach of Pacific cod specimen 00/83, which had a fork length of 70.5 cm and a weight of 4700 g, contained a Rockfish with a total length of 19.5 cm and a weight of 85.88 g. All four of these secondary fish were in very good condition, and had clearly not been in the stomachs of these Pacific cod for any appreciable length of time. In fact, the rockfish specimens were themselves processed as comparative specimens (specimens 00/80, 00/81, and 00/84). Clearly, the presence of such fish in the stomachs of even these intermediate-sized Pacific cod has implications for the total fish bone assemblages that ultimately comprise an archaeological site. Clausen, however, indicates that most of the Walleye pollock eaten by Pacific cod are juveniles, ranging from 9 to 25cm long (1981: 969). The good condition of these specimens, however, suggests that such secondary prey may still have contributed to the diet of the Aleut people who were harvesting the large Pacific cod. Of perhaps more concern is the presence of small numbers of bones of almost completely digested fish in the stomachs of these cod specimens as well. Such specimens may have also contributed to the total site assemblage without providing any direct source of food for the site inhabitants. This source of bias is somewhat lessened by Turner's indication that when Pacific cod are processed and dried for winter use, the stomachs are removed and discarded (1886: 90). It is unclear, however, whether the stomach contents would be discarded away from the habitation site or whether these materials may still ultimately form part of the site midden. Large Walleye pollock also feed largely on fish, and thus may also contribute to this potential bias (Dwyer et al. 1987). Similar issues arise from the fact that sea mammals also formed a major source of food for the Aleut people, and the fish taxa considered here were also eaten by sea mammals such as sea lions (Merrick et al. 1997; Yang 1999) and seals (Olesiuk et al. 1990). The stomach contents of these larger predators may also contribute to the

type of bias considered here.

The data and results presented in Chapter 6 can provide insight into Aleut subsistence activities even though several potential sources of error exist in making such interpretations based on the analysis of fish bones described here. At the very least, the relative proportions of the various taxa present in the site assemblages can be determined. It also seems highly likely, however, that these remains do in fact reflect Aleut subsistence activities, and thus the remains will be considered in that context.

7.2 Implications for Aleut Culture History

Ethnographic and archaeological sources of information on the Aleut were reviewed in some detail in Chapter 3. Information on subsistence practices are of particular interest for the interpretation and discussion of the results presented in Chapter 6. As discussed in Chapter 3, Aleut subsistence in prehistoric times was almost exclusively based on maritime resources, and marine fish such as those considered here played a major role in this subsistence. Lantis, for example, highlighted the use of "salmon, halibut, codfish, flounder, herring, sculpin" among a large variety of other resources (1984: 175, emphasis added). The importance of fish was also highlighted by other ethnographic sources such as Coxe (1970), Jochelson (1966), and Turner (1886). A variety of archaeological sources discuss the remains of fish found in other archaeological sites in the Aleutian Islands (Dall 1877b; Jochelson 1975; Laughlin 1963a, 1980; Lefèvre et al. 1997), though as outlined in Chapter 3 these analyses have only briefly discussed the fish remains, and very little work has considered in detail the contributions that various fish taxa have made to Aleut subsistence.

One of the most striking conclusions that can be drawn from the total weights and relative proportions presented in Table 6.19 (p. 60) is the overwhelming dominance of Pacific cod. In contrast to the importance of some of the other taxa when NISP or MNI values are considered (Tables 6.15 and 6.17, pp. 58 and 59), Pacific cod contributed far more to the diet of the occupants of these sites than any of the other taxa considered. This is perhaps not surprising given the large size attained by Pacific cod relative to the other taxa, and the abundance of Pacific cod in the waters surrounding the islands in question (Bakkala et al. 1984; Brown and Wilderbuer 1984; Kasahara 1961). Turner, writing in the late 19th century, indicates that "among the Aleutian Islands, especially on the north side, a hook can scarcely be thrown in the water without taking a Cod" (1886: 89). Despite the abundance of Pacific cod, however, Bakkala indicates that during a large scale survey in 1975 in the eastern Bering Sea, Pacific cod ranked seventh in abundance, falling far behind Walleye pollock (1984: 167; cf. Witherell 1996; Kasahara 1961: 75).

Furthermore, Yang states that "Atka mackerel (*Pleurogrammus monopterygius*) is presently the most abundant marine fish species in the Aleutian Islands" (1999: 1047). It must be emphasized, as discussed below in more detail, that modern distributions and abundances may be a result of pressures from commercial fishing. The particular importance of Pacific cod, however, was also highlighted in other ethnographic and previous archaeological sources as discussed in Chapter 3. Dall (1877b) and Jochelson (1975) indicate that Pacific cod (*Gadus macrocephalus*) are amongst the most common fish species encountered in their early excavations. More recently, Denniston (1974) also highlighted the importance of cod not only amongst the fish resources but amongst all sources of food. Interestingly, many of the sources discussed in Chapter 3 also list halibut as being an equally important fish resource. Halibut, however, is relatively uncommon or completely absent in the sites analyzed here and in other recently analyzed sites in the central and western Aleutian archipelago (Table 5.1, p. 24; Crockford n.d.).

Aside from the general dominance of Pacific cod in all of the sites, the only other generalization that can be made about the assemblages as a whole involves the relative absence of Walleye pollock. In all but one site (Adak 009) Walleye pollock represents the least common of the five taxa listed in Table 6.19 (p. 60), being absent from four of the seven assemblages. It is further possible, as discussed above, that these few specimens of Walleye pollock actually represent the stomach contents of some of the large Pacific cod that are also present in all of these assemblages. The remaining three taxa are all relatively variable in terms of their proportions of the total weight for each site. This variability is largely accounted for when the assemblages are examined along regional or geographic lines.

As indicated above (p. 42), Greenling is the only taxon, aside from Pacific cod, to consistently make a significant contribution to the Adak Island assemblages. Together, Greenling and Pacific cod account for greater than 94 percent of the total fish weight in all of the Adak assemblages. Considering MNI values, in fact, Greenling is for the most part more abundant than Pacific cod in these assemblages (Table 6.17, p. 59). Only very small amounts of Atka Mackerel, Rockfish, and Walleye pollock are present in the Adak sites. This suggests that although all five taxa appear to have been available in the waters surrounding Adak Island, Greenling and Pacific cod may have been available in larger quantities. Alternately, the inhabitants of Adak Island may have been selecting for these taxa through the harvesting techniques they were employing. The possibility of such selectivity is reflected by Jane Balme, who states that "[i]t is well known by fishermen and by fish biologists that different fishing methods select for both size and species" (1983:24). Size

selection is also mentioned by Stewart, who experimented with the use of traditional halibut fishing gear and noticed that "the size of the halibut to be caught could be controlled by the size and angle of the barb, and the size of the hook" (1982: 48). Such selectivity in harvesting techniques likely also existed among the Aleut. Ethnographic sources such as Turner (1886) and Jochelson (1966), for example, describe the techniques that were used by the Aleut to harvest Pacific cod, and Turner (1886) also discusses the harvesting of Greenling. These technological issues are discussed in more detail below.

The Buldir Island assemblage is the only site of the five at which Atka Mackerel makes a substantial contribution to the total fish weight. This suggests that Atka Mackerel may be more common in the vicinity of Buldir Island than in the other regions. Conversely, a relative shortage of other species may result in a greater reliance on Atka Mackerel. This latter possibility may be supported by the lower relative contribution of Pacific cod to the total estimated weight at Buldir, and by the also significant contributions made by both Greenling and Rockfish. It should be noted, however, that the total sample size for all taxa from the Buldir site is the lowest of all of the sites considered, with a total NISP of only 147 specimens. It is possible that the Buldir Island results are somewhat skewed by this small sample size.

Although the Shemya Island sites are again dominated by Pacific cod, they are also, as indicated in Chapter 6 (p. 42), the only two sites to contain all of the five taxa under consideration. It is also worth reiterating that in terms of NISP values, the Irish Lord taxon also makes significant contributions to the assemblages of both of the Shemya Island sites (Table 6.15, p. 58). Due to the comparatively small size of Irish Lords (Hart 1973: 502-504; Peden 1978), however, it is likely that Pacific cod would continue to dominate both assemblages in terms of total estimated weight even if Irish Lords were included in these calculations. Aside from Pacific cod and Rockfish, the assemblages of the two Shemya Island sites are virtually identical in terms of the relative contributions of the various taxa to the total estimated weight from each site. Rockfish is considerably more common at the Shemya 2 site than at Shemya 7, or at any of the other sites, contributing greater than 20 percent of the total estimated weight (Table 6.19, p. 60). This difference may relate to the slightly different locations of the two sites, with Sheyma 2 located on the northern coast of Shemya Island, and Shemya 7 located on the southern coast (p. 21; Corbett n.d.; Siegel-Causey *et al.* n.d.). Alternately, this may represent a slight temporal change in resource utilization, as there is a temporal gap between the oldest date of 1980±60 uncalibrated radiocarbon years B.P. for Shemya 2 and the youngest date of 2570±140 uncalibrated radiocarbon years B.P. for Sheyma 7 (Corbett n.d.).

Aside from this possible temporal variation, there is little basis for suggesting that major temporal changes occurred in the use of the five taxa under consideration. The radiocarbon dates for each of the sites are summarized in Table 7.2. The majority of the variability between sites appears to follow regional divisions quite well. The small amount of intra-island variability that is seen in the Adak Island assemblages does not appear to follow any obvious temporal trends. There is a slight indication that the use of Rockfish may be a recent development on Adak Island and that the use of Atka Mackerel may have decreased over time, though only small amounts of either taxa are present, and thus the trends may reflect sample size rather than true temporal trends. If the material from all five sites are considered purely along temporal lines, temporal trends remain scarce, with the use of the various taxa fluctuating somewhat but not showing any obvious trends. The only exception to this is that Walleye pollock is only present in sites older than roughly 1000 radiocarbon years B.P., but this is again based on a very small sample of Walleye pollock. Overall, it seem more likely that the variation between sites is a result of regional or geographic differences rather than temporal differences.

As discussed in Chapter 2 (section 2.5) it is often possible, through the type of faunal analysis presented here, to make conclusions about the technologies and methods that were employed by prehistoric populations for the harvesting of fish resources, and the seasons during which these species were harvested. Given the range of taxa and sizes of fish represented in the sites analyzed here, it is likely that a variety of techniques were employed in the harvesting of fish by the occupants of the sites under consideration. Ethnographic sources on the various fishing techniques employed by the Aleut people were discussed in Chapter 3 (pp. 14). Most of these sources focus on the use of hook and line technology from boats for the harvesting of deep sea fishes including Pacific cod (Jochelson 1966: 11; Veniaminov 1984: 361; Makarova 1975: 79), and do not specifically address the techniques used to harvest inshore fishes. Laughlin and Aigner briefly indicate that fishing was also done with lines from shore (1975: 184-185). Turner (1886) provides more detailed accounts of the techniques employed in the harvesting of specific taxa by the Aleut. The techniques described by Turner, however, involve those that he witnessed in the late 19th century, and may not represent the same techniques that were employed prehistorically. He indicates that cod are typically caught from boats at cod banks several miles from the shore (1886: 90). Greenling are generally harvested from shore, often by

Table 7.2 Summary of radiocarbon dates for the sites and assemblages under consideration. Only the oldest and most recent date available for each assemblage is listed, but dates do not necessarily represent the true maximum or minimum dates for the assemblage as a whole. Where no direct dates are available for the analyzed material, stratigraphically bounding dates are provided where possible. Dates are given as uncalibrated radiocarbon years B.P. (before present). All dates are from Corbett (n.d.).

Site/Assemblage		Minimum Date	Maximum Date
Adak 009		1040±70	1240±90 (1710±70 intrusive?)
Adak 011	HP1 - EU1		440±40*
	HP1 - EU2		< 2490±50**
	HP2	180±60	220±50
Buldir 008		220±60	390±80
Shemya 2		1700±70	1980±60
Shemya 7		2570±140	3096±155

* The date of 440±40 years B.P. for Adak 011 Housepit 1, Excavation Unit 1 is the only date from this assemblage, and it was taken from the lowest level of the assemblage.

** There are no direct dates from the levels analyzed from Adak 011 Housepit 1, Excavation Unit 2. The date of 2490±50 years B.P. comes from a level located stratigraphically below the material that was analyzed here.

women and children (Turner 1886: 95-96). Turner describes the harvesting of Atka Mackerel in some detail. He indicates that they are typically harvested in the spring and summer months, at which time they inhabit the passes between the islands of the Aleutians for spawning purposes (Turner 1886: 96). The techniques for harvesting the spawning Atka Mackerel involve the use of a gig or gaff to impale the fish that school in large numbers in the spawning grounds (Turner 1886: 97).

The use of biological and ecological information on the taxa being studied can contribute to interpretations about the technologies and approaches employed by the occupants of the sites being studied. Consideration of information on the biology and ecology of Pacific cod, for example, allows for seasonality of resource use to be evaluated. It is widely known and reported in the literature that Pacific cod follow seasonal migration patterns. During the winter, they migrate into deep water where spawning takes place, and in the spring and summer, they migrate into shallow waters to feed (Vinnikov 1996: 185). According to Vinnikov, Pacific cod in the Bering Sea concentrate at depths between 150 and 410 m during the winter (1996: 185). As surface waters warm in the spring and summer, these deep schools of fish begin to migrate into shallower waters. The timing of this migration depends on water temperatures, but by mid-May to early June cod may be caught at depths less than 100 m (Vinnikov 1996: 186).

It is highly unlikely that the prehistoric occupants of the sites were able to harvest the deep water winter fish, and thus the large numbers of cod that were harvested were likely taken in the summer months. Jochelson verifies this conclusion, indicating that the Aleut people went to sea in the summer months to harvest Pacific cod (1966: 11). This is significant in terms of seasonal changes in subsistence resources. Though schools of cod migrate into relatively shallow waters in the summer months, they remain quite deep. This is further emphasized when one considers the large size of many of the fish found in the analysed assemblages. According to Vinnikov, juvenile fish prefer shallow waters while larger fish are found at depths of 50 to 200 m during the summer (1996: 193). Alverson suggests that summer catches range from 11 to 90 fathoms, or roughly 20 to 165 m, but does not consider the distribution of fish of different sizes (1960: 22). In general, Aleutian Islands tend to be surrounded by shallow water and reefs which may extend for some distance from the shore (eg. Siegel-Causey *et al.* n.d.), and thus it is unlikely that larger Pacific Cod would be found particularly close to shore. It seems likely, therefore, that boats were a necessity for the prehistoric harvesting of Pacific cod. Also, lines or nets would have been required to reach the relatively deep fish.

Such technological implications derived from faunal remains may be particularly useful in making interpretations of the artifact assemblages at the sites being studied. As discussed in Chapter 2 (p. 9), for example, the selectivity of certain types of fishing gear for certain sizes or species of fish is common (Stewart 1982; Balme 1983; Greenspan 1998). When minimum technological requirements for the harvesting of certain sizes and/or taxa of fish are established, as described above for Pacific cod, it is likely that artifactual evidence of these technologies will also be present in the sites being analysed. I have not had access, however, to artifactual materials from the five sites being considered in this thesis.

Other taxa are somewhat less informative in these respects than are Pacific cod. As mentioned above, Turner (1886) indicated that Atka Mackerel were also harvested seasonally, being easily accessible in nearshore waters in the spring and summer months. This is supported by McDermott and Lowe, who state that "during much of the year, Atka mackerel are pelagic but migrate annually from the lower edge of the continental shelf to shallow coastal waters where they spawn demersally[19]" (1997: 321). They further add that the period of spawning for Atka mackerel

can last from July through October (McDermott and Lowe 1997: 331; cf. Zolotov 1993). A variety of techniques may have been employed for harvesting these seasonally abundant fish, though it is perhaps likely that a form of the gaffing technique, described by Turner (1886: 97) for the late 19th century, was used prehistorically as well.

Walleye pollock follow similar behavioural patterns to Pacific cod (Thompson 1981), and would likely be available through the same techniques, though the very small sample of pollock present in these assemblages suggests that they were not targeted as a major food source. Rather, the few Walleye pollock specimens that are present may have been harvested as a byproduct of the Pacific cod fishery, or may have been deposited in the sites as secondary prey items as discussed above. The various species of Greenling, Irish Lord, and Rockfish that are present in the Aleutian Island region occupy a variety of habitats, though these taxa are generally found in relatively nearshore waters and may be found from the surface to depths of several hundred metres (Hart 1973; Peden 1978). These taxa may thus have been obtained through a variety of methods, ranging from collection and line fishing from shore to the deep-sea fishing required for Pacific cod harvesting.

7.3 Biological Implications

In considering the biological implications of the results presented here, it is important to remember the warning of Wheeler, that modern distributions of fish may be a response to modern intensive harvesting (1978: 74). This warning is also of relevance to the discussions in the previous section, as many of the cultural implications of the results were made in relation to the distribution of the various fish taxa. Commercial fishing may have played a major role in the modern distributions of several of the taxa discussed here. For the Aleutian Islands, Alverson states that commercial exploitation began in that area in the latter part of the 19th Century, and Pacific cod has been one of the most important species taken in the trawl fishery (1960: 21-22). This is further emphasized by Brown and Wilderbuer (1984), who state that a commercial fishery for Pacific cod in the Aleutian region began in the 1870s and has continued in one form or another to the present (cf. Bakkala 1984; Kasahara 1961). Walleye pollock has also been a major target of commercial fisheries in the region (Bakkala 1984; Thompson 1981). Atka Mackerel has become an increasingly important commercial species in recent years (Lowe *et al.* 1998; McDermott and Lowe 1997; Efimov 1984), with the commercial Aleutian Island catch increasing from approximately 15,000 metric tons in 1980 to 81,000 metric tons in 1995 (Witherell 1996). Alverson (1960) also mentions that Rockfish have been targeted by commercial fisheries at times, and the Rockfish fishery is further emphasized by Witherell (1996).

---

19. Pelagic refers to species that live in the open ocean. Demersal refers to the bottom of the ocean. Atka Mackerel spawn on the sea floor in shallow coastal waters.

In considering the size of the archaeological fish specimens relative to modern data, Pacific cod again appear to be of the most interest. It is apparent from the estimated sizes of the archaeological samples that many of the Pacific cod specimens were quite large, some reaching and even surpassing the upper limits of the modern size distribution of Pacific cod. As mentioned above, Hart indicates that Pacific cod grow up to one metre in length (1973:223), while Vinnikov speaks of cod up to 118 centimeters in length (1996:188). It is possible, however, that the large size of the archaeological specimens represents a local variation in size that may still be present today. A study done by Wilimovsky, Peden and Peppar provides evidence that Pacific cod from the Aleutians are generally slightly larger than specimens from the Bering Sea, S. E. Alaska, or British Columbia (1967: 32). Ketchen states that the lifespan of cod in colder northern waters is longer than that of fish along the southern coast of British Columbia (1964: 1051), and that may account somewhat for the larger size seen in the area of the Aleutians.

The generally large size of the archaeological specimens of Pacific cod has important implications for the ecology of Pacific cod. Females are generally larger than males, due to the earlier maturation and shorter lifespan of males (Vinnikov 1996: 187). According to Vinnikov, "[f]emales make up about 50% of the 65 cm long fish; however, their proportion rapidly increases among larger fish, and fish 95-100 cm long are 100% female" (1996: 187). Based on these figures, a large proportion of the fish represented in the archaeological assemblages were likely female. Assuming that fish less than 65 cm were 50% female, fish greater than 95cm were 100% female, and fish between 65 and 95 cm were roughly 75% female, 69% of the archaeological Pacific cod individuals are female. This is significant as a larger proportion of the larger females are sexually mature, and larger females produce far more eggs, and thus produce more offspring, that do younger females. The scale of this is reflected by Hart, who states that "[a]t 60 centimeters a female may produce 1.2 million eggs, at 78 centimeters 3.3 million" (1973: 223). A total of 22 of the 215 archaeologically represented Pacific cod individuals are greater than 95 cm in length, and fish of such size are responsible for contributing a very large proportion of the total eggs during the spawning season. If many of the large females were being harvested, then this may have affected the size of fish or the size of cod populations on the local level. Similar patterns may also occur among some of the other taxa considered here, as DeMartini and Patten indicate that for the Red Irish Lord (*H. hemilepidotus*), "breeding females were longer...than breeding males...and twice as heavy as males" (1979). As estimated lengths and weights were not generated for Irish Lords, it is not possible to assess the implications of this sexual dimorphism. Zolotov (1993) also records an increase in egg production with increased body size for Atka mackerel.

Aside from Pacific cod, the taxa under consideration typically fall well within the expected size ranges, and are not particularly unusual in terms of their size or distributions. Atka Mackerel are listed by Jordan and Evermann as reaching a length of 18 inches (ca. 45cm) and a weight of 3 to 4 pounds (1.4 to 1.8kg) (1898: 1866). Other sources suggest that Atka Mackerel reach lengths of 50cm (Eschmeyer *et al.* 1983: 157). Jordan and Everman further indicate that Atka Mackerel are abundant around certain Aleutian Islands, particularly Atka (near Adak) and Attu (near Shemya) (1898: 1866). Others indicate that Atka Mackerel are found throughout the Aleutian Archipelago (Yang 1999; McDermott and Lowe 1997; Eschmeyer *et al.* 1983), and Lowe *et al.* state that the Aleutian Islands form the center of abundance for this species (1998: 502). McDermott and Lowe also found that for Atka Mackerel, size at 50% maturity ranged from 33cm to 38cm (1997: 329). The archaeological specimens of Atka Mackerel span this range, and thus may represent a mix of adult and sub-adult individuals.

Several Greenling species are found in the Aleutian Islands region, including *Hexagrammos octogrammus, H. decagrammus*, *H. lagocephalus*, *H. stelleri*, and *H. superciliosus* (Hart 1973: 461-467; Eschmeyer *et al.* 1983: 155-157; Lamb and Edgell 1986: 126-128; Jordan and Evermann 1898: 1867-1875; DeMartini 1986). The size attained by these species ranges from 28cm to 61cm according to Eschmeyer and colleagues (1983: 155-156; cf. Hart 1973: 461-467). It is relevant to note that Crockford (n.d.) suggests that the majority of the archaeological specimens of Greenling identified from the Aleutian sites under consideration represent the Rock Greenling, *H. lagocephalus*, which attains a length of up to 61cm according to Eschmeyer *et al.* (1983). The archaeological specimens of greenling generally fall below this maximum size, with only a single specimen from Buldir Island exceeding 61cm in estimated length.

A number of Irish Lord species are also common among the Aleutian Islands, including *Hemilepidotus jordani*, *H. hemilepidotus*, *H. zapus*, and *H. gilberti* (Peden 1978; Eschmeyer *et al.* 1983; Lamb and Edgell 1986: 166; Hart 1973: 502-503; Jordan and Evermann 1898: 1932-1936). In fact, Jordan and Evermann state that *H. jordani*, the Yellow Irish Lord, was "much valued by the Aleuts as a food-fish" (1898: 1935). As Irish Lord specimens were not included in size estimations, it is not possible to compare archaeological sizes to those reported from modern times.

As discussed above, Rockfish represent a very abundant and diverse taxon. Eschmeyer and colleagues identify 11 species of Rockfish that occur in the Aleutian Islands, with maximum sizes ranging from 32 to 96cm (1983: 132-152). Hart lists 9 Aleutian Islands species of Rockfish, with maximum lengths ranging from 32.4 to 71cm (1973: 388-

451). As is expected from this wide range of species present in the study region, the archaeological Rockfish specimens are very variable in terms of estimated lengths. The majority of the archaeological specimens fall well below the maximum published length for Rockfish, though a single specimen from the Shemya 2 site has an estimated length of 98.8cm.

Walleye pollock are also found throughout the Aleutian Islands, and are recorded as having a maximum size of 91cm (Eschmeyer *et al.* 1983: 98; Hart 1973: 228-229; Lamb and Edgell 1986: 43). As has been emphasized above, the archaeological sample of Walleye pollock is particularly small, and thus is not particularly informative, nor is it necessarily representative of the prehistoric populations that were being harvested. Nevertheless, it is interesting to note that the archaeological specimens all fall well below the maximum recorded size for pollock. This may provide additional support for the possibility that pollock entered the sites as secondary prey items as discussed above.

There is also some slight evidence for regional and temporal differences in the average size of the various taxa under consideration. This is evidenced through a comparison of the average weights of each taxon for each archaeological assemblage listed in Table 6.18 (p. 59) with the radiocarbon ages of these assemblages as summarized in Table 7.2 (p. 71). Pacific cod, for example, appear to be smaller on Adak Island, with the average weight being considerably larger on Buldir Island and somewhat intermediate in size on Shemya Island. This may be somewhat biased, however, by the particularly small sample size of Pacific cod from Buldir Island (Table 6.17, p. 59). There appear to be no general temporal trends visible in the Pacific cod data, though on Shemya Island there is an increase in the average weight of Pacific cod from the earlier Shemya 7 site to the more recent Shemya 2 site. The average size of Greenling also show some general trends, with Adak Island again showing the smallest average fish and Buldir representing the largest. Shemya Island is more variable in terms of average size. There also appears to be a general trend across all of the assemblages of an increase in the average size of Greenling in more recent times. Atka Mackerel do not show any obvious regional or temporal trends, though there is a very weak indication from Adak Island that Atka Mackerel in older deposits are slightly larger. Rockfish are equally uninformative, being variable in terms of average weight on both regional and temporal scales. The large degree of variability in average weight of Rockfish in the different assemblages may reflect the use of different species of Rockfish in different regions or at different times. As mentioned previously, the large number of Rockfish species present in the Aleutian Islands region vary considerably in terms of their size (Hart 1973: 394-447).

CHAPTER 8. SUMMARY AND CONCLUSIONS

The reconstruction of prehistoric human diet can provide insight into maritime adaptations and into the ecological role of the people involved. Faunal remains from archaeological sites comprise one of the best, and in many cases the only, source of data on prehistoric human diet. Despite this potential, faunal remains are often undervalued, and thus under analyzed, as an important source of cultural and biological information. Often faunal analyses do not go beyond the calculation of quantification figures such as the number of identified specimens present (NISP) and the minimum number of individuals (MNI), though more advanced techniques such as the one applied here hold much greater potential for contributing to archaeological interpretation. This project has applied statistical regression as a means of generating detailed size estimations of archaeological fish specimens. The regression technique was tested in the context of an Aleutian Islands case study.

The Aleutian Archipelago is unique in terms of its isolation and environment, and this environment formed the basis for much of the highly maritime adapted culture of the Aleut people. Thus, the Aleutian Islands form a particularly interesting region for the study of human adaptation, and particularly of human diet and resource exploitation. Ethnographic sources emphasize the extreme marine dependency of the Aleut people, and document the use of fish resources among other fauna. Previous archaeological research has further emphasized this maritime adaptation, though surprisingly fish remains have been largely under-studied.

This thesis attempted to take advantage of the greater potential of more advanced analytical methods of faunal analysis such as statistical regression to contribute to an understanding of Aleutian culture history. In particular, the relatively under analyzed fish remains from sites in the central and western Aleutians are considered. Specifically, five sites were analyzed, including two sites on Shemya Island, one site on Buldir Island, and two sites on Adak Island.

The methodology defined for this thesis problem involved two major components, namely the generation of regression formulae from comparative data and the archaeological application of those regression formulae. Comparative data were gathered for six fish taxa known to be particularly common in Aleutian Islands archaeological assemblages. These included Atka Mackerel (*Pleurogrammus monopterygius*), Greenling (*Hexagrammos* sp.), Irish Lords (*Hemilepidotus* sp.), Pacific cod (*Gadus macrocephalus*), Rockfish (*Sebastes* sp.), and Walleye pollock (*Theragra chalcogramma*). For each of these taxa, regression formulae were generated comparing length and weight to

specific bone measurements.

Archaeological materials from the five archaeological sites were first identified and then measured using the same variables applied to the comparative data. Irish Lords were excluded from further analysis due to small comparative sample size and the large size of the archaeological specimens compared to the comparative size range. For the remaining taxa, regression formulae were first used to estimate the original live length of each archaeological specimen, and these lengths were used to aid in the determination of MNI values for each taxon from each archaeological assemblage. Finally, for each individual fish contributing to the calculated MNI values, weight was estimated and these weights provided a basis for assessing the relative contributions that each taxon made to the diet of the inhabitants of each site.

The results of this analysis allowed for a number of interesting conclusions to be drawn. One of the most important conclusions of this research involves the comparison of the regression approach for calculating meat weight to the approach that has more typically been used (see Table 7.1, p. 68). From such a comparison it is clear that the regression approach provides a much more fine grained method for calculating weights. First, variability in the size of specimens caught at different sites is not accounted for by the traditional meat weight approach. The regression approach, however, avoids the assumption that only average sized fish were always harvested. Furthermore, the regression approach allows for an individual by individual comparison of the weight of different fish, which thus gives a view of the range of sizes harvested.

The results of this thesis analysis also provided insight into aspects of Aleut culture history. In terms of diet, the total estimated weight per taxon was used to compare the relative proportions of the analyzed taxa in the various archaeological assemblages (see Table 6.19, p. 60). From this comparison, Pacific cod dominated all of the analyzed assemblages. This is perhaps not surprising, however, given the large size of Pacific cod and the emphasis on this taxon in ethnographic accounts and previous archaeological work. The comparison of the total estimated weights also revealed some interesting regional differences. Aside from the dominance of Pacific cod, Greenling is the only taxon to make a significant contribution to Adak Island assemblages. On Buldir Island, Atka Mackerel makes a substantial contribution, followed by smaller, but significant amounts of Greenling and Rockfish. And finally, the Shemya Island Sites show the greatest diversity, being the only assemblages to contain all of the analyzed taxa. The two Shemya Island site also show some intra-island variability, with the Shemya 2 site containing much more Rockfish by weight than the Shemya 7 site, corresponding to relatively less Pacific cod at the Shemya 2 site. This may represent local ecological variability, as the two Shemya sites are located on opposite sides of the island. Alternately, the difference may represent temporal variability, as the Shemya 2 assemblage dates considerably younger than the Shemya 7 assemblage (see Table 7.2, p. 71). It is also significant that the relative contributions of the various taxa based on regression-estimated weights differ considerably from the relative contributions based on NISP or MNI.

A final major conclusion that follows from the analysis presented above involves the possibility that biological changes may be represented in the archaeological faunal assemblages. In particular, the very large size of many of the Pacific cod specimens is interesting, as the archaeological Pacific cod range up to and beyond the modern published size limits. There is some biological research that suggests that Aleutians Islands populations of Pacific cod may be larger than populations from elsewhere in the Bering Sea and North Pacific. Nevertheless, the large size of Pacific cod is significant as large Pacific cod tend to be female, and larger females produce far more eggs than smaller females. If a large number of large females were being harvested, as appears to be indicated archaeologically, then the effect on the reproductive potential of local cod populations may have resulted in changes to the local population structure.

Statistical regression, then, provides a technique for estimating weights that is far more fine grained than traditional meat weight approaches. The regression formulae and comparative data sets that have been compiled in this thesis provide a powerful analytical tool that may now be easily applied by subsequent researchers to the estimation of the lengths and weights of their own archaeological samples of these six taxa from contexts throughout the Northern Pacific. In addition, aside from the archaeological applicability of this approach, as demonstrated here, the detailed size estimation possible using the regression approach is also very valuable for other areas of study. Collaborative work between Tonya Zeppelin and Katherine Call of the National Marine Mammal Laboratory, Seattle, WA, and myself, for example, involves the application of the regression data presented in this thesis to the analysis of sea lion diet for the purposes of fisheries management. The technique would be equally valuable for other biological and paleontological studies. Ideally, comparative data sets of the type gathered and analyzed here will be compiled for all taxa that occur throughout the Aleutians and along the Northwest Coast. Such an expanded data set would facilitate the application of the methodology outlined here to *all* fish remains from faunal assemblages. The cautionary notes and

methodological conclusions presented here will aid in such future projects.

REFERENCES CITED

Acheson, Steven. (1998). *In the Wake of the* ya'aats' xaatgaay *['Iron People']: A study of changing settlement patterns among the Kunghit Haida.* Oxford: British Archaeological Reports International Series 711, BAR Publishing.

Aigner, Jean S. (1976). "Early Holocene Evidence for the Aleut Maritime Adaptation." *Arctic Anthropology* 13(2): 32-45.

(1985). "Early Arctic Settlements in North America." *Scientific American* 253(11): 160-169.

Aigner, Jean S., and Alan M. Bieber, Jr. (1976). "Preliminary Analysis of Stone Tool Distributions and Activity Zonation at Anangula, an 8500 B.P. Coastal Village in the Aleutian Islands, Alaska." *Arctic Anthropology* 13(2): 46-59.

Aigner, Jean S., Bruce Fullem, Douglas Veltre and Mary Veltre. (1976). "Preliminary Reports on Remains from Sandy Beach Bay, a 4300-5600 B.P. Aleut Village." *Arctic Anthropology* 13(2): 83-90.

Allen, Jim, and J. B. M. Guy. (1984). "Optimal estimations of individuals in archaeological faunal assemblages: how minimal is the MNI?" *Archaeology in Oceania* 19: 41-47.

Alverson, Dayton L. (1960). "A Study of Annual and Seasonal Bathymetric Catch Patterns for Commercially Important Groundfishes of the Pacific Northwest Coast of North America." *Pacific Marine Fisheries Commission Bulletin 4.*

Ames, Kenneth M. (1994). "The Northwest Coast: Complex Hunter-Gatherers, Ecology, and Social Evolution." *Annual Review of Anthropology* 23: 209-229.

(1998). "Economic Prehistory of the Northern British Columbia Coast." *Arctic Anthropology* 35(1): 68-87.

Bakkala, Richard G. (1984). "Pacific Cod of the Eastern Bering Sea." *International North Pacific Fisheries Commission, Bulletin* Number 42: 157-179.

Bakkala, R., S. Westrheim, S. Mishima, C. Zhang, and E. Brown. (1984). "Distribution of Pacific Cod (*Gadus macrocephalus*) in the North Pacific Ocean." *International North Pacific Fisheries Commission, Bulletin* Number 42: 111-115.

Balme, Jane. (1983). "Prehistoric Fishing in the Lower Darling, Western New South Wales," in Caroline Grigson and Juliet Clutton-Brock (eds.) *Animals and Archaeology: 2. Shell Middens, Fishes and Birds*, pp 19-32. Oxford: B.A.R.

Bank, Theodore P., II. (1953). "Cultural Succession in the Aleutians." *American Antiquity* 19(1): 40-49.

(1977). "The Aleuts: Clues to Their Origin." *Explorers Journal* 55(4): 168-171.

Barrett, James H. (1994). "Bone Weight and the Intra-class Comparison of Fish Taxa." in W. Van Neer (ed.) *Fish Exploitation in the Past: Proceedings of the 7th* meeting of the ICAZ Fish Remains Working Group, pp. 3-15. Annales du Musee Royal de l'Afrique Centrale, Sciences Zoologiques no. 274, Tervuren.

(1997). "Diagnostic elements and Diagnostic Zones for Recording Fish Assemblages." Paper presented at the North Atlantic Biocultural Organization, Zooarchaeological Working Group Meeting, January 1997, New York.

Bergsland, Knut. (1959). *Aleut Dialects of Atka and Attu.* Transactions of the American Philosophical Society (N.S.), Volume 49, Part 3. Philadelphia: The American Philosophical Society.

Berkh, Vasilii Nikolaevich. (1974). *A Chronological History of the Discovery of the Aleutian Islands or The Exploits of Russian Merchants.* Translation of the original Russian version published in 1823. Kingston: The Limestone Press.

Bernick, Kathryn, and Rebecca J. Wigen. (1990). "Seasonality of the Little Qualicum River West Site." *Northwest Anthropological Research Notes* 24(2): 153-159.

Bertram, Douglas F., and David W. Nagorsen. (1995). "Introduced Rats, *Rattus* spp., on the Queen Charlotte Islands: Implications for Seabird Conservation." *The Canadian Field-Naturalist* 109: 6-10.

Black, Lydia T. (1981). "Volcanism as a Factor in Human Ecology: The Aleutian Case." *Ethnohistory* 28(4): 313-340.

(1983). "Some Problems in the Interpretation of Aleut Prehistory." *Arctic Anthropology* 20(1): 49-78.

(1984). *Atka: An Ethnohistory of the Western Aleutians.* Alaska History, No. 24. Kingston: The Limestone Press.

(1998). "Animal World of the Aleuts." *Arctic Anthropology* 35(2): 126-135.

Black, Lydia T., and R. G. Liapunova. (1988). "Aleut: Islanders of the North Pacific," in William W. Fitzhugh and Aron Crowell (eds.) *Crossroads of Continents: Cultures of Siberia and Alaska*, pp. 52-57. Washington, D.C.: Smithsonian Institution Press.

Black, Robert F., and William S. Laughlin. (1964). "Anangula: A Geologic Interpretation of the Oldest Archeologic Site in the Aleutians." *Science* 143: 1321-1322.

Bökönyi, S. (1970). "A New Method for the Determination of the Number of Individuals in Animal Bone Material." *American Journal of Archaeology* 74: 291-292.

Bouchet, F., C. Lefevre, D. West, and D. Corbett. (1999). "First Paleoparasitological Analysis of a Midden in the Aleutian Islands (Alaska): Results and Limits." *Journal of Parasitology* 85: 369-372.

Bouchet, F., D. West, C. Lefevre, and D. Corbett. (2001). "Identification of Parsitoses in a Child Burial from

Adak Island (Central Aleutian Islands, Alaska)." *Comptes Rendus de l'Academie des Sciences, Series III, Sciences de la Vie* 324: 123-127.

Breen, Paul A., Trudy A. Carson, J. Bristol Foster, and E. Ann Stewart. (1982). "Changes in Subtidal Community Structure Associated with British Columbia Sea Otter Transplants." *Marine Ecology - Progress Series* 7: 13-20.

Brown, Eric S., and Thomas Wilderbuer. (1984). "Information on Pacific Cod from Results of a Trawl Survey of Groundfish in the Aleutian Islands Region." *International North Pacific Fisheries Commission, Bulletin* Number 42: 200-213.

Cannon, Debbi Yee. (1987). *Marine Fish Osteology: A Manual for Archaeologists*. Burnaby: Archaeology Press, Simon Fraser University.

Cannon, Aubrey. (1991). *The Economic Prehistory of Namu*. Burnaby: Archaeology Press, Simon Fraser University.

Cannon, Aubrey, Henry P. Schwarcz, and Martin Knyf. (1999). "Marine-based Subsistence Trends and the Stable Isotope Analysis of Dog Bones from Namu, British Columbia." *Journal of Archaeological Science* 26: 399-407.

Casteel, Richard W. (1971). "Differential Bone Destruction: Some Comments." *American Antiquity* 36(4): 466-469.

(1974a). "A Method for Estimation of Live Weight of Fish from the Size of Skeletal Elements." *American Antiquity* 39(1): 94-98.

(1974b). "Use of Pacific Salmon Otoliths for Estimating Fish Size, with a Note on the Size of Late Pleistocene and Pliocene Salmonids." *Northwest Science* 48(3): 175-179.

(1974c). "On the Number and Sizes of Animals in Archaeological Faunal Assemblages." *Archaeometry* 16(2): 238-243.

(1976). *Fish Remains in Archaeology and Paleo-environmental Studies*. New York: Academic Press Inc.

(1977a). "Characterization of Faunal Assemblages and the Minimum Number of Individuals Determined from Paired Elements: Continuing Problems in Archaeology." *Journal of Archaeological Science* 4: 125-134.

(1977b). "A comparison of methods for back-calculation of fish size from the size of scales found in archaeological sites." *OSSA* 3/4: 129-139.

(1977c). "A consideration of the behaviour of the minimum number of individuals index: A problem in faunal characterization." *OSSA* 3/4: 141-151.

(1978). "Faunal Assemblages and the "Wiegemethode" or Weight Method." *Journal of Field Archaeology* 5: 71-77.

Casteel, Richard W., and Donald K. Grayson. (1977). "Terminological Problems in Quantitative Faunal Analysis." *World Archaeology* 9(2): 235-242.

Chaplin, Raymond E. (1965). "Animals in Archaeology." *Antiquity* 39: 204-211.

(1971). *The Study of Animal Bones from Archaeological Sites*. London: Seminar Press.

Chisholm, Brian S., D. Erle Nelson, and Henry P. Schwarcz. (1982). "Stable-Carbon Isotope Ratios as a Measure of Marine Versus Terrestrial Protein in Ancient Diets." *Science* 216: 1131-1132.

Clason, A. T. (1986). "Fish and Archaeology," in D. C. Brinkhuizen and A. T. Clason (eds.) *Fish and Archaeology: Studies in Osteometry, Taphonomy, Seasonality and Fishing Methods*, pp 1-7. Oxford: B. A. R.

Clausen, David M. (1981). "Summer Food of Pacific Cod, *Gadus macrocephalus*, in Coastal Waters of Southeastern Alaska." *Fishery Bulletin* 78(4): 968-973.

Colley, Sarah. (1983). "Interpreting Prehistoric Fishing Strategies: An Orkney Case Study," in Caroline Grigson and Juliet Clutton-Brock (eds.) *Animals and Archaeology: 2. Shell Middens, Fishes and Birds*, pp. 157-171. Oxford: B.A.R.

Collins, Henry B., Jr. (1945). "The Islands and their People," in Henry B. Collins, Jr., Austin H. Clark, and Egbert H. Walker, *The Aleutian Islands: Their People and Natural History*. Smithsonian Institution War Background Studies Number Twenty-One, pp. 1-30. Washington: Smithsonian Institution.

(1977). "Eskimo Art," in *The Far North: 2000 Years of American Eskimo and Indian Art*, pp. 1-25. Bloomington: Indiana University Press.

Cook, S. F., and A. E. Treganza. (1950). "The Quantitative Investigation of Indian Mounds." *University of California Publications in American Archaeology and Ethnology* 40: 223-262.

Corbett, Debra G. (n.d.). Several written personal communications. February through April 2001.

Corbett, Debra G., Christine Lefevre, and Douglas Siegel-Causey. (1997a). "The Western Aleutians: Cultural Isolation and Environmental Change." *Human Ecology* 25(3): 459-479.

Corbett, Debra G., Christine Lefevre, Thomas J. Corbett, Dixie West, and Douglas Siegel-Causey. (1997b). "Excavations at KIS-008, Buldir Island: Evaluation and Potential." *Arctic Anthropology* 34(2): 100-117.

Coxe, William. (1970). *Account of the Russian Discoveries between Asia and America*. (Reprint of Third Edition, 1787.) New York: Augustus M. Kelley, Publishers.

Coy, Jennie. (1978). "Comparative Collections for Zooarchaeology," in D. R. Brothwell, K. D. Thomas, and Juliet Clutton-Brock (eds.) *Research Problems in Zooarchaeology*. Occasional Publication No. 3, pp. 143-145. London: Institute of Archaeology.

Crockford, Susan Janet. (1997). "Archeological Evidence

of Large Northern Bluefin Tuna, *Thunnus thynnus*, in Coastal Waters of British Columbia and Northern Washington." *Fishery Bulletin* 95: 11-24.

(n.d.). Unpublished data from analysis of fish remains from several sites in the western Aleutian Islands. Data in the possession of the author.

Croes, Dale R. (1992). "Exploring Prehistoric Subsistence Change on the Northwest Coast." *Research in Economic Anthropology*, Supplement 6, pp. 337-366.

Crowell, Aron L. (1997). *Archaeology and the Capitalist World System: A Study from Russian America.* New York: Plenum Press.

Dall, W. H. (1870). *Alaska and Its Resources.* London: Sampson Low, Son, and Marston.

(1877a). "On the Distribution and Nomenclature of the Native Tribes of Alaska and the Adjacent Territory." *Contributions to North American Ethnology, Vol. 1, Part 1: Tribes of the Extreme Northwest*, Pages 7-40. Department of the Interior, U. S. Geographical and Geological Survey of the Rocky Mountain Region. Washington: Government Printing Office.

(1877b). "On Succession in the Shell-Heaps of the Aleutian Islands." *Contributions to North American Ethnology, Vol. 1, Part 1: Tribes of the Extreme Northwest*, Pages 41-91. Department of the Interior, U. S. Geographical and Geological Survey of the Rocky Mountain Region. Washington: Government Printing Office.

(1885). "The Native Tribes of Alaska." An address before the Section of Anthropology of the American Association for the Advancement of Science, at Ann Arbor, August, 1885. From the *Proceedings of the American Association for the Advancement of Science*, Vol. 34, Pages 3-19. Salem: Salem Press.

Daly, Patricia. (1969). "Approaches to Faunal Analysis in Archaeology." *American Antiquity* 34(2): 146-153.

DeMartini, Edward E. (1986). "Reproductive Colorations, Paternal Behaviour and Egg Masses of Kelp Greenling, *Hexagrammos decagrammus*, and Whitespotted Greenling, *H. stelleri.*" *Northwest Science* 60(1): 32-35.

DeMartini, Edward E., and Benjamin G. Patten. (1979). "Egg guarding and reproductive biology of the red Irish lord, *hemilepidotus hemilepidotus* (Tilesius)." *Syesis* 12: 41-55.

Denniston, Glenda B. (1974). "The Diet of the Ancient Inhabitants of Ashishik Point, an Aleut Community." *Arctic Anthropology* 11(Supplement): 143-152.

Desse, Jean and Nathalie Desse-Berset. (1994). "Osteometry and Fishing Strategies in Cap Andreas Kastros, Cyprus (8th millennium BP)," in W. Van Neer (ed.) *Fish Exploitation in the Past: Proceedings of the 7th meeting of the ICAZ Fish Remains Working Group*, pp. 69-79. Annales du Musee Royal de l'Afrique Centrale, Sciences Zoologiques no. 274, Tervuren.

(1996a). "On the Boundaries of Osteometry Applied to Fish." *Archaeofauna* 5:171-179.

(1996b). "Archaeozoology of Groupers (Epinephelinae): Identification, Osteometry and Keys to Interpretation." *Archaeofauna* 5: 121-127.

Dixon, E. James. (1999). *Bones, Boats, & Bison: Archaeology and the First Colonization of Western North America.* Albuquerque: The University of New Mexico Press.

Driver, Jonathan C. (1993). "Zooarchaeology in British Columbia." *BC Studies* 99: 77-105.

Dumond, Don E. (1965). "On Eskaleutian Linguistics, Archaeology, and Prehistory." *American Anthropologist* 67: 1231-1257.

(1987a). "A Reexamination of Eskimo-Aleut Prehistory." *American Anthropologist* 89: 32-56.

(1987b). *The Eskimos and Aleuts.* Revised Edition. London: Thames and Hudson.

Dwyer, Deborah A., Kevin M. Bailey, and Patricia A. Livingston. (1987). "Feeding Habits and Daily Ration of Walleye Pollock (*Theragra chalcogramma*) in the Eastern Bering Sea, with Special Reference to Cannibalism." *Canadian Journal of Fisheries and Aquatic Sciences* 44: 1972-1984.

Efimov, Y. N. (1984). "Stock Condition and Assessment of Maximum Sustainable Yield of Atka Mackerel in the Gulf of Alaska." *International North Pacific Fisheries Commission, Bulletin* Number 42: 82-84.

Enghoff, Inge B. (1983). "Size Distribution of Cod (*Gadus morhua* L.) and Whiting (*Merlangus merlangus* (L.)) (Pisces, Gadidae) from a Mesolithic Settlement at Vedbæk, North Zealand, Denmark." *Videnskabelige Meddelelser fra Dansk Naturhistorisk Forening* 144: 83-97.

Erlandson, Jon M., Torben C. Rick, Rene L. Vellanoweth, and Douglas J. Kennett. (1999). "Maritime Subsistence at a 9300 Year Old Shell Midden on Santa Rosa Island, California." *Journal of Field Archaeology* 26: 255-265.

Eschmeyer, William N., Earl S. Herald, and Howard Hammann. (1983). *A Field Guide to Pacific Coast Fishes of North America.* Boston: Houghton Mifflin Company.

Eyerdam, Walter J. (1936). "Mammal Remains from an Aleut Stone Age Village." *Journal of Mammalogy* 17: 61.

Fedje, Daryl W., and Heiner Josenhans. (2000). "Drowned forests and archaeology on the continental shelf of British Columbia, Canada." *Geology* 28(2): 99-102.

Fieller, N. R. J., and A. Turner. (1982). "Number Estimation in Vertebrate Samples." *Journal of Archaeological Science* 9: 49-62.

Ford, Pamela J. (1989). "Archaeological and Ethnographic Correlates of Seasonality: Problems and Solutions on the Northwest Coast." *Canadian Journal of Archaeology* 13: 133-150.

Foucher, R. P. (1987). *Length Composition of Pacific Cod (Gadus macrocephalus) from Commercial Landings by Canadian Trawlers, 1974-85.* Canadian Data Report of Fisheries and Aquatic Sciences, No. 621. Nanaimo: Department of Fisheries, Fisheries Research Branch, Pacific Biological Station.

Furuhelm, J. (1877). "Notes on the Natives of Alaska." *Contributions to North American Ethnology, Vol. 1, Part 1: Tribes of the Extreme Northwest*, Pages 111-116. Department of the Interior, U. S. Geographical and Geological Survey of the Rocky Mountain Region. Washington: Government Printing Office.

Gilbert, Allan S., and Burton H. Singer. (1982). "Reassessing Zooarchaeological Quantification." *World Archaeology* 14(1): 21-40.

Golovin, Pavel N. (1983). *Civil and Savage Encounters.* Translation of letters published originally in 1863 in the Russian Naval Journal, Morskoi Sbornik. Portland: Western Imprints, The Press of the Oregon Historical Society.

Grayson, Donald K. (1973). "On the Methodology of Faunal Analysis." *American Antiquity* 38(4): 432-439.

(1978). "Minimum Numbers and Sample Size in Vertebrate Faunal Analysis." *American Antiquity* 43(1): 53-65.

(1979). "On the Quantification of Vertebrate Archaeofaunas." *Advances in Archaeological Method and Theory*, vol. 2, pp. 199-237.

(1981). "The Effects of Sample Size on Some Derived Measures in Vertebrate Faunal Analysis." *Journal of Archaeological Science* 8: 77-88.

(1984). *Quantitative Zooarchaeology: Topics in the Analysis of Archaeological Faunas.* Orlando: Academic Press, Inc.

Greenspan, Ruth L. (1998). "Gear Selectivity Models, Mortality Profiles and the Interpretation of Archaeological Fish Remains: A Case Study from the Harney Basin, Oregon." *Journal of Archaeological Science* 25: 973-984.

Gregory, William K. (1959). *Fish Skulls: A Study of the Evolution of Natural Mechanisms.* Laurel: Eric Lundberg. Originally published in the transactions of the American Philosophical Society, Volume Twenty-three, part two, 1933.

Hales, L. Stanton, Jr. and Elizabeth J. Reitz. (1992). "Historical Changes in Age and Growth of Atlantic Croaker, *Micropogonias undulatus* (Perciformes: Sciaenidae)." *Journal of Archaeological Science* 19: 73-99.

Harvey, James T., Thomas R. Loughlin, Michael A. Perez, and Dion S. Oxman. (1994). "Relationship Between Fish Size and Otolith Length for 62 Species of Fishes from the Eastern North Pacific Ocean." *NOAA Technical Report NMFS Circular.* Seattle: Alaska

Fisheries Science Center, National Marine Mammal Laboratory.

Hart, J. L. (1973). *Pacific Fishes of Canada.* Ottawa: Fisheries Research Board of Canada.

Hayden, Brian. (1997). *The Pithouses of Keatley Creek.* Fort Worth: Harcourt Brace College Publishers.

Heaton, Timothy H. (1995). "Interpretation of $\delta^{13}C$ Values from Vertebrate Remains of the Alexander Archipelago, S.E. Alaska." *Current Research in the Pleistocene* 12: 95-97.

Hoffman, Brian W. (1999). "Agayadan Village: Household Archaeology on Unimak Island, Alaska." *Journal of Field Archaeology* 26: 147-161.

Hoffman, Brian W., Jessica M. C. Czederpiltz and Megan A. Partlow. (2000). "Heads or Tails: The Zooarchaeology of Aleut Salmon Storage on Unimak Island, Alaska." *Journal of Archaeological Science* 27: 699-708.

Horton, D. R. (1984). "Minimum Numbers: a Consideration." *Journal of Archaeological Science* 11: 255-271.

Hrdlicka, Ales. (1941). "Exploration of Mummy Caves in the Aleutian Islands." *The Scientific Monthly* 52: 5-23, 113-130.

Hurt, Wesley R., Jr. (1950). "Artifacts from Shemya, Aleutian Islands." *American Antiquity* 16(1): 68-69.

Jochelson, Waldemar. (1927). "The Instrumental and the Comitative in the Aleut Language." *Language* 3: 9-11.

(1928). "People of the Foggy Seas." *Natural History* 28(4): 413-424.

(1966). *History, Ethnology and Anthropology of the Aleut.* Carnegie Institution of Washington, Publication No. 432. (Reprint of 1933 Edition.) Oosterhout N.B., The Netherlands: Anthropological Publications.

(1975). *Archaeological Investigations in the Aleutian Islands.* Carnegie Institutions of Washington, Publication No. 367. (Reprint of the 1925 Edition.) New York: AMS Press Inc.

Johnson, Lucille L. (1988). "Archaeological Surveys of the Outer Shumagin Islands, Alaska, 1984 and 1986." *Arctic Anthropology* 25(2): 139-170.

(1992). "Pre-contact and Contact-period Aleut Settlements in the Shumagin Islands," in O. W. Frost (ed.) *Bering and Chirikov: The American Voyages and Their Impact*, pp. 291-300. Anchorage: Alaska Historical Society.

Johnson, Lucille L., and Margaret A. Winslow. (1991). "Paleoshorelines and Prehistoric Settlement on Simeonof and Chernabura Islands, Outer Shumagin Islands, Alaska," in Lucille L. Johnson (ed.) *Paleoshorelines and Prehistory*, pp. 171-186. N.J.: Telford Press.

Johnson, Richard A., and Gouri K. Bhattacharyya. (1992). *Statistics: Principles and Methods.* Second Edition. New York: John Wiley & Sons, Inc.

Jordan, David S., and Barton W. Evermann. (1898). *The Fishes of North and Middle America.* Part 2. Reprinted 1963 for the Smithsonian Institution, Washington.

Kasahara, Hiroshi. (1961). *Fisheries Resources of the North Pacific Ocean.* Vancouver: Institute of Fisheries, The University of British Columbia.

Ketchen, K. S. (1964). "Preliminary Results of Studies on Growth and Mortality of Pacific Cod (*Gadus macrocephalus*) in Hecate Strait, British Columbia." *Journal of the Fisheries Research Board of Canada* 21(5):1051-1067.

Krantz, Grover S. (1968). "A New Method of Counting Mammal Bones." *American Journal of Archaeology* 72: 286-288.

Lamb, Andy, and Phil Edgell. (1986). *Coastal Fishes of the Pacific Northwest.* Madeira Park: Harbour Publishing.

Lantis, Margaret. (1970). "The Aleut Social System, 1750 to 1810, from Early Historical Sources," in Margaret Lantis (ed.) *Ethnohistory in Southwestern Alaska and the Southern Yukon*, pp. 139-301. Lexington: The University Press of Kentucky.
(1984). "Aleut," in David Damas (ed.) *Arctic. Handbook of North American Indians, Vol. 5*, pp. 119-135. Washington: Smithsonian Institution.

Laughlin, Sara B., William S. Laughlin, and Mary E. McDowell. (1975). "Anangula Blade Site Excavations, 1972 and 1973." *Anthropological Papers of the University of Alaska* 17(2): 39-48.

Laughlin, William S. (1951). "Notes on an Aleutian Core and Blade Industry." *American Antiquity* 17(1): 52-55.
(1952). "The Aleut-Eskimo Community." *Anthropological Papers of the University of Alaska* 1(1): 25-46.
(1963a). "Eskimos and Aleuts: Their Origins and Evolution." *Science* 142: 633-645.
(1963b). "The Earliest Aleuts." *Anthropological Papers of the University of Alaska* 10(2): 73-91.
(1966). "Aleutian Studies." *Arctic Anthropology* 3(2): 23-27.
(1975). "Aleuts: Ecosystem, Holocene History, and Siberian Origin." *Science* 189: 507-515.
(1980). *Aleuts: Survivors of the Bering Land Bridge.* New York: Holt, Rinehart and Winston.

Laughlin, William S., and Jean S. Aigner. (1975). "Aleut Adaptation and Evolution," in W. Fitzhugh (ed.) *Prehistoric Maritime Adaptations of the Circumpolar Zone*, pp. 181-201. The Hague, Paris: Mouton Publishers.

Laughlin, William S., and Gordon H. Marsh. (1951). "A New View of the History of the Aleutians." *Arctic* 4(2): 75-88.
(1954). "The Lamellar Flake Manufacturing Site on Anangula Island in the Aleutians." *American Antiquity* 20(1): 27-39.

Laughlin, W. S., G. H. Marsh, and J. W. Leach. (1952). "Supplementary Note on the Aleutian Core and Blade Industry." *American Antiquity* 18(1): 69-70.

Leach, Foss. (1997). *A Guide to the Identification of Fish Remains from New Zealand Archaeological Sites.* New Zealand Journal of Archaeology Special Publication. Kilbirnie: New Zealand Journal of Archaeology.

Leach, Foss, and Janet Davidson. (2000). "Pre-European Catches of Snapper (*Pagrus auratus*) in Northern New Zealand." *Journal of Archaeological Science* 27: 509-522.

Leach, B. F., J. M. Davidson, L. M. Horwood, and A. J. Anderson. (1996). "The Estimation of Live Fish Size from Archaeological Cranial Bones of the New Zealand Barracouta *Thyrsites atun*." *Tuhinga: Records of the Museum of New Zealand Te Papa Tongarewa* 6: 1-25.

Lefevre, Christine, Debra G. Corbett, Dixie West, and Douglas Siegel-Causey. (1997). "A Zooarchaeological Study at Buldir Island, Western Aleutians, Alaska." *Arctic Anthropology* 34(2):118-131.

Lepofsky, Dana, Karla D. Kusmer, Brian Hayden, and Kenneth P. Lertzman. (1996). "Reconstructing Prehistoric Socioeconomies from Paleoethnobotanical and Zooarchaeological Data: An Example from the British Columbia Plateau." *Journal of Ethnobiology* 16(1): 31-62.

Lie, Rolf W. (1980). "Minimum Number of Individuals from Osteological Samples." *Norwegian Archaeological Review* 13(1): 24-30.
(1983). "Reply to Wild and Nichol." *Norwegian Archaeological Review* 16(1): 49.

Lippold, Lois K. (1966). "Chaluka: The Economic Base." *Arctic Anthropology* 3(2): 125-131.
(1972). "Mammalian Remains from Aleutian Archaeological Sites: A Preliminary Report." *Arctic Anthropology* 9(2): 113-114.

Lowe, Sandra A., Donald M. Van Doornik, and Gary A. Winans. (1998). "Geographic Variation in Genetic and Growth Patterns of Atka Mackerel, *Pleurogrammus monopterygius* (Hexagrammidae), in the Aleutian Archipelago." *Fishery Bulletin* 96: 502-515.

Lyman, R. Lee. (1979). "Available Meat from Faunal Remains: A Consideration of Techniques." *American Antiquity* 44(3): 536-546.
(1985). "Bone Frequencies: Differential Transport, *In Situ* Destruction, and the MGUI." *Journal of Archaeological Science* 12: 221-236.
(1994). "Quantitative Units and Terminology in Zooarchaeology." *American Antiquity* 59(1): 36-71.
(1996). "Applied zooarchaeology: the relevance of faunal analysis to wildlife management." *World*

Archaeology 28(1): 110-125.

Lyon, Patricia J. (1970). "Differential Bone Destruction: An Ethnographic Example." *American Antiquity* 35(2): 213-215.

Mackie, Quentin, Trevor J. Orchard, and Martina Steffen. (2001). "Environmental Archaeology of the Late Precontact and Early Contact Periods in Gwaii Haanas." Paper presented at the 34th annual meeting of the Canadian Archaeological Association, Banff, Alberta, May 2001.

Makarova, Raisa V. (1975). *Russians on the Pacific: 1743-1799.* Translation of the original Russian version published in 1968. Kingston: The Limestone Press.

Marsh, Gordon H., and William S. Laughlin. (1954). "A Comparative Survey of Eskimo-Aleut Religion." *Anthropological Papers of the University of Alaska* 3(1): 21-36.

(1956). "Human Anatomical Knowledge Among the Aleutian Islanders." *Southwestern Journal of Anthropology* 12(1): 38-78.

Maschner, Herbert D. G., and Katherine L. Reedy-Maschner. (1998). "Raid, Retreat, Defend (Repeat): The Archaeology and Ethnohistory of Warfare on the North Pacific Rim." *Journal of Anthropological Archaeology* 17: 19-51

Matson, R. G. (1992). "The Evolution of Northwest Coast Subsistence." *Research in Economic Anthropology*, Supplement 6, pp. 367-428.

McCartney, Allen P. (1971). "A Proposed Western Aleutian Phase in the Near Islands, Alaska." *Arctic Anthropology* 8(2): 92-142.

(1974). "Maritime Adaptations on the North Pacific Rim." *Arctic Anthropology* 11(Suppl.): 153-162.

(1975). "Maritime Adaptations in Cold Archipelagos: An Analysis of Environment and Culture in the Aleutian and Other Island Chains," in W. Fitzhugh (ed.) *Prehistoric Maritime Adaptations of the Circumpolar Zone*, pp. 281-338. The Hague, Paris: Mouton.

(1984). "Prehistory of the Aleutian Region," in David Damas (ed.) *Arctic. Handbook of North American Indians, Vol. 5*, pp. 119-135. Washington: Smithsonian Institution.

McCartney, Allen P., and Douglas W. Veltre. (1999). "Aleutian Island Prehistory: Living in Insular Extremes." *World Archaeology* 30(3): 503-515.

McDermott, Susanne F. and Sandra A. Lowe. (1997). "The Reproductive Cycle and Sexual Maturity of Atka Mackerel, *Pleurogrammus monopterygius*, in Alaska Waters." *Fishery Bulletin* 95: 321-333.

McHugh, J. L. (1942). "Variation of Vertebral Centra in Young Pacific Herring (*Clupea pallasii*)." *Journal of the Fisheries Research Board of Canada* 5(4): 347-360.

McKenzie, John, Robert L. Schaefer, and Elizabeth Farber.

(1995). *The Student Edition of MINITAB® for Windows.* Reading: Addison-Wesley Publishing Company, Inc.

Merrick, Richard L., M. Kathryn Chumbley, and G. Vernon Byrd. (1997). "Diet diversity of Steller sea lions (*Eumetopias jubatas*) and their population decline in Alaska: a potential relationship." *Canadian Journal of Fisheries and Aquatic Sciences* 54: 1342-1348.

Mitchell, Donald. (1988). "Changing Patterns of Resource Use in the Prehistory of Queen Charlotte Strait, British Columbia." *Research in Economic Anthropology*, Supplement 3: 245-290.

(1990). "Coast Salish Subsistence Studies and a Methodological Barrier." *Northwest Anthropological Research Notes* 24(2): 239-247.

Morlan, Richard E. (1983). "Counts and Estimates of Taxonomic Abundance in Faunal Remains: Microtine Rodents from Bluefish Cave I." *Canadian Journal of Archaeology* 7(1): 61-76.

Moss, Madonna L., and Jon M. Erlandson. (1992). "Forts, Refuge Rocks, and Defensive Sites: The Antiquity of Warfare along the North Pacific Coast of North America." *Arctic Anthropology* 29(2): 73-90.

Mujib, Khwaja A. (1967). "The Cranial Osteology of the Gadidae." *Journal of the Fisheries Research Board of Canada* 24(6): 1315-1375.

Nelson, Willis H., and Frank Barnett. (1955). "A Burial Cave on Kanaga Island, Aleutian Islands." *American Antiquity* 20(4): 387-392.

Nichol, R. K., and C. J. Wild. (1984). "'Numbers of Individuals' in Faunal Analysis: the Decay of Fish Bone in Archaeological Sites." *Journal of Archaeological Science* 11: 35-51.

Noe-Nygaard, Nanna. (1983). "The Importance of Aquatic Resources to Mesolithic Man at Inland Sites in Denmark," in Caroline Grigson and Juliet Clutton-Brock (eds.) *Animals and Archaeology: 2. Shell Middens, Fishes and Birds*, pp. 125-142. Oxford: B. A. R.

Olesiuk, Peter F., Michael A. Bigg, Graeme M. Ellis, Susan J. Crockford, and Rebecca J. Wigen. (1990). An assessment of the feeding habits of harbour seals (*Phoca vitulina*) in the Strait of Georgia, British Columbia, based on scat analysis. *Canadian Technical Report of Fisheries and Aquatic Sciences* 1730: 135 p.

Olsen, Stanley J. (1971). *Zooarchaeology: Animal Bones in Archaeology and their Interpretation.* Reading: Addison-Wesley Publishing Company, Inc.

Orchard, Trevor J. (1998). "A Case Study in Faunal Analysis: Analysis of Pacific Cod *(Gadus macrocephalus)* Remains from Shemya Island." Poster presented at the 8th International Congress of the International Council for Archaeozoology, August 1998, Victoria.

(2000). "Problems and Prospects of Quantitative

Zooarchaeology: The Use of Statistical Regression in the Analysis of Fish Remains." *Cultural Reflections* 2: 26-33.

——— (2001). "Environmental Archaeology in Gwaii Haanas." *Canadian Zooarchaeology* 19: 2-8.

Owen, Jennifer F. and John R. Merrick. (1994a). "Analysis of Coastal Middens in South-Eastern Australia: Sizing of Fish Remains in Holocene Deposits." *Journal of Archaeological Science* 21: 3-10.

——— (1994b). "Analysis of Coastal Middens in South-Eastern Australia: Selectivity of Angling and Other Fishing Techniques Related to Holocene Deposits." *Journal of Archaeological Science* 21: 11-16.

Payne, Sebastian. (1972). "On the Interpretation of Bone Samples from Archaeological Sites," in E. S. Higgs (ed.) *Papers in economic prehistory*, pp. 65-82. Cambridge: Cambridge University Press.

Peden, Alex E. (1978). "A systematic revision of the hemilepidotine fishes (Cottidae)." *Syesis* 11:11-49.

Perkins, Dexter, Jr., and Patricia Daly. (1968). "A Hunter's Village in Neolithic Turkey." *Scientific American* 219(5): 96-106.

Purdue, James R. (1987). "Estimation of Body Weight of White-Tailed Deer (*Odocoileus virginianus*) from Bone Size." *Journal of Ethnobiology* 7(1): 1-12.

Ransom, Ellis. (1946). "Aleut Natural-Food Economy." *American Anthropologist* 48: 607-623.

Rau, Charles. (1884). "Prehistoric Fishing in Europe and North America." *Smithsonian Contributions to Knowledge*, Vol. 25, Pages 1-342. Washington: Smithsonian Institution.

Reimchen, T. E. (2000). "Some Ecological and Evolutionary Aspects of Bear-Salmon Interactions in Coastal British Columbia." *Canadian Journal of Zoology* 78: 448-457.

Reitz, Elizabeth J. and Dan Cordier. (1983). "Use of Allometry in Zooarchaeological Analysis," in Caroline Grigson and Juliet Clutton-Brock (eds.) *Animals and Archaeology: 2. Shell Middens, Fishes and Birds*, pp. 237-252. Oxford: B. A. R.

Reitz, Elizabeth J., Lee A. Newsom, and Sylvia J. Scudder. (1996). "Issues in Environmental Archaeology," in Elizabeth J. Reitz, Lee A. Newsom, and Sylvia J. Scudder (eds.) *Case Studies in Environmental Archaeology*, pp. 3-16. New York: Plenum Press.

Reitz, Elizabeth J., Irvy R. Quitmyer, H. Stephen Hale, Sylvia J. Scudder, and Elizabeth S. Wing. (1987). "Application of Allometry to Zooarchaeology." *American Antiquity* 52(2): 304-317.

Reitz, Elizabeth J. and Elizabeth S. Wing. (1999). *Zooarchaeology*. Cambridge: Cambridge University Press.

Renfrew, Colin, and Paul Bahn. (2000). *Archaeology: Theories Methods and Practice*. Third Edition. New York: Thames & Hudson.

Reynolds, William W., and William J. Karlotski. (1977). "The Allometric Relationship of Skeleton Weight to Body Weight in Teleost Fishes: A Preliminary Comparison with Birds and Mammals." *Copeia* 1977(1): 160-163.

Ricker, W. E. (1973). "Linear Regressions in Fishery Research." *Journal of the Fisheries Research Board of Canada* 30(3): 409-434.

Ringrose, T. J. (1993). "Bone Counts and Statistics: A Critique." *Journal of Archaeological Science* 20: 121-157.

Rojo, Alfonso L. (1986). "Live Length and Weight of Cod (*Gadus morhua*) Estimated from Various Skeletal Elements." *North American Archaeologist* 7(4): 329-351.

——— (1987). "Excavated Fish Vertebrae as Predictors in Bioarchaeological Research." *North American Archaeologist* 8(3): 209-225.

——— (1991). *Dictionary of Evolutionary Fish Osteology.* Boca Raton: CRC Press, Inc.

Sandweiss, Daniel H., Heather McInnis, Richard L. Burger, Asunción Cano, Bernardino Ojeda, Rolando Paredes, María del Carmen Sandweiss, and Michael D. Glascock. (1998). "Quebrada Jaguay: Early South American Maritime Adaptations." *Science* 281: 1830-1832.

Schuck, Howard A. (1949). "Problems in Calculating Size of Fish at Various Ages from Proportional Measurements of Fish and Scale Sizes." *Journal of Wildlife Management* 13(3): 298-303.

Shotwell, J. Arnold. (1955). "An Approach to the Paleoecology of Mammals." *Ecology* 36(2): 327-337.

Siegel-Causey, Douglas, Debra Corbett, and Christine Lefevre. (n.d.). "Report of the Western Aleutian Archaeological Project Shemya Island Excavations." Unpublished preliminary site report of Shemya Island excavations. Manuscript in the possession of the author.

Smith, Pippa. (1995). "A Regression Equation to Determine the Total Length of Hake (*Merluccius merluccius*) from Selected Measurements of the Bones." *International Journal of Osteoarchaeology* 5: 93-95.

Spaulding, Albert C. (1953). "The Current Status of Aleutian Archaeology." *Memoirs of the Society for American Archaeology* 9: 29-31.

Sternberg, Myriam. (1992). *Fiches D'osteologie Animale pour L'archeologie. Serie A: Poissons*. Centre de Recherches Archeologiques du CNRS.

Stewart, Frances L., and Peter W. Stahl. (1977). "Cautionary Note on Edible Meat Poundage Figures." *American Antiquity* 42(2): 267-270.

Stewart, Hilary. (1982). *Indian Fishing: Early Methods on the Northwest Coast*. Vancouver: Douglas & McIntyre.

Thompson, J. M. (1981). "Preliminary Report on the

Population Biology and Fishery of Walleye Pollock (*Theragra Chalcogramma*) Off the Pacific Coast of Canada." *Canadian Technical Report of Fisheries and Aquatic Sciences*, No. 1031. 157 pages.

Turner, Alan. (1982). "Minimum number estimation offers minimal insight in faunal analysis." *OSSA* 7: 199-201.

Turner, Christy G., II. (1970). "Archaeological Reconnaissance of Amchitka Island, Alaska." *Arctic Anthropology* 7(2): 118-128.

(1972). "Preliminary Report of Archaeological Survey and Test Excavations in the Eastern Aleutian Islands, Alaska." *Arctic Anthropology* 9(2): 32-35.

(1976). "The Aleuts of Akun Island." *The Alaska Journal* 6(1): 25-31.

Turner, Christy G., II, Jean S. Aigner, and Linda R. Richards. (1974). "Chaluka Stratigraphy, Umnak Island, Alaska." *Arctic Anthropology* 11, Supplement: 125-142.

Turner, L. M. (1886). *Results of Investigations Made Chiefly in the Yukon District and the Aleutian Islands; Conducted Under the Auspices of the Signal Service, United States Army, Extending from May, 1874, to August, 1881*. Contributions to the History of Alaska, No. II. Washington: Government Printing Office.

Uerpmann, Hans-Peter. (1973). "Animal Bone Finds and Economic Archaeology: a Critical Study of 'Osteoarchaeological' Method." *World Archaeology* 4(3): 307-322.

Veltre, Douglas W. (1990). "Perspectives on Aleut Culture Change during the Russian Period," in Barbara S. Smith and Redmond J. Barnett (eds.) *Russian America: The Forgotten Frontier*, pp. 175-183. Tacoma: Washington State Historical Society.

(1994). "Precontact Aleut Culture." *Alaska Geographic* 21(4): 86-89.

(1998). "Prehistoric Maritime Adaptations in the Western and Central Aleutian Islands, Alaska." *Arctic Anthropology* 35(1): 223-233.

Veniaminov, Ivan. (1984). *Notes on the Islands of the Unalashka District*. Alaska History, No. 27. Kingston: The Limestone Press. (Translation of 1840 Edition.)

Vinnikov, Andrei V. (1996). "Pacific Cod (*Gadus macrocephalus*) of the Western Bering Sea." Pp 183-202 in Ole A. Methisen and Kenneth O. Coyle (eds.) *Ecology of the Bering Sea: A Review of Russian Literature*. Fairbanks: University of Alaska Fairbanks.

Wheeler, A. (1978). "Problems of Identification and Interpretation of Archaeological Fish Remains," in D. R. Brothwell, K. D. Thomas, and Juliet Clutton-Brock (eds.) *Research Problems in Zooarchaeology*, pp. 69-75. London: Institute of Archaeology.

Wheeler, Alwyne and Andrew K. G. Jones. (1989). *Fishes*. Cambridge: Cambridge University Press.

Wheeler, Jane C., and Elizabeth J. Reitz. (1987).

"Allometric Prediction of Live Weight in the Alpaca (*Lama pacos* L.)." *Archaeozoologia* 1(1): 31-46.

White, Theodore E. (1952). "Observations on the Butchering Technique of Some Aboriginal Peoples: I." *American Antiquity* 17(4): 337-338.

(1953a). "Observations on the Butchering Technique of Some Aboriginal Peoples No. 2." *American Antiquity* 19(2): 160-164.

(1953b). "A Method of Calculating the Dietary Percentage of Various Food Animals Utilized by Aboriginal Peoples." *American Antiquity* 18(4): 396-398.

Wigen, R. J. S. (1980). *A Faunal Analysis of Two Middens on the East Coast of Vancouver Island*. M.A. thesis, University of Victoria.

Wild, C. J., and R. K. Nichol. (1983a). "Estimation of the Original Number of Individuals from Paired Bone Counts Using Estimators of the Krantz Type." *Journal of Field Archaeology* 10: 337-344.

(1983b). "A Note on Rolf W. Lie's Approach to Estimating Minimum Numbers from Osteological Samples." *Norwegian Archaeological Review* 16(1): 45-48.

Wilimovsky, N. J., A. Peden, and J. Peppar. (1967). "Systematics of Six Demersal Fishes of the North Pacific Ocean." *Fisheries Research Board of Canada: Technical Report* No. 34

Wing, Elizabeth S. and Antoinette B. Brown. (1979). *Paleonutrition: Method and Theory in Prehistoric Foodways*. New York: Academic Press.

Winslow, Margaret A. (1991). "Modeling Paleoshorelines in Geologically Active Regions: Applications to the Shumagin Islands, Southwest Alaska," in Lucille L. Johnson (ed.) *Paleoshorelines and Prehistory*, pp. 151-169. N.J.: Telford Press.

Witherell, David. (1996). "Groundfish of the Bering Sea and Aleutian Islands Area: A Species Profile." Anchorage: North Pacific Fishery Management Council [Online] Available http://www.fakr.noaa.gov/npfmc/grdsum.htm (November 4, 1998).

Woodbury, Anthony C. (1984). "Eskimo and Aleut Languages," in David Damas (ed.) *Arctic. Handbook of North American Indians*, Vol. 5, pp. 49-63. Washington: Smithsonian Institution.

Yang, Mei-Sun. (1999). "The trophic role of Atka mackerel, *Pleurogrammus monopterygius*, in the Aleutian Islands area." *Fishery Bulletin* 97(4): 1047-1057.

Yesner, D. R. (1980). "Nutrition and Cultural Evolution: Patterns in Prehistory." Ch. 4 in Norge W. Jerome, Randy F. Kandel, and Gretel H. Pelto (eds.) *Nutritional Anthropology: Contemporary Approaches to Diet & Culture*. Pleasantville: Redgrave Publishing Company.

Yesner, David R. and Jean S. Aigner. (1976).

"Comparative Biomass Estimates and Prehistoric Cultural Ecology of the Southwest Umnak Region, Aleutian Islands." *Arctic Anthropology* 13(2): 91-112.

Zolotov, O. G. (1993). "Notes on the Reproductive Biology of *Pleurogrammus monopterygius* in Kamchatkan Waters." *Journal of Ichthyology* 33(4): 25-37.

APPENDIX 1. COMPARATIVE DATA

The tables on the following pages contain the comparative data which formed the basis for the regression analysis described above. All length data and skeletal element dimensions are given in millimetres, while weights are given in grams. Many of the Atka Mackerel specimens listed were donated by National Marine Mammal Lab, Seattle, Washington, and currently reside in the permanent collection of the Department of Anthropology, University of Victoria, Victoria, British Columbia. As such, these specimens have been given identification numbers from both the National Marine Mammal Lab (NMML) and the University of Victoria (UVIC), and both sets of identifications are listed. For other taxa, only a single specimen number is listed. Specimens with a BN, GM, TC, or REF# designation are from the collection of the NMML. All other specimens are from the UVIC collection. The following abbreviations are used for the identification of skeletal elements, with the measurement number following the element identification:

VOME:	Vomer	HYH2:	Hypohyal #2
DENT:	Dentary	INPH:	Inferior Pharyngeal
ANGU:	Angular	PHA2:	Pharyngobranchial #2
ARTI:	Articular	HYB3:	Hypobranchial #3
PREM:	Premaxilla	EPB3:	Epibranchial #3
QUAD:	Quadrate	EPB4:	Epibranchial #4
INTE:	Interhyal	VER1:	Vertebra #1 (Atlas)
EPIH:	Epihyal	VER9:	Vertebra #9
BASI:	Basihyal	PEVE:	Penultimate Vertebra
HYOM:	Hyomandibular	OTOL:	Otolith

Measurements that are represented by "n/a" were unattainable due to missing skeletal elements, while those represented by "n/m" were unmeasurable due to the anomalous or fragmentary nature of the elements present.

Atka Mackerel Comparative Specimens

UVIC	NMML	Lab FL	Lab SL	Lab Wt	Boat L	Boat Wt	Sex
92/45		294.0	274.0	353.0	n/a	n/a	n/a
95/21		n/a	n/a	658.9	390.0	n/a	n/a
99/23	PM-001-99	360.0	320.0	652.0	n/a	n/a	M
99/24	PM-002-99	415.0	380.0	1020.0	n/a	n/a	M
99/25	PM-003-99	420.0	390.0	974.0	n/a	n/a	F
99/26	PM-004-99	365.0	330.0	759.0	n/a	n/a	F
99/27	PM-005-99	n/a	n/a	1797.0	500.0	1830.0	F
99/28	PM-006-99	n/a	n/a	1281.0	480.0	1320.0	F
99/29	PM-007-99	n/a	n/a	615.0	350.0	630.0	F
99/30	PM-008-99	360.0	325.0	631.0	370.0	650.0	M
99/31	PM-009-99	390.0	370.0	775.0	410.0	780.0	F
99/32	PM-010-99	360.0	320.0	637.0	370.0	650.0	F
99/33	PM-011-99	485.0	450.0	1810.0	500.0	1820.0	F
99/34	PM-012-99	405.0	370.0	834.0	420.0	850.0	M
99/35	PM-013-99	410.0	370.0	935.0	430.0	950.0	M
99/36	PM-014-99	**485.0**	**465.0**	986.0	400.0	1000.0	M
99/37	PM-015-99	390.0	370.0	856.0	400.0	850.0	M
99/38	PM-016-99	420.0	390.0	843.0	440.0	850.0	M
99/39	PM-017-99	365.0	350.0	670.0	370.0	700.0	M
99/40	PM-018-99	425.0	395.0	920.0	430.0	950.0	F
99/41	PM-019-99	385.0	355.0	870.0	390.0	900.0	M
99/42	PM-020-99	390.0	365.0	785.0	390.0	800.0	F
99/43	PM-021-99	455.0	435.0	881.0	470.0	900.0	F
99/44	PM-022-99	360.0	340.0	686.0	370.0	700.0	F
99/45	PM-023-99	405.0	385.0	957.0	420.0	1000.0	M
99/46	PM-024-99	355.0	330.0	671.0	380.0	700.0	F
99/47	PM-025-99	500.0	450.0	1972.0	500.0	2100.0	M
99/48	PM-026-99	400.0	370.0	888.0	410.0	900.0	M
99/49	PM-027-99	410.0	385.0	1000.0	440.0	950.0	F
99/50	PM-028-99	410.0	375.0	1106.0	430.0	1150.0	M
99/51	PM-029-99	210.0	185.0	89.0	220.0	50.0	F
99/52	PM-030-99	335.0	300.0	456.0	350.0	410.0	F
99/53	PM-031-99	210.0	190.0	93.0	210.0	60.0	M
99/54	PM-032-99	350.0	320.0	591.0	360.0	580.0	F
99/55	PM-033-99	350.0	325.0	629.0	370.0	630.0	M
99/56	PM-034-99	420.0	390.0	953.0	430.0	1000.0	M
99/57	PM-035-99	430.0	400.0	887.0	450.0	900.0	F
99/58	PM-036-99	410.0	390.0	878.0	420.0	800.0	F
99/59	PM-037-99	380.0	355.0	778.0	390.0	700.0	F
99/60	PM-038-99	430.0	395.0	1026.0	440.0	1100.0	M
99/61	PM-039-99	310.0	290.0	352.0	310.0	400.0	F
99/62	PM-040-99	325.0	310.0	451.0	330.0	500.0	F
99/63	PM-041-99	480.0	445.0	1592.0	490.0	1600.0	M
99/64	PM-042-99	410.0	375.0	863.0	410.0	850.0	M
99/65	PM-043-99	395.0	380.0	950.0	410.0	876.0	F
99/66	PM-044-99	375.0	350.0	770.0	390.0	700.0	M
99/67	PM-045-99	345.0	320.0	618.0	350.0	550.0	M
99/68	PM-046-99	375.0	350.0	775.0	390.0	750.0	M

Atka Mackerel Comparative Specimens

UVIC	NMML	Lab FL	Lab SL	Lab Wt	Boat L	Boat Wt	Sex
99/69	PM-047-99	360.0	335.0	616.0	380.0	600.0	F
99/70	PM-048-99	350.0	330.0	618.0	360.0	600.0	F
99/71	PM-049-99	340.0	320.0	614.0	340.0	600.0	F
99/72	PM-050-99	360.0	335.0	672.0	360.0	600.0	M
99/73	PM-051-99	395.0	360.0	886.0	410.0	860.0	M
99/74	PM-052-99	405.0	375.0	931.0	420.0	920.0	F
99/75	PM-053-99	410.0	380.0	775.0	430.0	830.0	F
99/76	PM-054-99	430.0	395.0	972.0	460.0	920.0	F
99/77	PM-055-99	390.0	365.0	801.0	420.0	800.0	F
99/78	PM-056-99	430.0	390.0	1150.0	440.0	1150.0	F
99/79	PM-057-99	255.0	235.0	156.0	260.0	150.0	F
99/80	PM-058-99	350.0	320.0	644.0	350.0	660.0	M
99/81	PM-059-99	315.0	290.0	448.0	330.0	420.0	M
99/82	PM-060-99	430.0	400.0	803.0	450.0	810.0	F
99/83	PM-061-99	305.0	280.0	336.0	420.0	360.0	M
99/84	PM-062-99	385.0	360.0	760.0	400.0	710.0	F
99/85	PM-063-99	410.0	380.0	1098.0	420.0	1870.0	M
99/86	PM-064-99	425.0	390.0	869.0	440.0	840.0	M
99/87	PM-065-99	295.0	280.0	312.0	310.0	300.0	M
99/88	PM-066-99	440.0	410.0	1263.0	460.0	1570.0	M
99/89	PM-067-99	340.0	320.0	643.0	n/a	690.0	F
99/90	PM-068-99	220.0	205.0	92.0	220.0	90.0	M
99/91	PM-069-99	300.0	275.0	291.0	310.0	290.0	F
99/92	PM-070-99	280.0	260.0	259.0	290.0	260.0	M
99/93	PM-071-99	430.0	400.0	940.0	440.0	n/a	M
99/94	PM-072-99	370.0	340.0	776.0	380.0	800.0	M
99/95	PM-073-99	400.0	370.0	940.0	n/a	n/a	M
99/96	PM-074-99	420.0	390.0	1054.0	n/a	n/a	M
99/97	PM-075-99	345.0	325.0	626.0	350.0	650.0	M
99/98	PM-076-99	340.0	310.0	487.0	340.0	500.0	F
99/99	PM-077-99	425.0	400.0	834.0	440.0	800.0	F
99/100	PM-078-99	400.0	375.0	891.0	420.0	909.0	F
99/101	PM-079-99	360.0	335.0	666.0	370.0	700.0	n/a
99/102	PM-080-99	370.0	345.0	638.0	n/a	650.0	F
99/113	PM-081-99	210.0	195.0	78.0	220.0	100.0	F
99/114	PM-082-99	265.0	250.0	169.0	270.0	110.0	F
99/115	PM-083-99	200.0	190.0	73.0	210.0	50.0	F
99/116	PM-084-99	270.0	250.0	201.0	280.0	160.0	F
99/117	PM-085-99	220.0	210.0	112.0	230.0	100.0	M
99/118	PM-086-99	305.0	285.0	319.0	320.0	290.0	M
99/119	PM-087-99	265.0	240.0	152.0	270.0	100.0	M
99/120	PM-088-99	440.0	410.0	743.0	440.0	800.0	F
99/121	PM-089-99	425.0	390.0	913.0	440.0	870.0	F
99/122	PM-090-99	230.0	210.0	108.0	240.0	100.0	F
99/123	PM-091-99	190.0	175.0	56.0	100.0	50.0	M
99/124	PM-092-99	185.0	170.0	47.0	190.0	50.0	F
99/125	PM-093-99	200.0	185.0	57.0	190.0	50.0	M
99/126	PM-094-99	185.0	170.0	52.0	190.0	50.0	M

Atka Mackerel Comparative Specimens

UVIC	VOME-1	VOME-2	DENT-1	DENT-2	DENT-3	ANGU-1	ANGU-2	ARTI-1
92/45	5.41	2.46	19.39	3.55	10.26	3.76	2.99	21.91
95/21	6.84	3.48	24.80	4.49	13.82	4.77	4.07	28.02
99/23	7.10	3.66	23.93	4.62	12.52	5.13	3.73	26.49
99/24	9.54	4.06	31.84	7.72	16.04	6.14	4.87	33.32
99/25	8.38	4.33	28.42	5.55	14.51	5.43	4.28	33.13
99/26	7.09	3.48	23.93	4.59	12.67	4.57	3.63	28.21
99/27	11.10	5.37	37.09	7.45	18.43	6.35	5.32	41.33
99/28	8.84	4.33	32.28	6.11	16.35	5.66	5.09	36.25
99/29	6.42	3.29	22.87	4.16	12.26	4.79	3.52	28.11
99/30	6.88	3.78	23.93	4.48	12.95	5.41	3.73	28.87
99/31	7.12	3.97	25.81	5.35	13.87	5.15	4.23	31.61
99/32	6.74	3.51	23.85	4.31	12.63	4.44	3.39	27.90
99/33	11.05	5.63	36.27	7.44	18.03	6.90	5.85	39.87
99/34	7.60	3.70	27.24	5.23	14.21	4.75	4.32	31.21
99/35	9.42	5.16	31.88	6.91	16.56	6.15	4.60	34.69
99/36	7.54	3.60	28.89	5.62	14.43	5.23	4.68	31.59
99/37	8.13	4.00	29.20	6.37	15.50	5.45	4.16	31.10
99/38	8.15	4.23	30.97	7.07	15.75	5.68	4.72	32.97
99/39	6.93	3.63	23.95	4.04	12.52	5.18	3.73	27.01
99/40	9.04	4.65	29.10	6.21	15.33	5.83	4.54	33.48
99/41	7.31	4.08	25.19	4.75	13.35	4.96	3.81	28.70
99/42	6.76	3.68	26.17	4.67	13.34	5.22	3.71	31.14
99/43	9.03	4.48	32.82	6.03	16.61	6.63	5.21	37.14
99/44	6.78	3.31	22.44	4.50	11.71	4.58	3.73	26.14
99/45	8.71	4.54	29.99	5.90	15.68	6.28	4.30	33.19
99/46	6.64	3.45	22.61	4.17	11.66	4.62	3.65	26.32
99/47	10.41	4.66	34.75	7.83	18.65	6.55	5.30	38.01
99/48	9.17	3.83	29.87	6.10	14.97	5.93	5.02	33.17
99/49	7.45	3.85	28.38	5.72	14.57	5.53	4.34	31.91
99/50	8.54	4.18	30.62	6.34	15.52	5.57	5.06	32.76
99/51	3.85	1.69	12.79	2.24	6.72	2.47	1.76	15.22
99/52	6.62	3.60	23.11	4.34	11.97	4.53	3.59	26.70
99/53	3.86	1.92	12.85	2.36	6.77	2.31	1.82	15.98
99/54	6.95	4.17	23.64	4.81	12.46	4.83	3.39	27.68
99/55	6.59	3.72	23.36	4.45	12.39	4.75	3.58	27.43
99/56	8.59	5.07	30.52	7.32	16.60	6.55	4.79	34.56
99/57	8.50	4.94	29.24	6.14	15.24	6.20	5.09	34.72
99/58	7.75	4.49	28.27	5.31	14.74	5.40	4.59	33.14
99/59	7.14	3.33	24.09	4.57	12.32	4.86	4.00	28.34
99/60	8.72	4.69	31.63	6.50	15.54	5.74	4.61	34.04
99/61	5.73	2.93	20.30	4.25	10.39	3.93	3.40	23.70
99/62	5.77	3.38	22.16	3.75	11.79	4.56	3.52	26.99
99/63	10.04	4.86	35.12	7.45	17.04	7.67	5.96	40.95
99/64	8.28	3.76	28.29	6.28	15.25	5.94	4.62	31.80
99/65	7.34	3.95	27.41	5.39	14.33	4.69	4.27	31.34
99/66	7.15	3.92	24.74	4.79	12.82	4.99	4.18	28.01
99/67	6.67	3.73	23.72	4.69	12.73	5.15	3.52	27.75
99/68	6.87	3.50	25.32	5.00	13.52	4.89	3.61	28.67

Atka Mackerel Comparative Specimens

UVIC	VOME-1	VOME-2	DENT-1	DENT-2	DENT-3	ANGU-1	ANGU-2	ARTI-1
99/69	6.69	3.37	21.99	4.01	12.13	4.33	3.60	26.43
99/70	6.87	3.69	22.97	4.40	12.38	4.57	3.44	26.57
99/71	6.73	3.63	22.45	4.31	11.72	4.50	3.13	27.15
99/72	6.90	3.87	24.67	4.65	13.53	5.16	3.72	27.28
99/73	7.97	4.57	29.59	5.94	15.22	5.52	4.36	32.62
99/74	7.58	3.48	27.85	5.23	13.80	4.75	4.25	32.19
99/75	8.40	4.15	27.25	5.31	14.66	6.98	4.22	31.98
99/76	7.84	4.16	27.91	5.91	14.27	5.87	4.26	32.57
99/77	8.04	4.23	27.95	5.88	15.16	5.83	4.31	31.13
99/78	9.63	4.60	32.38	5.80	16.56	6.21	4.84	35.40
99/79	4.73	2.90	16.89	3.14	9.11	3.52	2.48	21.53
99/80	6.33	2.93	24.19	4.49	12.48	4.81	3.60	27.19
99/81	6.33	3.60	21.74	4.32	11.38	4.10	3.56	25.23
99/82	9.23	4.90	30.45	5.91	15.59	5.70	4.68	33.98
99/83	5.89	3.12	20.88	3.86	11.30	4.36	3.06	25.20
99/84	6.61	3.53	24.99	4.84	13.60	5.34	3.77	28.81
99/85	8.75	3.99	30.89	6.31	15.25	5.49	4.69	32.91
99/86	8.17	4.44	29.57	6.49	14.73	5.92	4.15	32.19
99/87	5.29	2.84	19.91	3.70	10.94	4.44	2.88	23.97
99/88	9.84	4.74	33.69	6.66	16.41	6.39	5.06	36.34
99/89	6.53	3.45	24.46	4.41	12.61	4.60	3.32	28.52
99/90	3.81	2.01	13.87	2.49	7.31	2.98	1.80	16.27
99/91	5.90	2.86	20.09	3.65	10.86	3.90	3.03	24.28
99/92	5.38	2.85	19.63	3.74	10.43	3.80	3.03	22.82
99/93	8.94	3.95	29.44	6.10	15.28	5.72	4.23	33.32
99/94	7.29	3.94	24.95	4.80	12.86	4.71	3.56	28.04
99/95	8.12	3.94	27.39	5.46	14.04	4.85	3.74	29.48
99/96	8.72	4.11	29.60	6.87	14.90	6.29	4.64	31.80
99/97	6.92	3.53	23.06	4.50	11.82	4.65	3.54	26.97
99/98	6.48	3.76	21.85	4.05	11.25	4.59	2.95	26.96
99/99	9.81	4.13	30.42	6.34	16.18	6.19	4.85	37.58
99/100	7.87	4.57	27.65	5.99	14.46	5.23	4.20	32.63
99/101	6.81	3.32	23.40	4.38	12.25	4.85	3.70	27.36
99/102	6.65	3.49	23.37	4.28	12.22	4.82	3.56	27.57
99/113	3.90	2.10	13.19	2.32	7.22	2.74	1.76	15.87
99/114	4.59	2.72	17.93	3.10	9.41	3.53	2.56	21.37
99/115	3.83	2.07	12.96	2.27	6.94	2.51	1.70	15.56
99/116	5.31	2.99	18.40	3.62	9.47	3.51	2.92	21.68
99/117	4.16	2.14	14.24	2.50	7.60	2.90	2.15	16.75
99/118	5.75	3.33	21.09	3.85	10.95	4.62	3.24	25.33
99/119	4.98	2.61	17.06	3.18	9.27	3.59	2.95	21.03
99/120	8.70	5.06	31.04	6.19	16.54	6.07	5.11	35.89
99/121	8.00	4.25	28.00	5.29	14.30	5.88	4.18	32.30
99/122	3.93	2.15	14.29	2.66	7.21	2.51	2.14	16.60
99/123	3.32	1.88	12.02	2.21	6.09	2.34	1.79	14.93
99/124	3.13	1.66	11.08	1.92	5.90	1.97	1.62	13.85
99/125	3.57	1.92	11.35	2.07	5.87	2.11	1.65	13.78
99/126	3.12	1.54	11.20	2.00	6.11	2.26	1.58	13.57

Atka Mackerel Comparative Specimens

UVIC	ARTI-2	ARTI-3	ARTI-4	PREM-1	PREM-2	PREM-3	QUAD-3	QUAD-4
92/45	8.27	3.17	2.31	17.80	8.80	5.93	2.57	13.35
95/21	11.63	4.08	3.09	24.23	11.87	7.83	3.73	15.71
99/23	9.80	4.19	3.21	22.26	11.12	6.87	3.36	16.80
99/24	12.85	5.18	4.65	32.00	15.37	9.68	5.28	19.85
99/25	12.48	4.98	3.92	27.72	13.62	8.70	4.58	18.14
99/26	10.55	4.10	3.04	21.45	11.26	7.34	3.52	16.24
99/27	14.38	6.05	4.87	33.67	17.86	10.49	5.50	23.04
99/28	13.86	5.66	4.52	31.06	14.91	9.60	4.92	19.91
99/29	11.04	4.23	2.73	21.91	11.29	7.24	3.42	16.18
99/30	11.47	4.36	3.40	22.80	11.15	7.54	3.54	16.86
99/31	11.49	4.49	3.74	24.24	12.57	7.56	4.23	18.28
99/32	10.44	4.21	3.30	21.97	11.89	7.57	3.36	16.85
99/33	15.36	5.83	5.04	33.71	17.78	10.05	5.63	24.69
99/34	12.40	4.92	3.63	25.65	12.16	8.25	4.17	18.08
99/35	13.41	5.40	4.14	31.14	14.76	9.34	4.60	20.74
99/36	11.96	4.59	3.62	27.52	11.93	8.08	4.48	18.68
99/37	11.58	4.98	4.54	27.96	12.20	7.63	4.62	20.21
99/38	12.32	5.00	4.15	30.25	14.58	8.96	4.65	18.43
99/39	10.72	3.99	3.07	22.66	11.11	7.30	3.67	16.40
99/40	12.50	5.56	3.99	28.34	13.04	8.72	4.67	19.51
99/41	10.79	4.07	3.31	24.42	11.99	7.96	3.87	16.24
99/42	11.46	4.76	3.58	23.11	11.93	7.77	3.87	17.55
99/43	14.00	5.47	4.50	30.64	14.89	9.96	5.03	21.77
99/44	9.49	3.60	3.39	21.08	11.14	6.90	3.48	15.37
99/45	12.05	5.01	4.32	29.08	14.34	9.38	4.83	19.77
99/46	10.13	3.80	2.97	21.11	11.16	7.19	3.41	15.81
99/47	15.25	5.50	5.30	33.64	17.48	11.24	6.09	24.11
99/48	13.42	5.24	4.41	28.80	13.30	8.70	5.06	19.31
99/49	12.35	4.83	3.94	26.11	13.86	9.21	4.61	19.00
99/50	12.73	5.45	4.48	30.50	13.35	8.87	4.85	20.07
99/51	5.37	2.25	1.51	11.89	5.97	4.11	1.73	9.16
99/52	9.86	3.90	2.92	21.33	11.49	7.22	3.15	15.58
99/53	5.87	2.33	1.63	11.98	6.59	4.27	1.68	8.67
99/54	10.91	4.42	2.93	22.22	11.64	7.39	3.37	15.60
99/55	10.25	4.15	3.04	22.72	11.94	7.66	3.76	16.71
99/56	13.15	4.95	4.29	28.31	14.87	8.94	5.06	19.97
99/57	13.63	5.09	3.90	27.58	14.24	8.98	4.83	20.16
99/58	12.60	4.61	3.67	26.47	11.89	7.77	4.26	18.67
99/59	10.74	4.08	3.23	22.47	11.86	7.67	3.52	17.11
99/60	13.21	5.72	4.29	29.90	13.90	8.76	4.80	21.85
99/61	9.00	3.58	2.63	18.54	9.74	6.06	2.97	14.56
99/62	10.47	3.84	2.66	19.79	10.00	6.64	3.25	15.34
99/63	14.86	6.30	4.93	33.39	17.60	10.94	5.83	21.65
99/64	12.46	5.08	3.97	29.08	12.99	8.50	4.68	19.21
99/65	11.34	4.82	3.76	26.75	13.41	8.42	4.16	17.54
99/66	10.82	3.96	3.47	24.25	11.82	7.97	3.95	17.52
99/67	10.91	4.06	3.01	22.30	11.21	7.36	3.62	15.40
99/68	10.55	4.51	3.21	23.08	11.50	7.37	3.70	17.75

Atka Mackerel Comparative Specimens

UVIC	ARTI-2	ARTI-3	ARTI-4	PREM-1	PREM-2	PREM-3	QUAD-3	QUAD-4
99/69	10.18	4.26	2.97	21.15	11.18	7.10	3.20	15.77
99/70	9.96	3.78	2.85	21.57	10.98	6.90	3.27	15.70
99/71	10.47	4.07	2.90	20.34	11.08	7.04	3.27	14.81
99/72	10.74	4.41	3.22	23.25	11.91	7.51	3.79	17.00
99/73	12.72	5.18	3.96	27.74	12.59	8.45	4.28	18.68
99/74	10.81	4.62	3.70	25.43	13.10	8.35	4.16	19.08
99/75	13.10	4.90	3.79	26.08	12.99	8.03	4.54	18.46
99/76	12.61	5.29	3.84	27.32	13.99	8.74	4.62	19.82
99/77	12.02	4.84	3.76	26.30	13.43	8.59	4.29	19.15
99/78	13.89	5.93	4.57	30.83	15.25	9.58	5.25	23.03
99/79	8.21	3.18	2.06	15.41	7.87	5.32	2.47	12.08
99/80	10.41	4.10	3.10	22.41	11.16	7.47	3.56	16.84
99/81	9.26	3.49	2.74	20.74	9.95	6.53	3.03	15.31
99/82	12.15	5.05	4.06	28.97	12.90	8.14	4.54	19.78
99/83	8.62	3.51	2.73	19.05	10.03	6.32	3.05	14.74
99/84	11.04	4.73	3.44	23.30	12.04	7.52	3.76	17.35
99/85	13.36	4.90	3.92	29.22	13.07	8.36	4.57	19.05
99/86	12.83	5.81	4.12	29.31	13.46	8.84	4.67	20.48
99/87	8.89	3.22	2.57	18.53	9.14	6.00	2.83	13.76
99/88	13.87	6.13	4.78	33.44	14.12	9.12	6.19	21.80
99/89	10.82	3.82	2.90	22.57	11.00	7.22	3.35	15.58
99/90	6.45	2.73	1.75	12.79	7.19	4.15	1.83	9.64
99/91	9.66	3.77	2.50	19.14	9.60	5.85	2.97	13.34
99/92	8.90	3.36	2.41	17.28	9.73	6.23	2.73	13.43
99/93	12.80	4.81	4.15	30.46	13.94	8.33	4.73	19.30
99/94	10.53	4.24	3.48	22.95	11.70	7.59	3.97	16.46
99/95	11.38	4.70	3.78	25.87	12.70	8.59	4.12	18.29
99/96	12.28	4.93	4.24	30.20	14.47	8.90	4.98	19.12
99/97	9.85	4.09	3.21	22.23	11.18	7.36	3.47	15.18
99/98	10.22	3.97	2.96	20.21	11.00	6.59	3.50	15.22
99/99	14.42	5.58	4.33	29.95	14.50	9.34	5.00	20.37
99/100	12.65	4.70	3.82	26.99	13.20	8.48	4.19	19.12
99/101	10.48	3.91	3.05	22.22	11.21	7.30	3.39	16.41
99/102	10.06	4.25	3.06	21.93	11.36	7.35	3.60	15.81
99/113	6.16	2.34	1.46	11.91	6.59	4.40	1.69	9.22
99/114	7.91	3.13	2.08	16.79	8.67	5.64	2.47	12.15
99/115	5.65	2.31	1.56	11.48	6.22	4.17	1.85	8.77
99/116	7.68	3.28	2.35	16.97	9.12	6.03	2.58	12.47
99/117	6.58	2.54	1.78	12.77	7.35	4.60	2.06	9.97
99/118	10.05	3.91	2.63	19.37	10.10	6.16	2.97	14.49
99/119	7.70	3.31	2.11	15.87	8.44	5.20	2.50	12.37
99/120	15.09	5.36	3.79	28.68	15.40	8.79	4.67	20.38
99/121	13.10	5.46	3.74	25.94	12.88	7.86	4.22	18.10
99/122	6.47	2.51	1.62	12.67	6.97	4.56	1.92	9.52
99/123	5.56	2.37	1.40	11.07	5.64	3.85	1.62	8.42
99/124	4.98	2.06	1.33	9.95	5.35	3.59	1.52	8.22
99/125	5.33	1.97	1.27	10.31	5.48	3.70	1.49	8.15
99/126	5.15	2.10	1.32	10.19	5.77	3.85	1.47	7.90

Atka Mackerel Comparative Specimens

UVIC	INTE-1	EPIH-1	EPIH-2	EPIH-3	BASI-1	BASI-2	HYOM-1	HYOM-2
92/45	3.93	9.87	1.88	7.52	10.10	1.10	9.72	20.28
95/21	4.81	12.55	2.01	9.53	13.13	1.50	12.28	26.76
99/23	4.12	12.21	2.31	9.25	11.96	1.43	11.60	25.59
99/24	5.68	17.03	2.56	12.06	15.76	2.72	16.20	32.96
99/25	4.81	15.39	2.81	11.34	14.76	1.76	14.71	31.58
99/26	4.47	12.02	2.21	9.47	12.20	1.96	12.08	25.58
99/27	6.30	17.91	3.18	13.27	17.32	3.80	17.30	36.03
99/28	5.63	16.98	2.63	12.43	14.61	1.88	15.49	33.88
99/29	4.61	11.49	2.43	8.79	11.13	1.85	10.95	24.35
99/30	4.74	12.20	2.61	9.27	12.71	1.75	12.43	25.93
99/31	5.17	13.71	3.11	10.46	13.11	2.31	13.44	28.42
99/32	4.57	12.18	2.77	8.81	11.55	2.29	11.58	25.31
99/33	7.42	19.17	4.27	13.67	17.18	2.57	18.07	38.01
99/34	4.90	13.13	3.27	10.16	13.06	2.09	13.27	28.42
99/35	5.47	15.22	3.60	11.85	14.20	2.87	14.73	32.73
99/36	5.70	14.71	3.72	11.34	14.81	2.15	14.62	29.23
99/37	5.40	14.85	2.17	11.39	15.34	1.62	14.47	30.97
99/38	5.14	14.79	2.47	10.75	14.50	2.41	14.73	30.81
99/39	4.69	12.57	2.07	9.24	11.85	1.42	11.98	25.41
99/40	5.32	15.74	2.76	11.51	14.54	2.54	14.41	32.38
99/41	4.51	12.59	2.10	9.85	12.35	1.73	12.40	27.10
99/42	4.76	12.66	1.98	9.55	12.16	1.95	12.82	26.62
99/43	6.01	16.54	3.23	12.87	16.20	2.51	16.51	34.77
99/44	4.19	12.25	2.15	9.01	11.70	1.57	11.57	24.35
99/45	6.50	15.28	2.19	11.12	14.31	3.21	14.77	30.74
99/46	4.72	12.20	2.10	9.21	11.95	1.62	11.80	26.08
99/47	7.01	18.57	3.05	13.02	17.17	2.69	17.01	37.56
99/48	5.95	15.03	2.60	11.63	14.85	2.22	13.86	29.90
99/49	5.30	14.61	2.41	10.63	13.98	1.94	14.05	30.16
99/50	6.05	15.28	2.60	12.19	15.02	1.58	15.09	33.04
99/51	2.15	6.32	1.07	5.14	6.67	0.90	6.59	14.45
99/52	4.36	11.23	2.16	8.56	11.49	1.52	11.47	23.53
99/53	2.51	6.17	0.95	4.86	6.76	0.97	6.52	14.13
99/54	4.42	11.06	1.98	8.84	11.63	2.08	10.97	24.27
99/55	4.37	12.02	2.46	9.35	11.76	1.46	11.35	25.28
99/56	5.00	15.88	2.23	11.88	15.41	2.91	16.28	32.92
99/57	5.92	15.26	2.29	11.37	14.00	2.35	14.98	31.39
99/58	4.85	14.92	2.91	11.07	14.12	2.60	14.79	30.66
99/59	4.59	13.30	2.75	9.93	12.96	1.91	12.80	25.43
99/60	5.97	16.19	2.85	12.78	15.63	3.26	16.10	33.23
99/61	3.45	10.55	2.11	8.08	10.35	1.38	10.17	22.01
99/62	4.23	11.28	2.21	8.75	11.25	1.39	10.64	23.96
99/63	5.29	17.39	3.10	12.56	16.70	1.81	17.13	36.06
99/64	6.09	14.40	2.29	10.90	14.19	1.60	13.91	29.90
99/65	5.47	14.10	2.27	10.76	13.56	1.37	14.40	29.18
99/66	4.60	12.84	2.07	9.45	13.30	1.66	12.51	26.65
99/67	4.40	11.69	1.78	9.06	12.00	1.36	11.63	24.05
99/68	4.36	12.84	2.70	9.80	12.55	1.79	12.47	26.14

Atka Mackerel Comparative Specimens

UVIC	INTE-1	EPIH-1	EPIH-2	EPIH-3	BASI-1	BASI-2	HYOM-1	HYOM-2
99/69	3.56	11.73	2.23	8.66	12.05	1.53	11.54	24.02
99/70	4.53	11.97	1.93	9.15	11.22	1.65	11.47	24.72
99/71	3.77	10.90	2.47	9.25	11.23	1.26	10.97	24.60
99/72	5.11	11.88	2.17	9.35	11.64	1.78	12.10	25.56
99/73	5.34	14.94	2.47	11.08	14.16	1.44	14.38	29.56
99/74	5.16	14.78	2.43	10.54	13.83	2.61	13.93	30.05
99/75	5.53	14.48	2.85	11.12	14.03	2.62	14.42	30.04
99/76	4.70	14.54	2.69	10.96	14.33	2.51	14.06	30.13
99/77	5.25	14.03	2.40	10.57	14.60	1.43	13.84	29.78
99/78	5.77	16.63	2.51	13.11	15.61	2.60	16.20	33.34
99/79	3.45	8.61	1.54	6.61	8.97	1.63	8.68	18.82
99/80	5.06	12.26	2.18	9.47	11.96	1.62	11.96	25.27
99/81	4.27	11.33	2.04	8.79	10.68	1.63	10.74	23.81
99/82	5.95	15.30	1.82	11.29	15.19	2.00	15.44	32.13
99/83	4.23	10.50	2.11	8.29	10.81	1.68	11.08	22.67
99/84	4.86	12.63	2.22	9.87	12.53	1.76	11.79	26.71
99/85	6.17	15.64	2.38	11.58	14.29	1.88	15.06	32.58
99/86	5.69	15.40	2.39	11.59	15.10	2.46	14.94	31.07
99/87	3.49	10.18	1.44	7.63	9.84	1.53	9.79	21.55
99/88	5.49	17.85	2.21	13.26	17.86	2.54	16.15	35.31
99/89	4.22	11.99	1.70	9.05	11.75	1.96	11.99	25.54
99/90	2.43	6.98	1.33	5.70	7.36	1.48	6.80	15.09
99/91	3.84	10.11	1.76	8.10	10.13	1.81	9.91	21.43
99/92	3.31	9.45	1.68	7.54	9.55	2.07	9.52	20.16
99/93	5.02	15.65	3.08	11.66	15.16	2.41	15.18	30.41
99/94	4.51	12.80	2.24	9.39	12.09	1.89	12.19	25.36
99/95	5.68	14.20	2.87	10.61	13.65	1.95	13.55	28.57
99/96	5.78	15.41	2.91	11.60	14.17	2.43	14.48	32.25
99/97	4.28	11.32	1.94	9.09	11.81	2.11	11.59	24.91
99/98	3.77	10.98	2.31	8.70	10.98	1.21	10.70	22.91
99/99	6.02	16.51	2.49	12.35	15.69	1.73	16.20	33.75
99/100	6.15	14.21	2.26	11.01	13.61	2.04	14.57	30.02
99/101	4.30	12.19	1.89	9.45	11.60	1.51	11.86	25.10
99/102	4.57	12.04	1.84	9.18	12.60	1.49	11.64	25.24
99/113	2.32	6.42	1.18	5.09	6.84	0.79	6.89	13.81
99/114	3.46	9.08	1.54	6.71	9.22	1.19	9.01	18.78
99/115	2.21	6.23	1.20	5.07	6.37	0.97	6.67	13.82
99/116	3.41	9.43	1.64	7.42	9.36	1.10	9.41	19.82
99/117	2.65	7.29	1.60	5.78	7.33	1.11	7.46	15.84
99/118	4.27	10.62	2.00	8.28	10.10	2.07	10.38	21.50
99/119	3.22	9.11	2.07	7.08	9.68	1.73	9.12	19.28
99/120	5.71	16.25	1.87	12.34	15.93	2.81	16.50	32.70
99/121	4.88	14.24	2.63	10.58	14.18	2.06	14.20	28.60
99/122	2.64	6.79	1.29	5.53	7.28	0.90	7.12	15.64
99/123	2.23	5.95	1.22	4.79	6.54	1.12	6.26	13.45
99/124	2.09	5.63	1.06	4.56	5.71	0.95	6.07	12.79
99/125	1.89	5.83	0.97	4.65	5.83	1.02	5.86	12.68
99/126	1.80	5.10	1.23	4.46	5.73	0.85	5.73	12.16

94

Atka Mackerel Comparative Specimens

UVIC	HYOM-3	HYH2-1	INPH-1	INPH-2	PHA2-1	PHA2-2	HYB3-1	VER1-1
92/45	4.54	3.83	15.22	2.40	6.24	3.05	5.42	3.83
95/21	5.30	4.84	19.08	3.19	8.69	3.67	7.25	4.61
99/23	4.72	4.89	19.14	2.99	8.42	3.58	6.93	4.40
99/24	5.52	6.27	23.72	3.82	10.49	4.73	9.40	5.71
99/25	5.91	6.09	21.86	3.20	10.80	4.32	8.54	5.85
99/26	4.99	5.04	19.13	2.65	8.54	3.66	6.99	5.19
99/27	7.19	7.37	26.33	4.45	11.94	4.70	10.04	7.31
99/28	5.91	6.71	24.21	3.91	10.70	4.16	9.14	6.47
99/29	5.17	4.43	18.28	3.01	7.84	3.34	6.81	4.60
99/30	4.83	4.83	18.84	2.91	9.25	3.20	6.85	4.49
99/31	4.81	5.62	20.92	3.46	9.35	3.88	7.97	5.49
99/32	4.65	4.38	18.26	2.93	8.47	3.41	7.30	4.32
99/33	6.60	7.16	27.99	4.21	12.16	5.43	10.50	7.27
99/34	5.14	5.41	21.12	3.35	9.95	4.15	8.16	5.72
99/35	5.99	6.10	22.43	4.07	10.71	4.63	8.84	5.75
99/36	5.85	5.55	21.75	3.53	9.62	4.36	8.70	5.30
99/37	5.50	6.15	23.12	3.57	9.95	3.75	8.52	5.23
99/38	4.99	5.90	23.36	4.08	9.90	4.65	8.84	5.49
99/39	4.87	4.61	19.13	2.83	8.49	3.62	6.89	4.82
99/40	5.38	5.83	23.59	3.71	9.76	3.51	8.91	5.62
99/41	5.00	5.23	18.97	3.70	9.46	3.69	6.96	4.94
99/42	4.90	4.65	19.01	3.19	8.78	3.65	7.62	5.23
99/43	6.61	6.41	24.60	4.20	10.74	4.49	10.24	6.38
99/44	4.92	4.63	17.56	2.87	8.30	3.04	6.88	4.50
99/45	5.28	5.92	22.16	3.68	9.73	4.49	8.44	5.58
99/46	5.10	4.62	18.64	2.92	7.85	3.42	6.86	4.72
99/47	7.03	7.43	26.24	4.72	12.76	5.14	11.07	7.06
99/48	6.09	6.05	22.51	3.53	9.58	4.07	8.49	5.49
99/49	5.24	5.32	21.28	3.69	9.84	4.12	8.33	5.76
99/50	5.71	6.07	23.08	3.58	10.17	4.44	8.77	5.54
99/51	3.07	2.52	9.98	1.39	4.25	1.78	3.61	2.53
99/52	5.10	4.40	17.71	2.60	7.94	3.18	6.69	4.40
99/53	3.14	2.44	10.35	1.41	4.67	2.08	3.49	2.66
99/54	4.87	4.65	17.77	3.01	8.05	3.27	6.58	4.58
99/55	4.98	5.16	18.82	3.15	7.89	3.66	6.70	4.68
99/56	5.89	6.41	22.70	3.75	10.48	4.08	9.33	5.55
99/57	5.55	6.00	21.83	3.84	10.36	4.64	8.87	6.47
99/58	4.97	5.36	21.89	3.40	9.71	3.93	8.38	5.91
99/59	4.54	5.25	19.50	2.88	8.52	3.71	7.64	4.83
99/60	5.90	6.32	24.02	3.76	11.13	4.61	9.45	5.54
99/61	4.15	3.93	15.85	2.27	7.65	2.80	6.26	4.13
99/62	4.62	4.26	17.89	2.81	7.96	3.26	6.43	4.35
99/63	6.54	6.52	24.63	4.27	11.46	5.09	10.37	6.82
99/64	5.48	5.75	22.07	3.83	10.10	4.01	8.29	5.47
99/65	5.51	5.71	20.43	3.69	9.41	4.20	7.87	5.43
99/66	4.98	5.08	19.70	3.10	8.64	3.60	7.44	4.70
99/67	4.64	4.62	18.40	2.78	7.79	3.62	7.04	4.58
99/68	4.63	4.71	18.79	3.10	8.91	3.33	7.30	4.96

Atka Mackerel Comparative Specimens

UVIC	HYOM-3	HYH2-1	INPH-1	INPH-2	PHA2-1	PHA2-2	HYB3-1	VER1-1
99/69	4.68	4.55	17.28	2.88	7.76	2.89	6.66	4.62
99/70	5.11	4.72	17.71	3.16	8.35	3.61	6.95	4.52
99/71	4.78	4.72	17.41	2.56	8.36	3.54	6.40	4.47
99/72	5.29	4.67	18.70	2.90	8.69	3.52	6.77	4.52
99/73	5.42	5.62	22.19	3.52	10.00	4.04	8.40	5.59
99/74	5.74	5.84	20.36	2.80	9.21	3.80	8.61	5.43
99/75	5.71	5.93	21.28	3.56	10.02	4.09	8.80	5.94
99/76	5.11	5.38	21.38	3.53	10.46	4.09	8.49	5.77
99/77	5.23	5.47	21.53	3.77	9.95	3.49	9.06	5.42
99/78	5.72	6.44	25.02	4.32	11.49	4.98	9.67	6.17
99/79	4.11	3.63	13.38	1.87	5.35	2.39	5.14	3.08
99/80	5.34	4.71	18.09	3.16	7.98	3.44	6.07	4.68
99/81	4.95	4.36	16.93	2.65	6.98	3.26	6.47	4.33
99/82	5.82	5.69	22.43	3.19	10.75	4.23	8.77	5.59
99/83	4.21	4.20	16.96	2.53	7.27	3.14	6.24	4.24
99/84	4.96	5.07	19.10	3.26	8.75	3.62	7.41	4.91
99/85	5.61	5.52	22.91	3.73	9.81	4.29	8.63	5.38
99/86	5.34	6.24	22.58	3.50	10.58	4.12	8.83	6.05
99/87	4.08	4.07	15.63	2.36	6.95	2.77	5.56	3.85
99/88	5.50	6.09	25.58	4.42	11.51	4.17	9.30	6.03
99/89	4.85	4.60	18.90	3.17	8.39	3.36	7.20	4.68
99/90	3.65	2.69	10.31	1.57	4.82	1.94	3.82	2.49
99/91	4.83	4.19	16.30	2.61	6.99	2.76	6.04	4.13
99/92	3.99	3.85	14.51	2.24	6.52	2.80	5.18	3.42
99/93	5.89	6.13	22.59	3.61	10.41	4.28	8.32	6.16
99/94	5.07	5.10	19.14	3.18	8.50	3.81	6.99	4.96
99/95	5.04	5.24	20.52	3.01	9.10	3.66	7.84	5.64
99/96	5.27	5.80	22.33	3.75	10.79	4.20	8.95	5.40
99/97	4.97	4.69	18.68	2.79	7.69	3.51	6.70	4.51
99/98	4.34	4.39	16.56	2.66	6.77	2.97	5.92	4.33
99/99	6.12	6.29	24.05	4.22	10.53	4.36	9.69	6.44
99/100	5.75	5.31	21.92	3.73	9.82	4.15	8.46	5.69
99/101	4.72	4.75	18.78	3.11	7.57	3.35	7.04	4.74
99/102	4.58	4.62	18.39	3.00	7.97	3.50	6.93	4.91
99/113	3.01	2.87	10.37	1.45	4.22	2.08	3.85	2.45
99/114	3.95	3.61	13.48	2.37	6.07	2.54	5.50	3.28
99/115	2.93	2.32	10.02	1.43	4.43	1.86	3.51	2.33
99/116	4.10	3.76	14.07	2.05	5.97	2.59	5.33	3.46
99/117	3.47	2.94	11.47	1.62	5.06	2.29	4.29	2.71
99/118	4.57	4.05	16.17	2.38	6.06	3.03	5.81	3.99
99/119	3.86	3.45	13.78	2.11	5.90	2.65	5.16	3.27
99/120	5.92	6.64	25.29	4.01	11.92	4.95	9.77	5.99
99/121	5.63	5.65	20.32	3.08	8.65	4.00	8.02	5.60
99/122	3.45	2.85	11.35	1.42	4.85	2.05	3.92	2.71
99/123	2.91	2.43	9.71	1.26	3.96	1.65	3.29	2.10
99/124	2.75	2.28	8.47	1.22	3.92	1.64	3.01	2.07
99/125	2.82	2.32	n/a	n/a	4.07	1.61	3.41	2.15
99/126	2.79	2.08	8.56	1.29	3.90	1.74	2.71	2.13

Atka Mackerel Comparative Specimens

UVIC	VER1-2	VER1-3	PEVE-1	PEVE-2	PEVE-3	OTOL-1	OTOL-2
92/45	4.50	2.25	3.39	3.39	2.81	4.33	2.04
95/21	5.70	2.25	3.90	4.23	3.57	n/a	n/a
99/23	5.81	2.48	3.90	4.26	3.58	5.19	2.47
99/24	7.03	2.78	4.76	5.47	3.88	6.11	2.62
99/25	6.83	2.33	4.38	4.73	3.73	6.66	2.60
99/26	6.35	2.53	4.45	4.65	3.86	5.18	2.25
99/27	8.06	2.66	5.98	5.66	4.32	6.71	2.89
99/28	7.66	2.93	5.05	5.55	4.30	6.41	2.81
99/29	5.31	2.21	3.95	4.18	3.30	4.80	2.05
99/30	5.31	2.35	4.20	4.39	3.50	5.31	2.27
99/31	6.31	2.67	4.60	4.92	3.67	5.69	2.45
99/32	5.58	2.44	3.91	4.31	3.67	5.11	2.40
99/33	8.27	2.49	5.69	6.00	4.90	7.11	2.85
99/34	6.59	2.36	4.48	4.57	3.48	5.20	2.56
99/35	7.09	2.74	4.73	5.01	4.25	6.61	2.71
99/36	6.18	2.31	4.42	4.57	3.92	6.31	2.41
99/37	6.58	2.29	4.31	4.58	3.64	6.59	2.39
99/38	6.84	2.75	4.52	5.22	4.04	6.28	2.62
99/39	5.97	2.31	4.00	4.36	3.59	4.90	2.24
99/40	7.22	2.01	4.65	5.22	4.10	6.67	2.62
99/41	5.83	2.87	4.26	4.49	3.22	5.50	2.31
99/42	6.49	2.34	4.29	4.39	3.45	5.41	2.43
99/43	7.49	3.25	5.03	5.04	4.27	6.72	2.58
99/44	5.47	2.68	3.77	4.24	3.13	5.15	2.15
99/45	6.85	2.69	4.62	4.83	3.69	6.24	2.69
99/46	5.82	2.29	4.01	3.95	3.13	5.23	2.31
99/47	8.32	3.01	5.83	6.11	4.70	6.59	2.74
99/48	6.78	2.30	4.39	4.87	3.61	6.45	2.35
99/49	6.82	2.08	4.55	4.72	3.69	n/a	2.76
99/50	7.09	2.93	4.66	4.79	3.93	6.80	2.50
99/51	3.18	1.47	2.45	2.36	2.04	3.45	1.58
99/52	5.48	2.14	3.60	4.07	3.15	4.64	2.29
99/53	3.23	1.66	2.45	2.28	2.08	3.37	1.74
99/54	5.61	2.09	3.86	4.35	3.46	5.26	2.34
99/55	5.70	2.36	4.06	4.09	3.33	5.13	2.30
99/56	6.55	2.41	4.75	5.04	3.94	6.05	2.28
99/57	7.53	2.43	4.80	5.24	4.02	6.59	2.86
99/58	6.57	2.54	4.53	4.58	3.78	5.80	2.55
99/59	5.83	2.20	4.12	4.83	3.51	5.01	2.39
99/60	7.32	2.64	4.46	5.22	4.12	6.26	2.32
99/61	5.19	2.06	3.47	3.66	2.96	4.70	1.97
99/62	5.51	2.33	3.80	3.56	2.97	5.36	2.43
99/63	7.64	2.64	5.88	5.67	4.19	6.75	2.73
99/64	6.56	1.91	4.70	4.72	3.65	5.60	2.58
99/65	7.00	2.43	4.65	4.62	3.85	6.82	2.53
99/66	6.03	2.20	3.88	4.46	3.48	4.99	2.33
99/67	5.43	2.28	3.94	4.14	3.41	4.89	2.28
99/68	6.12	2.41	4.05	4.42	3.69	5.30	2.28

Atka Mackerel Comparative Specimens

UVIC	VER1-2	VER1-3	PEVE-1	PEVE-2	PEVE-3	OTOL-1	OTOL-2
99/69	5.44	2.70	3.80	4.21	3.37	4.69	2.15
99/70	5.55	2.59	4.11	3.98	3.48	5.08	2.21
99/71	5.84	2.35	3.66	4.11	2.84	5.49	2.29
99/72	6.13	2.30	3.94	4.54	3.25	5.40	2.35
99/73	6.67	2.55	4.43	4.83	3.69	6.35	2.37
99/74	6.29	2.07	4.32	4.91	3.66	6.73	2.39
99/75	6.88	2.76	4.65	5.09	4.04	6.08	2.62
99/76	6.96	2.67	4.59	4.66	3.87	6.01	2.52
99/77	5.86	2.64	4.12	4.34	3.41	5.88	2.48
99/78	7.48	2.58	5.14	5.08	4.12	6.82	2.86
99/79	3.63	1.82	2.73	2.70	2.59	4.16	1.94
99/80	5.66	2.34	4.13	4.17	3.36	4.98	2.47
99/81	5.48	1.83	4.04	3.75	2.98	4.69	2.19
99/82	6.98	2.56	4.59	4.87	3.79	5.84	2.40
99/83	5.10	2.10	3.67	3.63	n/a	4.95	2.09
99/84	6.10	2.34	4.18	4.17	3.21	5.67	2.31
99/85	6.58	2.54	4.59	4.71	3.84	6.06	2.56
99/86	7.01	2.69	4.59	4.75	3.93	5.51	2.64
99/87	4.51	1.88	3.38	3.38	2.92	4.89	2.01
99/88	6.96	1.96	4.66	4.95	3.86	6.77	2.95
99/89	5.54	2.30	4.01	4.35	3.07	5.12	2.09
99/90	3.40	1.45	2.48	2.56	2.18	3.63	1.74
99/91	5.05	2.11	3.49	3.57	2.73	4.94	2.14
99/92	4.34	1.84	3.10	2.95	2.50	4.27	2.09
99/93	7.14	2.86	4.89	5.31	4.07	6.35	2.41
99/94	5.66	2.36	4.16	4.33	3.28	5.53	2.43
99/95	6.83	2.77	4.65	4.68	3.97	6.45	2.61
99/96	6.58	2.71	4.78	5.35	3.91	6.26	2.73
99/97	5.71	2.40	3.88	4.17	3.28	5.18	2.18
99/98	5.44	2.23	3.67	4.01	3.35	4.59	2.10
99/99	6.97	2.67	4.90	4.87	4.18	5.86	2.29
99/100	7.02	2.64	4.52	4.78	3.70	6.66	2.67
99/101	5.69	2.27	3.91	4.45	3.32	5.25	2.34
99/102	5.53	2.26	3.88	4.38	3.17	5.64	2.41
99/113	3.22	1.40	2.44	2.34	2.12	3.31	1.64
99/114	4.16	1.72	3.02	2.81	2.46	4.14	2.03
99/115	2.93	1.41	2.23	2.36	2.09	3.42	1.60
99/116	4.41	1.88	3.08	3.06	2.69	4.74	2.16
99/117	3.35	1.54	2.61	2.71	2.27	3.72	1.74
99/118	4.71	2.12	3.53	3.56	n/a	4.76	2.33
99/119	4.17	1.73	2.97	2.85	2.54	3.99	2.02
99/120	7.04	3.15	4.75	5.03	4.09	5.87	2.88
99/121	6.80	2.56	4.72	4.65	3.71	5.98	2.28
99/122	3.46	1.54	2.64	2.63	2.16	3.24	1.62
99/123	2.79	1.33	2.22	2.16	1.82	3.15	1.57
99/124	2.80	1.33	2.12	1.97	1.95	2.78	1.51
99/125	2.69	1.30	2.16	2.04	1.99	3.00	1.50
99/126	2.63	1.35	2.08	2.01	1.96	2.80	1.54

Greenling Comparative Specimens

Specimen	Species	TL	SL	Wt
82/07	*H. decagrammus*	395		966.60
83/08	*H. stelleri*	140		29.00
83/87	*H. decagrammus*	180		74.50
83/88	*H. decagrammus*	220		135.60
83/89	*H. decagrammus*	150		68.40
84/28	*H. stelleri*	265		374.30
84/29	*H. stelleri*	308		376.60
88/78	*H. stelleri*			226.25
88/105	*H. decagrammus*	142		34.90
93/77	*H. decagrammus*	230		115.10
97/16	*H. octagrammus*	92		6.72
99/03	*H. decagrammus*	355	318	615.90
00/07	*H. octagrammus*	163	145	47.02
00/08	*H. octagrammus*	173	155	61.75
00/09	*H. lagocephalus*	169	150	54.16
00/11	*Hexagrammos sp.*	69	60	4.04
00/12	*Hexagrammos sp.*	74	64	4.43
00/13	*Hexagrammos sp.*	68	58	3.56
00/14	*Hexagrammos sp.*	70	60	3.67
00/15	*Hexagrammos sp.*	69	59	3.46
00/16	*Hexagrammos sp.*	89	76	7.84
BN REF#328	*H. lagocephalus*	470	420	2000.00

Specimen	VOME-1	VOME-2	DENT-1	DENT-2	DENT-3	ANGU-1	ANGU-2	ARTI-1
82/07	11.11	4.60	22.70	5.91	13.00	6.36	5.38	23.86
83/08	3.17	1.65	n/a	n/a	n/a	n/a	n/a	9.42
83/87	4.37	1.99	9.65	2.55	5.76	2.66	2.02	11.12
83/88	n/a	n/a	11.49	3.42	6.54	n/a	n/a	n/a
83/89	4.25	2.19	9.88	2.69	5.83	3.19	2.04	11.10
84/28	6.82	3.27	17.94	3.68	10.10	4.83	3.63	18.12
84/29	6.83	3.42	18.19	4.19	10.84	5.03	3.95	18.70
88/78	5.71	3.08	14.68	3.77	8.24	4.24	2.97	15.88
88/105	3.22	1.33	8.00	2.09	4.55	2.04	1.57	9.10
93/77	5.40	2.78	13.02	2.89	7.19	3.85	2.65	13.62
97/16	1.90	1.07	5.38	1.29	2.71	1.32	0.93	5.80
99/03	9.16	3.79	20.14	5.09	11.28	5.77	4.48	21.42
00/07	3.37	1.76	8.73	2.31	4.80	2.62	1.90	10.11
00/08	3.86	1.94	9.65	2.67	5.05	2.77	2.06	10.58
00/09	3.70	1.67	9.68	2.68	5.27	2.82	2.11	10.90
00/11	1.52	0.66	3.98	0.93	1.94	0.88	0.76	4.64
00/12	1.59	0.79	4.20	1.11	2.53	1.06	0.77	4.97
00/13	1.55	0.74	3.97	1.04	2.31	n/a	n/a	4.58
00/14	1.49	0.73	3.90	0.94	2.07	n/a	n/a	4.48
00/15	1.42	0.67	3.71	0.90	2.00	n/a	n/a	4.37
00/16	1.74	0.89	4.99	1.21	2.84	1.25	0.96	5.56
BN REF#328	15.75	5.11	34.74	11.17	17.79	8.29	7.89	34.85

Greenling Comparative Specimens

Specimen	ARTI-3	ARTI-4	PREM-1	PREM-2	PREM-3	QUAD-3	QUAD-4	INTE-1
82/07	4.39	4.26	21.03	18.85	10.75	4.21	15.07	5.86
83/08	1.54	1.37	7.29	6.50	3.55	1.41	5.49	1.50
83/87	1.94	1.66	8.50	7.94	4.06	1.82	6.63	1.99
83/88	n/a	n/a	9.15	9.41	5.08	2.24	7.94	n/a
83/89	2.00	1.67	8.61	8.55	4.46	1.90	7.07	1.91
84/28	3.44	3.08	15.95	12.48	7.23	3.26	11.40	4.23
84/29	3.36	3.06	16.58	13.70	8.17	3.23	11.64	3.84
88/78	3.01	2.81	12.17	10.80	6.45	2.71	9.78	3.33
88/105	1.59	1.34	6.55	6.56	3.47	1.44	5.39	1.47
93/77	2.32	2.25	11.15	9.31	5.20	2.34	8.38	2.73
97/16	1.07	0.89	3.89	4.14	2.12	0.93	3.60	n/a
99/03	4.12	3.99	17.95	15.80	8.52	3.80	13.29	4.48
00/07	1.76	1.66	7.14	6.95	3.48	1.81	6.16	1.86
00/08	1.94	1.78	8.18	7.59	3.87	1.96	6.52	2.04
00/09	1.93	1.74	7.59	7.48	3.76	1.95	6.13	1.94
00/11	0.69	0.56	2.75	2.99	1.59	0.68	2.72	n/a
00/12	0.98	0.65	3.26	3.25	1.68	0.70	2.87	n/a
00/13	0.83	0.56	3.10	3.12	1.55	0.73	2.73	n/a
00/14	0.80	0.63	3.17	2.92	1.46	0.67	2.59	n/a
00/15	0.74	0.64	2.89	2.70	1.47	0.66	2.54	n/a
00/16	1.02	0.84	3.82	n/a	1.96	0.89	3.20	n/a
BN REF#328	7.03	7.70	32.58	22.76	12.71	7.10	18.06	6.75

Specimen	EPIH-1	EPIH-2	EPIH-3	BASI-1	BASI-2	HYOM-1	HYOM-2	HYOM-3
82/07	13.08	3.87	8.89	n/a	n/a	14.86	25.17	4.88
83/08	4.50	1.21	3.35	n/a	n/a	4.53	9.04	1.97
83/87	5.23	1.44	4.15	4.94	1.33	5.78	11.16	2.45
83/88	n/a	n/a	n/a	n/a	n/a	n/a	n/a	n/a
83/89	5.53	1.82	4.27	5.03	1.25	5.66	11.11	2.31
84/28	9.92	2.20	7.36	n/a	n/a	10.63	19.12	3.76
84/29	10.03	2.55	7.32	7.91	1.93	10.78	19.30	3.89
88/78	8.41	2.04	6.22	n/a	n/a	8.80	16.20	3.13
88/105	4.25	1.30	3.41	4.07	0.88	4.52	9.21	1.98
93/77	7.20	1.70	5.22	6.54	1.01	7.75	14.47	2.67
97/16	2.57	0.89	2.31	2.67	0.63	2.99	6.24	1.44
99/03	11.67	3.53	8.85	10.03	1.70	11.71	21.72	4.36
00/07	4.49	1.59	3.84	4.83	1.24	5.09	10.10	1.91
00/08	4.76	1.73	4.13	5.12	1.44	5.24	10.36	2.24
00/09	4.71	1.71	3.96	4.60	1.27	5.45	10.09	2.09
00/11	1.82	0.60	1.69	1.78	0.44	1.88	4.76	0.98
00/12	1.95	0.68	1.82	1.89	0.54	2.28	5.19	1.14
00/13	1.84	0.58	1.66	1.89	0.54	2.07	4.83	0.99
00/14	1.81	0.70	1.68	n/a	n/a	2.16	4.79	1.05
00/15	1.75	0.58	1.71	1.89	0.34	2.14	4.74	0.89
00/16	2.36	0.88	2.11	2.45	0.55	2.49	6.02	1.20
BN REF#328	18.41	5.05	12.80	14.14	4.35	19.59	36.20	7.31

Greenling Comparative Specimens

Specimen	HYH2-1	INPH-1	INPH-2	PHA2-1	PHA2-2	HYB3-1	VER1-1	VER1-2
82/07	5.87	17.60	3.27	n/a	n/a	n/a	6.05	5.79
83/08	1.89	n/a	n/a	n/a	n/a	n/a	1.75	1.93
83/87	2.55	n/a	n/a	3.80	1.76	3.06	2.28	2.78
83/88	2.61	n/a	n/a	n/a	n/a	n/a	2.62	2.83
83/89	n/a	n/a	n/a	n/a	n/a	n/a	2.16	2.51
84/28	4.09	n/a	n/a	n/a	n/a	n/a	3.94	4.17
84/29	4.12	n/a	n/a	n/a	n/a	n/a	3.95	4.35
88/78	3.62	11.51	1.79	5.51	2.57	n/a	n/a	n/a
88/105	1.85	5.58	0.96	2.57	1.27	2.41	1.78	1.95
93/77	2.65	9.92	1.61	4.38	2.43	3.99	3.04	3.62
97/16	1.12	3.95	0.63	1.96	0.97	1.71	1.16	1.52
99/03	5.45	14.97	2.44	6.80	3.80	6.73	4.91	5.02
00/07	2.06	6.62	1.18	3.10	1.55	2.87	2.31	2.71
00/08	2.27	6.88	1.23	3.35	1.87	3.01	2.45	2.69
00/09	2.11	7.00	1.21	3.16	1.84	n/a	2.21	2.63
00/11	0.81	2.81	0.35	1.30	0.70	n/a	n/a	n/a
00/12	0.84	3.17	0.54	1.43	0.75	n/a	0.92	1.14
00/13	0.79	2.86	0.46	1.34	0.86	n/a	0.85	1.08
00/14	0.79	2.85	0.47	1.33	0.62	n/a	0.87	1.08
00/15	0.78	2.83	0.51	1.32	0.63	1.08	0.82	1.11
00/16	1.05	3.50	0.64	1.72	0.95	1.43	1.12	1.29
BN REF#328	8.62	24.96	5.78	8.79	6.34	10.80	8.96	7.88

Specimen	VER1-3	PEVE-1	PEVE-2	PEVE-3	OTOL-1	OTOL-2
82/07	2.29	4.78	4.51	3.95	n/a	n/a
83/08	1.31	1.76	1.29	1.12	3.04	1.30
83/87	1.19	1.99	1.90	1.77	3.33	1.44
83/88	1.62	2.29	2.46	2.08	n/a	n/a
83/89	1.09	2.00	1.94	1.76	n/a	n/a
84/28	2.36	3.07	4.10	2.97	4.19	1.95
84/29	2.22	n/a	n/a	n/a	4.26	2.06
88/78	n/a	2.48	2.68	2.11	n/a	n/a
88/105	0.88	1.63	1.50	1.44	n/a	n/a
93/77	1.92	2.45	2.70	2.15	3.70	1.79
97/16	0.70	1.11	0.98	0.80	1.90	0.89
99/03	2.14	4.06	4.09	3.41	5.32	2.24
00/07	1.20	2.08	1.76	1.44	2.85	1.26
00/08	1.38	2.19	2.11	1.72	2.97	1.36
00/09	1.25	2.16	1.80	1.71	2.70	1.27
00/11	n/a	0.80	0.67	0.64	1.38	0.70
00/12	0.55	0.87	0.77	0.60	1.55	0.77
00/13	0.53	0.80	0.78	0.64	1.44	0.69
00/14	0.48	0.77	0.66	0.63	1.57	0.80
00/15	0.47	n/a	n/a	n/a	1.67	0.75
00/16	0.61	1.02	0.87	0.77	1.69	0.86
BN REF#328	2.92	5.91	5.83	4.37	n/a	n/a

Irish Lord Comparative Specimens

Specimen	Species	TL	Wt
91/124	*H. hemilepidotus*	190	109.90
91/125	*H. hemilepidotus*	155	54.48
91/126	*H. hemilepidotus*	130	36.85
94/26	*H. jordani*	225	132.55
97/43	*H. papilio*	330	411.99
97/60	*H. papilio*	375	643.00
97/61	*H. papilio*	372	604.40
00/87	*H. papilio*	359	582.90

Specimen	VOME-1	VOME-2	DENT-1	DENT-2	DENT-3	ANGU-1	ANGU-2	ARTI-1
91/124	6.13	2.66	21.46	3.73	9.40	4.60	3.65	18.75
91/125	4.69	1.95	17.08	2.71	6.73	3.71	n/a	14.97
91/126	n/a	n/a	n/a	n/a	n/a	n/a	n/a	n/a
94/26	6.43	2.84	20.85	3.46	8.90	4.19	3.24	18.89
97/43	8.49	4.23	36.35	5.23	15.48	5.19	5.96	30.17
97/60	11.19	4.83	38.38	6.74	16.51	5.47	6.70	34.20
97/61	10.00	4.28	39.56	6.72	15.82	5.68	6.40	33.05
00/87	9.96	4.60	37.86	7.00	16.62	7.04	6.57	30.36

Specimen	ARTI-2	ARTI-3	ARTI-4	PREM-1	PREM-2	PREM-3	QUAD-3	QUAD-4
91/124	10.30	3.74	3.37	14.11	11.32	6.79	2.29	11.08
91/125	7.06	2.78	2.18	10.56	9.25	5.27	1.89	9.00
91/126	n/a	n/a	n/a	n/a	n/a	n/a	n/a	n/a
94/26	10.59	3.48	3.46	13.06	11.76	6.99	2.59	11.68
97/43	15.86	5.05	4.85	26.19	16.22	9.97	4.15	18.27
97/60	18.11	5.54	4.86	28.07	14.94	9.47	4.63	20.66
97/61	16.71	5.80	6.19	28.96	16.25	10.69	4.95	21.67
00/87	17.53	6.28	5.87	28.56	16.27	11.04	5.14	20.56

Specimen	INTE-1	EPIH-1	EPIH-2	EPIH-3	HYOM-1	HYOM-2	HYOM-3	HYH2-1
91/124	n/a	11.62	1.61	7.12	9.30	14.60	3.95	2.54
91/125	4.23	n/a	n/a	n/a	n/a	n/a	n/a	2.04
91/126	n/a	n/a	n/a	n/a	n/a	n/a	n/a	n/a
94/26	5.30	11.42	1.54	7.18	9.18	14.37	3.15	2.83
97/43	7.29	19.71	2.28	12.28	14.27	23.61	3.80	3.90
97/60	7.78	21.68	2.43	10.78	15.56	26.69	3.89	4.74
97/61	8.24	24.31	2.72	12.49	16.30	28.00	4.55	4.54
00/87	8.20	23.74	2.62	12.54	15.33	28.51	3.80	4.66

Irish Lord Comparative Specimens

Specimen	INPH-1	INPH-3	INPH-4	PHA2-1	PHA2-2	HYB3-1	VER1-1	VER1-2
91/124	11.92	2.86	2.78	n/a	n/a	n/a	3.10	3.55
91/125	n/a	2.28	1.39	4.33	3.41	n/a	2.43	2.67
91/126	n/a	n/a	n/a	n/a	n/a	n/a	n/a	n/a
94/26	11.29	3.01	3.27	5.37	3.86	7.91	3.28	3.56
97/43	16.26	4.02	3.43	7.47	5.84	14.00	4 .00	4.33
97/60	19.00	5.30	4.38	9.41	6.95	17.94	4.85	6.07
97/61	19.38	5.71	6.15	9.76	7.52	18.77	5.30	6.88
00/87	20.73	4.91	4.30	9.21	7.14	17.71	5.03	5.85

Specimen	VER1-3	PEVE-1	PEVE-2	PEVE-3	OTOL-1	OTOL-2
91/124	2.25	2.31	3.14	2.32	5.69	2.43
91/125	1.71	1.94	2.23	2.02	4.34	2.05
91/126	n/a	n/a	n/a	n/a	3.99	1.78
94/26	2.06	2.64	2.67	2.67	n/a	n/a
97/43	2.54	3.32	4.15	3.15	n/a	n/a
97/60	3.83	3.97	4.71	3.27	7.21	4.07
97/61	3.71	4.46	4.87	3.29	7.94	3.68
00/87	3.25	5.00	5.30	3.57	7.81	4.03

Pacific Cod Comparative Specimens

Specimen	FL	SL	TL	Wt
83/76			600	
90/145			335	429.91
83/55			280	220.00
83/56			350	460.00
93/27			290	247.54
93/28			325	374.36
98/12	645		655	3250.00
98/13	320		325	339.62
BN138	320	285		410.00
BN136	335	285		371.00
BN137	330	280		490.00
BN141	690	650		3811.00
98/43	550	510		1915.00
00/65	855	800	865	8100.00
00/79	800	750	805	7200.00
00/83	705	665	715	4700.00
GM-001	610	560		2717.00
GM-002	470	440		1304.00
GM-003	260	245		207.00
GM-004	590	550		2750.00
GM-005	580	550		2400.00
GM-006	650	605		3600.00
GM-007	290	270		227.40
GM-008	490	460		1296.60
GM-009	320	300		322.60
GM-010	500	470		1454.80
GM-011	340	320		410.70
GM-012	640	590		3619.00
GM-013	880	830		10900.00
GM-014	360	330		515.00
GM-015	745	690		6200.00

Pacific Cod Comparative Specimens

Specimen	VOME-1	VOME-2	DENT-1	DENT-2	DENT-3	ANGU-1	ANGU-2	PREM-1
83/76	19.75	10.90	58.25	5.65	34.95	n/a	n/a	42.25
90/145	10.70	5.70	30.05	3.05	20.60	6.05	4.80	22.10
83/55	9.70	5.00	26.15	2.70	17.00	4.30	3.80	19.85
83/56	11.35	5.90	31.45	3.40	20.80	n/a	n/a	24.95
93/27	9.40	4.85	26.70	2.60	18.10	4.60	4.40	20.15
93/28	10.80	5.45	29.10	2.95	19.50	4.80	4.35	21.75
98/12	22.10	11.40	60.30	6.25	40.30	10.50	11.00	46.65
98/13	9.05	4.90	26.35	2.60	18.35	4.90	4.40	21.00
BN138	12.10	6.35	30.60	3.20	20.60	5.60	5.00	24.05
BN136	10.45	5.60	28.90	2.85	19.45	5.10	4.70	22.80
BN137	11.70	6.10	30.40	3.00	20.55	5.00	4.75	24.10
BN141	25.35	13.05	69.60	7.35	46.05	12.45	12.70	50.90
98/43	19.60	10.45	52.20	5.20	33.75	10.05	9.40	42.20
00/65	27.30	13.32	72.54	8.94	47.25	14.34	14.46	54.57
00/79	27.58	13.66	74.23	8.23	48.33	15.56	13.66	57.08
00/83	22.96	11.62	63.83	7.29	41.32	12.62	11.81	49.49
GM-001	20.17	10.29	60.53	5.57	36.83	12.09	9.55	45.69
GM-002	16.32	8.44	43.11	4.23	28.39	8.81	7.76	34.75
GM-003	8.22	4.41	23.05	2.13	14.98	3.91	3.53	17.94
GM-004	17.70	10.00	53.81	5.31	36.27	10.24	9.82	42.09
GM-005	19.83	9.33	52.11	5.33	32.96	9.49	9.43	40.67
GM-006	21.29	10.58	60.60	6.08	38.81	11.87	10.94	49.55
GM-007	8.91	4.79	24.76	2.44	16.83	4.05	3.69	18.92
GM-008	15.65	8.32	44.51	4.14	28.39	8.00	7.35	36.27
GM-009	10.08	5.31	28.52	2.59	18.51	4.98	4.47	21.24
GM-010	16.63	8.46	47.10	4.84	30.25	9.29	7.59	36.01
GM-011	11.48	6.20	31.59	3.04	20.77	6.06	4.79	24.84
GM-012	20.39	10.92	59.22	5.63	38.41	8.21	11.10	45.15
GM-013	28.01	13.27	79.13	8.38	48.82	16.99	15.18	58.92
GM-014	11.67	6.13	32.01	2.97	21.63	5.28	5.06	26.63
GM-015	27.84	13.06	73.62	8.37	47.94	14.86	14.04	59.49

Pacific Cod Comparative Specimens

Specimen	PREM-2	PREM-3	QUAD-3	QUAD-4	INTE-1	EPIH-1	EPIH-2	EPIH-3
83/76	14.60	11.80	7.95	29.55	15.80	20.05	4.25	15.45
90/145	7.80	6.20	4.75	16.90	7.65	11.00	3.05	8.60
83/55	6.50	5.05	3.80	13.75	5.50	9.35	2.25	6.85
83/56	8.15	6.00	4.80	16.40	n/a	11.30	3.10	8.90
93/27	6.60	5.30	3.80	14.90	7.05	9.10	2.45	6.70
93/28	7.70	6.15	4.45	17.85	7.60	10.50	2.65	7.65
98/12	15.40	10.65	9.65	37.40	16.45	22.70	6.55	17.70
98/13	7.15	5.80	4.00	15.55	7.25	9.45	2.20	7.20
BN138	7.80	6.50	4.40	17.70	8.70	11.00	2.75	8.85
BN136	7.15	5.90	4.00	17.60	7.85	10.45	3.00	8.40
BN137	7.60	6.10	4.15	18.00	8.55	11.35	2.40	9.00
BN141	16.75	12.50	10.35	40.70	20.95	27.10	6.40	19.95
98/43	13.35	10.05	7.80	29.30	14.35	19.00	5.25	14.30
00/65	19.69	15.72	14.70	43.71	21.64	28.27	7.94	20.59
00/79	17.63	14.42	11.27	40.48	21.63	28.28	8.66	20.72
00/83	16.08	13.54	9.93	38.62	17.46	23.67	6.38	18.90
GM-001	14.54	11.31	9.14	31.04	15.64	19.21	5.88	14.89
GM-002	10.57	8.73	6.35	23.31	11.97	15.67	4.32	12.37
GM-003	5.31	4.36	3.40	13.81	5.84	7.92	2.24	6.11
GM-004	13.34	11.02	7.85	27.17	13.32	19.33	5.49	15.46
GM-005	13.47	10.99	7.63	29.52	14.43	19.50	6.23	14.62
GM-006	14.58	12.34	9.12	34.48	17.41	23.08	6.55	17.29
GM-007	6.17	4.98	3.80	13.92	6.08	8.67	2.22	6.81
GM-008	11.45	8.91	6.33	25.94	11.28	15.38	4.54	12.38
GM-009	6.82	5.20	4.21	15.42	7.17	9.40	3.00	7.66
GM-010	11.10	9.38	6.24	24.97	11.72	15.50	4.77	12.17
GM-011	7.73	6.21	4.46	17.42	7.94	10.05	2.61	8.01
GM-012	13.11	10.76	8.13	29.99	18.15	21.39	6.58	15.78
GM-013	20.76	15.70	12.86	44.62	22.13	30.59	8.82	23.25
GM-014	8.02	6.47	4.57	17.82	8.29	10.97	3.06	8.32
GM-015	17.87	14.35	12.83	43.07	21.18	28.81	8.54	20.71

Pacific Cod Comparative Specimens

Specimen	PHA2-1	PHA2-2	HYP3-1	EPB4-1	EPB3-1	VER1-1	VER1-2	VER1-3
83/76	15.65	10.05	13.70	23.40	9.95	9.20	n/a	5.75
90/145	7.75	5.50	7.60	12.10	4.50	4.60	n/a	2.85
83/55	6.65	5.10	n/a	n/a	n/a	4.05	n/a	2.25
83/56	7.70	5.80	8.65	12.85	5.95	4.65	n/a	2.85
93/27	7.10	4.90	6.80	10.10	4.00	3.90	n/a	2.45
93/28	7.60	4.55	7.50	12.00	4.30	4.85	n/a	2.85
98/12	15.85	11.00	18.20	24.35	10.40	10.20	n/a	6.10
98/13	6.85	5.00	7.45	11.00	4.40	3.95	n/a	2.30
BN138	7.50	5.50	9.05	12.00	4.95	4.75	n/a	2.50
BN136	7.65	4.85	7.85	11.55	4.45	4.60	n/a	2.95
BN137	8.10	5.15	8.35	12.05	4.90	4.85	n/a	2.40
BN141	19.00	13.50	18.80	29.45	12.25	12.20	n/a	6.40
98/43	13.55	8.75	13.50	20.45	8.70	8.40	n/a	4.95
00/65	18.20	10.67	20.00	30.44	12.81	13.68	14.14	6.61
00/79	18.11	10.11	18.62	30.73	12.40	12.76	n/a	6.78
00/83	16.44	8.94	17.73	27.67	10.62	10.77	11.55	6.39
GM-001	14.25	10.24	14.65	23.61	8.64	9.49	11.06	5.68
GM-002	10.95	7.88	12.44	18.34	6.77	7.37	7.37	3.66
GM-003	5.92	4.18	6.14	8.88	3.41	3.57	3.57	1.94
GM-004	14.21	9.26	13.91	22.48	8.59	8.54	9.95	5.38
GM-005	14.44	8.20	15.22	22.19	9.08	9.43	9.83	4.07
GM-006	15.44	11.46	17.00	25.11	10.37	10.59	11.74	5.92
GM-007	6.52	3.65	6.33	10.12	3.80	3.86	4.25	2.29
GM-008	10.38	6.89	11.36	18.33	7.07	7.09	7.77	4.32
GM-009	6.66	4.90	6.96	11.18	3.73	4.45	4.65	2.38
GM-010	11.99	7.64	12.34	18.85	7.39	7.52	8.21	4.27
GM-011	7.89	4.95	7.78	12.32	4.47	4.79	5.21	2.53
GM-012	15.36	8.74	15.94	24.41	10.61	9.47	10.90	5.34
GM-013	21.28	15.36	23.37	36.24	14.80	14.25	17.19	8.26
GM-014	7.72	5.29	8.15	12.64	4.66	5.20	5.42	3.17
GM-015	20.49	12.02	20.87	30.29	13.08	12.74	13.69	6.81

Pacific Cod Comparative Specimens

Specimen	VER9-1	VER9-2	VER9-3
83/76	10.25	11.80	8.75
90/145	4.90	5.10	4.70
83/55	4.10	4.25	3.95
83/56	5.15	5.35	4.85
93/27	4.15	4.20	3.80
93/28	5.05	5.25	4.85
98/12	11.80	12.60	9.20
98/13	4.35	4.70	3.95
BN138	5.05	5.35	4.80
BN136	4.80	4.80	4.75
BN137	5.10	5.20	4.80
BN141	13.10	14.10	11.20
98/43	9.60	9.95	7.85
00/65	15.31	15.31	12.16
00/79	15.83	15.13	12.15
00/83	12.99	12.93	10.61
GM-001	11.46	11.24	8.76
GM-002	7.83	7.56	6.47
GM-003	3.56	3.80	3.42
GM-004	10.03	9.96	8.17
GM-005	10.50	10.96	8.22
GM-006	12.24	11.76	9.23
GM-007	3.99	4.43	3.75
GM-008	7.93	8.40	6.63
GM-009	4.55	4.83	4.17
GM-010	8.05	8.08	6.87
GM-011	5.01	5.49	4.52
GM-012	11.34	11.74	9.32
GM-013	17.62	17.08	13.69
GM-014	5.45	5.34	4.59
GM-015	15.56	14.21	10.97

Rockfish Comparative Specimens

Specimen	Species	TL	Wt
82/08	S. melanops	320	532.00
82/09	S. maliger	280	401.30
82/10	S. caurinus	325	558.40
82/12	S. nigrocinctus	270	362.80
82/13	Sebastes sp.	410	n/a
83/09	S. caurinus	260	375.00
83/10	S. caurinus	295	585.00
83/24	S. caurinus	380	819.50
83/65	S. paucispinis	640	3370.00
83/66	S. pinniger	460	1370.00
83/67	S. pinniger	450	1350.00
83/68	S. pinniger	410	1365.00
83/69	S. melanops	430	1830.00
83/70	S. flavidus	340	1060.00
83/74	S. babcocki	560	2774.00
83/77	S. nebulosus	310	685.00
83/78	S. pinniger	410	2360.00
83/79	S. flavidus	380	920.00
83/80	S. paucispinis	560	2265.00
83/81	S. paucispinis	560	n/a
83/83	S. caurinus	450	1795.00
83/84	S. borealis	600	3335.00
83/85	S. paucispinis	570	2199.00
83/86	S. brevispinis	330	1627.00
84/17	S. auriculatus	126	34.70
84/19	S. proriger	288	303.16
88/137	S. caurinus	208	162.53
95/24	S. aleutianus	230	144.00
95/25	S. diploproa	310	364.00
95/27	S. babcocki	290	405.00
95/28	S. helvomaculatus	295	318.00
00/10	S. melanops	280	309.38
00/80	S. proriger	250	188.00
00/81	S. proriger	205	102.80
00/84	S. proriger	195	85.88

Rockfish Comparative Specimens

Specimen	VOME-1	VOME-2	DENT-1	DENT-2	DENT-3	ANGU-1	ANGU-2	ARTI-1
82/08	9.50	4.54	34.58	6.23	17.04	5.47	5.44	31.58
82/09	8.19	4.43	33.70	5.86	16.12	5.73	6.95	28.68
82/10	10.03	5.53	39.78	6.82	19.69	6.43	7.09	34.67
82/12	8.82	4.87	30.65	6.22	16.48	6.85	6.80	28.95
82/13	n/a	n/a	45.54	8.30	22.42	7.20	6.65	41.77
83/09	8.42	4.39	31.88	5.23	15.96	5.64	5.87	27.25
83/10	9.43	5.45	36.73	6.13	17.90	6.07	7.15	33.18
83/24	9.18	5.13	38.52	6.92	18.49	7.04	7.05	35.00
83/65	17.49	8.49	88.99	12.52	36.43	12.31	9.97	85.68
83/66	12.95	5.87	54.80	11.79	29.17	7.78	8.60	50.04
83/67	12.83	5.30	54.52	10.19	28.11	7.44	8.44	48.21
83/68	13.02	5.57	52.21	10.64	27.32	8.80	8.57	47.82
83/69	13.96	7.13	53.02	9.82	25.52	n/a	n/a	48.64
83/70	12.09	6.32	47.41	8.80	23.09	n/a	n/a	42.51
83/74	14.26	7.94	n/a	n/a	n/a	11.03	11.74	n/a
83/77	9.15	4.87	37.52	7.29	18.04	6.42	7.95	32.69
83/78	17.00	6.27	61.49	10.50	30.26	9.39	9.14	52.50
83/79	10.72	5.84	44.49	8.42	21.57	n/a	n/a	40.84
83/80	15.30	7.75	79.33	11.23	32.65	11.62	8.61	77.94
83/81	18.68	8.09	93.57	14.50	38.70	13.93	11.16	88.49
83/83	14.40	6.25	52.45	9.88	26.07	n/a	n/a	44.47
83/84	19.24	9.79	72.64	12.89	35.59	14.38	13.93	61.83
83/85	16.97	6.78	n/a	14.49	n/a	n/a	n/a	64.34
83/86	15.92	7.01	55.88	11.17	27.19	7.99	9.10	50.93
84/17	3.96	1.68	14.11	2.05	7.55	2.16	2.04	12.15
84/19	11.37	6.05	42.19	7.42	21.44	7.88	7.57	37.32
88/137	6.92	3.51	n/a	n/a	n/a	n/a	n/a	n/a
95/24	6.70	3.39	28.59	4.42	14.56	n/a	n/a	25.22
95/25	9.25	3.94	n/a	6.94	n/a	6.21	5.83	34.88
95/27	8.98	4.37	32.00	5.08	16.37	5.94	6.14	28.71
95/28	7.25	4.34	35.41	6.28	17.90	n/a	n/a	28.34
00/10	7.64	3.91	29.03	5.10	14.19	4.32	4.63	28.29
00/80	6.59	3.28	26.98	5.09	13.93	4.46	3.67	24.88
00/81	5.56	2.43	21.84	3.86	11.13	3.23	2.92	19.40
00/84	4.97	2.31	19.46	3.19	10.35	3.23	2.94	17.75

Rockfish Comparative Specimens

Specimen	ARTI-2	ARTI-4	PREM-1	PREM-2	PREM-3	QUAD-3	QUAD-4	INTE-1
82/08	20.31	3.15	26.62	13.31	9.63	4.19	16.73	n/a
82/09	21.10	3.45	26.20	15.54	11.03	4.60	18.32	11.04
82/10	24.09	4.14	29.91	16.32	11.53	5.39	19.71	n/a
82/12	18.91	3.78	24.22	17.16	10.98	4.26	16.39	10.65
82/13	25.41	4.24	33.53	18.00	12.90	n/a	n/a	11.93
83/09	19.35	3.21	24.92	13.44	10.28	4.17	15.83	9.78
83/10	23.76	3.54	28.50	15.82	11.02	n/a	n/a	12.12
83/24	23.98	3.84	29.73	18.00	12.13	5.51	19.32	n/a
83/65	51.16	7.18	62.72	19.35	16.34	8.80	31.64	16.63
83/66	32.12	4.96	45.94	17.77	14.51	6.71	25.48	15.33
83/67	31.16	4.92	43.54	17.89	13.92	6.30	23.39	14.67
83/68	31.78	4.72	42.26	17.83	14.62	6.98	23.13	15.11
83/69	30.39	5.75	40.78	20.08	14.67	6.31	24.10	15.55
83/70	25.51	3.96	37.06	17.62	13.50	4.81	21.72	11.05
83/74	n/a	n/a	44.74	24.78	17.87	10.03	31.72	20.18
83/77	23.91	4.23	27.84	18.13	12.19	5.49	17.93	n/a
83/78	37.42	5.10	49.85	19.77	15.31	7.60	28.60	17.50
83/79	24.59	4.24	33.98	16.56	11.78	5.15	21.13	10.75
83/80	47.26	5.50	55.60	15.51	14.13	7.48	31.05	15.48
83/81	51.57	8.05	65.25	22.45	17.75	9.73	38.75	18.75
83/83	30.84	6.35	41.64	24.00	17.12	8.30	27.41	n/a
83/84	44.94	9.32	51.78	30.71	21.95	11.36	36.54	n/a
83/85	41.09	6.84	54.89	20.77	16.45	8.38	30.19	n/a
83/86	30.47	5.90	44.77	21.34	15.71	7.20	24.96	16.11
84/17	8.46	1.34	11.80	6.36	4.45	1.64	6.83	4.42
84/19	26.93	4.40	32.49	18.70	13.68	5.94	21.25	n/a
88/137	n/a	n/a	n/a	n/a	n/a	n/a	n/a	n/a
95/24	15.64	2.19	22.30	10.26	8.21	3.28	14.55	n/a
95/25	21.08	3.68	32.22	n/a	12.98	4.55	20.62	n/a
95/27	19.18	3.16	26.82	14.34	10.09	4.29	17.41	9.51
95/28	21.03	3.78	28.85	n/a	11.37	4.98	15.78	n/a
00/10	17.94	2.50	24.63	12.35	8.75	3.49	13.40	7.17
00/80	15.13	2.05	20.81	10.41	7.60	3.02	12.16	6.23
00/81	11.89	1.63	16.56	9.13	6.40	2.39	10.54	5.33
00/84	10.93	1.60	15.13	8.28	5.75	2.32	9.94	4.81

Rockfish Comparative Specimens

Specimen	EPIH-1	EPIH-2	EPIH-3	BASI-1	BASI-2	HYOM-1	HYOM-2	HYOM-3
82/08	18.26	1.64	12.07	n/a	n/a	13.67	26.21	4.44
82/09	19.16	2.77	12.40	n/a	n/a	15.57	27.08	4.67
82/10	21.12	2.44	14.32	n/a	n/a	18.69	30.05	5.85
82/12	17.82	2.18	11.23	n/a	n/a	13.77	22.78	4.06
82/13	23.32	2.42	15.23	15.96	3.71	18.19	35.61	5.07
83/09	17.40	2.36	11.72	n/a	n/a	14.45	24.99	4.50
83/10	21.44	2.35	13.58	n/a	n/a	n/a	23.76	3.56
83/24	21.17	2.35	13.74	n/a	n/a	19.16	31.04	6.11
83/65	38.94	5.22	24.73	31.81	4.99	31.94	53.56	9.13
83/66	28.58	3.69	18.09	n/a	n/a	21.87	41.07	7.16
83/67	27.78	3.10	17.15	n/a	n/a	21.73	40.05	6.08
83/68	27.76	3.24	17.66	16.58	3.60	21.63	39.84	6.73
83/69	29.19	2.80	18.54	n/a	n/a	21.71	40.49	6.55
83/70	23.11	2.58	15.42	n/a	n/a	18.25	35.07	5.59
83/74	36.15	6.67	25.62	n/a	n/a	27.45	48.37	9.98
83/77	22.31	2.78	15.15	n/a	n/a	17.93	30.51	6.15
83/78	34.23	3.42	21.76	n/a	n/a	23.96	49.71	8.61
83/79	23.07	2.15	14.91	n/a	n/a	17.87	35.23	5.14
83/80	36.81	4.72	22.63	30.71	4.76	28.34	47.26	7.64
83/81	43.03	6.60	26.03	n/a	n/a	31.42	56.12	9.23
83/83	31.63	3.92	20.77	n/a	n/a	24.54	41.85	7.49
83/84	41.53	6.27	26.02	n/a	n/a	31.08	48.24	9.41
83/85	33.45	4.88	21.17	27.95	4.32	27.29	45.76	9.32
83/86	31.03	2.85	19.53	19.93	3.80	24.46	45.52	6.80
84/17	n/a	1.04	5.57	n/a	n/a	6.14	10.52	1.73
84/19	23.35	3.14	16.39	n/a	n/a	19.60	31.62	5.93
88/137	n/a	n/a	n/a	n/a	n/a	n/a	n/a	n/a
95/24	14.23	1.25	9.42	n/a	n/a	10.62	20.00	3.19
95/25	21.00	2.18	14.38	n/a	n/a	15.78	34.65	5.18
95/27	18.70	2.58	12.59	n/a	n/a	14.41	25.71	4.66
95/28	19.39	1.90	12.26	n/a	n/a	14.03	26.18	4.21
00/10	15.24	1.48	10.01	9.34	1.83	11.44	22.60	3.99
00/80	12.98	1.08	8.59	n/a	n/a	9.66	19.23	3.09
00/81	10.94	0.92	7.03	6.99	1.21	8.20	16.27	2.79
00/84	9.93	0.83	6.23	6.95	1.16	7.40	15.18	2.43

Rockfish Comparative Specimens

Specimen	HYH2-2	INPH-1	INPH-3	INPH-4	PHA1-1	PHA1-2	HYB1-1	VER1-1
82/08	6.63	18.48	3.89	4.06	10.38	4.55	n/a	5.26
82/09	6.23	19.56	3.68	5.40	11.25	5.34	n/a	5.77
82/10	7.10	22.88	4.82	5.95	n/a	n/a	n/a	6.49
82/12	6.13	n/a	n/a	n/a	9.85	4.33	8.32	5.48
82/13	8.50	24.41	4.54	5.77	n/a	n/a	11.70	7.16
83/09	5.85	19.77	3.67	4.83	n/a	n/a	n/a	4.87
83/10	n/a	23.23	4.16	5.03	n/a	n/a	n/a	n/a
83/24	6.50	n/a	n/a	n/a	n/a	n/a	n/a	6.54
83/65	14.31	43.47	7.67	7.54	23.56	8.96	21.09	10.90
83/66	8.72	n/a	n/a	n/a	15.90	6.62	n/a	8.65
83/67	9.11	n/a	n/a	n/a	n/a	n/a	14.71	8.15
83/68	9.36	26.96	5.40	6.14	15.06	6.93	14.26	8.41
83/69	9.73	n/a	n/a	n/a	15.91	6.97	n/a	n/a
83/70	8.53	24.74	4.83	6.03	13.90	6.06	n/a	7.59
83/74	10.97	38.42	7.95	9.25	19.72	10.98	17.76	12.09
83/77	7.18	21.93	5.20	5.72	12.73	6.46	n/a	6.33
83/78	10.97	36.83	6.66	8.67	20.30	9.09	n/a	9.28
83/79	7.98	23.73	4.56	5.36	n/a	n/a	n/a	6.81
83/80	13.53	38.04	5.82	5.71	21.77	8.81	18.26	9.74
83/81	15.00	n/a	n/a	n/a	n/a	n/a	n/a	11.91
83/83	10.13	n/a	6.58	n/a	n/a	n/a	n/a	9.03
83/84	14.06	37.60	9.15	10.61	23.48	9.77	18.01	11.30
83/85	n/a	34.24	6.05	7.54	20.89	7.13	n/a	10.60
83/86	11.05	31.68	6.32	7.23	19.41	8.20	16.95	10.30
84/17	n/a	n/a	n/a	n/a	n/a	n/a	n/a	1.95
84/19	n/a	26.14	4.79	6.24	n/a	n/a	n/a	n/a
88/137	n/a	n/a	n/a	n/a	n/a	n/a	n/a	4.05
95/24	n/a	14.65	2.85	3.68	n/a	n/a	n/a	3.75
95/25	6.65	n/a	n/a	n/a	n/a	n/a	n/a	n/a
95/27	5.53	18.63	3.72	4.31	9.12	5.49	8.59	5.00
95/28	n/a	18.57	4.28	4.61	n/a	n/a	n/a	5.56
00/10	5.29	16.03	3.29	4.15	8.90	3.99	8.15	4.87
00/80	4.40	12.49	2.46	2.62	6.13	3.13	6.73	3.82
00/81	3.57	10.71	2.12	1.75	5.60	2.44	5.79	2.89
00/84	3.49	9.96	1.90	2.08	5.01	2.39	5.17	2.69

Rockfish Comparative Specimens

Specimen	VER1-2	VER1-3	PEVE-1	PEVE-2	PEVE-3	OTOL-1	OTOL-2
82/08	5.44	4.19	4.67	4.59	5.68	12.93	6.64
82/09	5.57	3.99	4.16	4.13	4.10	11.50	6.31
82/10	6.54	4.56	4.58	4.51	4.75	12.42	5.97
82/12	5.93	3.27	3.87	3.93	4.19	10.96	5.44
82/13	7.93	4.94	5.88	6.44	6.87	17.22	7.21
83/09	5.68	3.45	3.87	3.72	3.56	11.11	5.44
83/10	n/a	n/a	4.47	4.65	4.68	12.09	5.73
83/24	6.62	4.58	n/a	n/a	n/a	12.63	5.82
83/65	12.42	8.09	9.65	10.24	11.50	16.62	8.11
83/66	8.84	6.20	7.35	7.15	7.92	16.20	8.54
83/67	8.15	5.81	6.87	6.84	7.22	16.08	8.50
83/68	7.56	5.93	6.87	7.20	7.28	16.42	8.22
83/69	n/a	n/a	n/a	n/a	n/a	17.27	8.16
83/70	7.52	5.61	6.33	6.47	7.41	17.16	7.72
83/74	11.94	6.97	8.02	8.26	9.43	17.13	7.77
83/77	7.02	4.69	4.31	4.36	4.94	11.96	6.56
83/78	10.60	4.81	7.02	8.24	8.02	20.00	9.76
83/79	6.46	4.87	5.97	5.70	6.51	n/a	n/a
83/80	10.93	8.24	8.10	9.17	9.75	15.67	7.29
83/81	12.55	8.45	9.71	11.32	12.30	17.36	8.27
83/83	9.98	6.76	6.51	6.73	6.12	15.49	8.13
83/84	12.68	7.27	8.03	9.20	9.04	19.15	9.58
83/85	11.47	6.85	7.74	8.41	8.17	18.03	7.60
83/86	9.15	8.39	7.93	8.59	8.01	21.14	8.51
84/17	2.15	1.61	1.71	1.53	1.89	n/a	n/a
84/19	n/a	n/a	n/a	n/a	n/a	12.66	5.84
88/137	3.96	2.91	3.06	2.88	2.89	8.91	4.51
95/24	3.84	2.49	3.07	2.47	3.52	10.07	5.58
95/25	n/a	n/a	5.41	4.56	4.95	14.50	8.78
95/27	5.30	3.18	4.21	3.56	4.51	12.20	6.56
95/28	5.33	3.42	4.21	4.15	4.90	n/a	n/a
00/10	4.70	3.14	4.25	3.79	4.57	11.29	5.29
00/80	4.20	2.70	3.47	3.13	4.40	9.27	4.84
00/81	3.33	2.35	2.77	2.56	3.82	7.95	4.17
00/84	3.18	2.24	2.80	2.48	3.04	7.61	3.86

Walleye Pollock Comparative Specimens

Specimen	FL	Wt		Specimen	FL	Wt
93/33	135.00	16.80		BN196	84.00	3.90
95/36	480.00	939.00		BN210	85.00	5.00
95/44	465.00	1269.00		BN211	87.50	5.00
96/45	100.00	5.60		TC001	460.00	672.00
96/46	92.00	4.00		TC002	480.00	703.00
96/47	95.00	4.00		TC003	390.00	449.00
96/48	93.00	4.00		TC004	370.00	372.00
96/49	89.00	4.00		TC005	410.00	484.00
96/50	200.00	n/a		TC006	295.00	197.00
96/51	202.50	65.00		TC007	435.00	559.00
96/52	162.50	28.00		TC008	410.00	471.00
96/53	152.50	35.00		TC009	445.00	530.00
96/55	223.00	77.10				
96/56	260.00	138.00				
96/57	220.00	75.00				
96/58	320.00	322.00				
BN22	90.00	2.90				
BN23	111.00	8.30				
BN24	83.00	4.10				
BN71	219.00	70.40				
BN72	107.00	6.70				
BN96	315.00	288.00				
BN143	365.00	455.00				
BN156	90.00	3.00				
BN157	91.00	3.10				
BN158	135.00	10.00				
BN159	130.00	10.20				
BN160	147.50	21.00				
BN161	185.00	47.00				
BN162	140.00	16.00				
BN165	95.00	5.00				
BN166	185.00	43.00				
BN167	187.00	54.00				
BN168	195.00	54.00				
BN169	165.00	37.00				
BN170	205.00	60.00				
BN171	185.00	50.00				
BN172	175.00	44.00				
BN173	177.50	37.00				
BN179	270.00	174.00				
BN180	260.00	154.00				
BN182	190.00	51.00				
BN186	230.00	91.00				
BN187	195.00	64.00				
BN188	189.00	52.00				
BN189	189.00	50.00				
BN194	90.00	4.80				

Walleye Pollock Comparative Specimens

Specimen	VOME-1	VOME-2	DENT-1	DENT-2	DENT-3	ANGU-1	ANGU-2	PREM-1
93/33	3.91	2.10	12.22	1.40	8.86	1.91	1.50	9.41
95/36	17.86	8.39	55.03	7.06	39.34	8.87	7.95	38.19
95/44	16.50	8.70	50.60	5.60	30.20	9.20	n/a	36.15
96/45	2.76	1.56	9.30	1.01	6.73	1.28	0.96	7.06
96/46	2.49	1.40	n/a	0.89	n/a	n/a	n/a	6.19
96/47	2.44	1.15	7.80	0.87	5.47	1.26	0.91	6.18
96/48	2.36	1.33	8.06	0.87	5.30	n/a	n/a	6.53
96/49	2.38	1.23	7.96	0.90	5.84	1.17	0.90	6.32
96/50	4.11	2.34	16.17	1.63	11.45	2.57	1.80	11.46
96/51	5.01	2.94	15.49	1.64	11.06	2.64	1.88	12.52
96/52	n/a	n/a	13.40	1.43	9.60	2.37	1.70	10.10
96/53	n/a	n/a	13.72	1.46	9.79	2.25	1.59	10.47
96/55	6.24	3.62	20.87	2.16	14.91	3.50	2.42	14.93
96/56	7.47	3.92	23.96	2.41	16.59	4.01	3.16	17.83
96/57	5.45	3.08	17.99	1.86	12.76	3.29	1.94	13.93
96/58	9.98	4.91	30.40	3.09	20.49	5.26	4.00	22.30
BN22	2.29	1.25	6.92	0.80	4.77	n/a	n/a	5.62
BN23	3.13	1.87	10.01	1.07	6.80	1.61	1.17	7.56
BN24	2.40	1.41	7.87	0.83	5.22	n/a	n/a	5.91
BN71	5.95	3.19	20.79	2.17	14.08	3.19	2.43	15.10
BN72	2.71	1.64	10.02	0.96	6.70	1.41	1.11	7.72
BN96	8.65	4.64	26.84	2.72	19.99	4.92	3.97	18.96
BN143	n/a	n/a	32.96	3.31	23.45	4.83	4.46	n/a
BN156	2.38	1.33	7.87	0.93	5.27	1.07	0.90	6.15
BN157	2.48	1.39	8.00	0.90	5.35	1.17	0.89	6.37
BN158	3.81	2.18	12.67	1.19	8.89	n/a	n/a	9.48
BN159	3.61	2.01	11.96	1.15	8.40	n/a	n/a	9.08
BN160	4.07	2.37	12.98	1.22	9.07	1.80	1.53	9.90
BN161	4.80	3.07	16.04	1.80	11.16	2.40	1.93	11.80
BN162	3.68	2.06	12.02	1.20	8.40	1.80	1.37	9.24
BN165	2.51	1.35	8.01	0.97	5.52	n/a	n/a	6.67
BN166	5.28	2.81	17.03	1.76	11.57	2.71	2.10	12.37
BN167	4.98	3.14	17.54	1.79	11.97	2.72	2.07	12.76
BN168	5.45	2.91	17.71	1.75	12.82	2.58	2.05	12.91
BN169	4.66	2.67	15.04	1.58	10.72	2.12	1.66	11.47
BN170	5.59	3.16	17.28	1.89	11.83	3.01	2.24	12.63
BN171	5.22	2.72	16.96	1.80	11.17	2.45	1.94	12.10
BN172	4.85	2.79	16.47	1.65	11.18	2.27	1.78	12.29
BN173	4.93	2.91	15.84	1.55	11.67	2.59	1.92	12.52
BN179	7.98	4.91	26.16	2.82	18.71	4.36	3.51	19.71
BN180	7.30	4.05	24.14	2.39	16.39	3.58	2.85	16.99
BN182	5.19	3.19	16.65	1.64	11.65	2.44	2.07	12.30
BN186	6.23	3.83	19.87	1.96	14.17	3.63	2.68	15.21
BN187	5.05	3.03	18.03	1.77	12.08	2.63	2.16	13.16
BN188	5.06	2.96	17.06	1.78	11.72	2.57	2.06	12.73
BN189	5.17	3.10	17.74	1.83	11.58	2.86	2.08	12.71
BN194	2.45	1.25	8.13	0.87	5.44	n/a	n/a	6.21

Walleye Pollock Comparative Specimens

Specimen	VOME-1	VOME-2	DENT-1	DENT-2	DENT-3	ANGU-1	ANGU-2	PREM-1
BN196	n/a	n/a	n/a	0.73	n/a	n/a	n/a	5.48
BN210	2.50	1.23	8.04	0.95	5.51	1.13	0.93	6.61
BN211	n/a	n/a	7.46	0.84	5.28	n/a	n/a	6.18
TC001	11.94	6.10	38.27	4.35	27.83	6.41	5.29	30.05
TC002	11.81	7.01	37.73	4.25	25.42	6.12	5.29	27.79
TC003	10.56	5.65	32.05	3.71	21.95	6.39	4.26	24.16
TC004	9.85	5.58	31.84	3.26	21.84	4.60	4.30	23.54
TC005	10.42	6.15	33.58	3.64	23.21	5.42	3.75	24.96
TC006	7.79	4.78	25.09	2.85	17.15	4.32	3.19	19.80
TC007	11.62	6.83	36.33	4.06	25.54	5.81	5.24	28.11
TC008	11.22	6.00	35.08	3.66	22.49	6.18	4.44	26.26
TC009	11.51	6.93	37.79	4.07	25.88	6.07	4.68	27.18

Walleye Pollock Comparative Specimens

Specimen	PREM-2	PREM-3	QUAD-3	QUAD-4	INTE-1	EPIH-1	EPIH-2	EPIH-3
93/33	2.39	2.29	1.30	7.75	2.70	4.13	1.48	2.98
95/36	9.83	9.25	8.16	30.45	13.06	21.68	6.33	13.23
95/44	9.20	8.45	7.10	28.35	13.20	18.45	4.30	12.15
96/45	1.75	1.70	0.99	5.69	1.82	3.14	1.05	2.19
96/46	1.55	1.45	0.92	4.95	1.70	2.70	0.85	1.81
96/47	1.58	1.50	1.05	5.06	n/a	2.67	0.91	1.87
96/48	1.47	1.27	0.92	4.85	n/a	n/a	n/a	n/a
96/49	1.55	1.42	0.93	4.63	1.59	2.70	0.85	1.95
96/50	2.91	2.70	1.97	9.24	3.39	5.31	1.63	3.68
96/51	3.28	2.93	2.10	10.25	3.71	5.62	1.98	4.39
96/52	2.60	2.36	1.77	8.66	2.87	4.41	1.56	3.47
96/53	2.56	2.51	1.77	8.40	3.07	4.87	1.61	3.60
96/55	3.75	3.34	2.39	13.36	4.71	7.29	2.47	5.02
96/56	4.82	4.41	3.00	13.52	5.55	8.57	2.37	5.94
96/57	3.35	3.12	2.20	10.94	4.15	6.08	1.72	4.42
96/58	5.55	5.26	4.10	18.89	7.59	11.46	3.85	7.94
BN22	1.40	1.13	0.84	4.54	1.40	2.46	0.59	1.75
BN23	1.91	1.77	1.18	6.16	2.23	3.43	0.93	2.29
BN24	1.54	1.33	0.93	4.91	n/a	2.70	0.68	1.80
BN71	4.20	3.67	2.30	11.31	4.38	7.09	2.19	4.85
BN72	1.79	1.66	1.06	6.34	2.10	3.23	0.90	2.36
BN96	5.38	4.73	3.58	15.01	6.23	9.44	2.34	6.55
BN143	n/a	n/a	n/a	n/a	7.14	12.45	3.85	8.42
BN156	1.53	1.45	0.90	4.64	1.78	2.63	0.67	1.97
BN157	1.57	1.36	1.01	5.01	n/a	2.60	0.83	1.95
BN158	2.24	2.04	1.43	7.88	2.83	4.31	1.36	2.79
BN159	2.06	1.90	1.40	7.07	2.48	4.05	1.16	2.80
BN160	2.49	2.31	1.70	7.56	2.80	4.11	1.21	3.31
BN161	3.08	2.88	2.04	9.51	3.63	5.58	1.87	3.81
BN162	2.28	2.02	1.51	7.56	2.48	4.00	1.12	2.95
BN165	1.63	1.43	1.00	5.06	n/a	n/a	n/a	n/a
BN166	3.19	2.86	2.02	10.29	3.63	6.19	1.92	4.23
BN167	3.05	2.79	1.91	9.39	3.74	5.69	1.85	4.00
BN168	3.30	2.92	2.12	10.35	n/a	6.15	1.95	4.39
BN169	2.84	2.79	1.90	9.47	3.38	4.98	1.46	3.76
BN170	3.21	3.02	2.25	10.19	4.04	6.13	2.09	4.29
BN171	3.04	2.70	2.23	9.68	3.74	5.63	1.87	4.26
BN172	2.87	2.74	2.03	9.98	3.43	5.45	1.49	3.76
BN173	3.01	2.82	1.95	10.19	3.62	5.54	1.85	3.96
BN179	5.12	4.50	3.09	15.17	6.11	9.11	2.58	6.73
BN180	4.51	4.21	2.99	13.99	5.50	8.33	2.60	6.19
BN182	3.05	2.93	2.04	10.39	3.68	6.01	1.65	4.08
BN186	3.82	3.44	2.37	12.41	4.62	7.05	2.11	4.87
BN187	3.14	2.68	2.14	10.31	4.03	6.25	1.92	4.42
BN188	3.18	2.83	2.01	9.99	3.60	5.78	1.59	4.08
BN189	3.19	2.97	2.03	10.30	3.94	5.81	1.63	4.20
BN194	1.54	1.50	0.90	4.15	n/a	2.70	0.97	2.02

Walleye Pollock Comparative Specimens

Specimen	PREM-2	PREM-3	QUAD-3	QUAD-4	INTE-1	EPIH-1	EPIH-2	EPIH-3
BN196	1.39	1.29	0.80	4.47	n/a	2.46	0.86	1.70
BN210	1.66	1.43	0.88	4.91	n/a	2.67	0.95	2.00
BN211	1.44	1.32	0.89	4.92	n/a	2.40	0.66	1.85
TC001	7.19	6.73	5.00	20.51	8.79	13.57	3.84	9.79
TC002	7.00	6.25	4.91	21.06	9.06	14.29	3.99	10.53
TC003	6.21	5.27	4.25	19.23	7.39	11.78	3.57	8.39
TC004	5.73	5.57	4.00	17.94	7.21	10.96	3.04	7.95
TC005	5.89	5.51	4.47	21.12	7.86	12.42	3.21	9.06
TC006	4.79	4.28	3.19	14.66	5.26	8.75	2.67	6.15
TC007	6.49	6.03	4.77	20.79	8.32	12.64	3.88	9.33
TC008	7.03	6.31	4.46	19.02	8.03	12.26	3.80	9.16
TC009	6.78	6.34	4.76	21.03	8.50	13.96	3.83	9.78

Walleye Pollock Comparative Specimens

Specimen	PHA2-1	PHA2-2	HYP3-1	EPB4-1	EPB3-1	VER1-1	VER1-2	VER1-3
93/33	2.26	1.74	2.87	3.95	1.51	1.64	1.75	0.89
95/36	12.24	8.50	14.27	20.13	8.62	8.04	9.51	4.03
95/44	10.10	7.20	12.40	17.25	7.75	7.55	8.90	4.45
96/45	1.85	1.45	2.16	2.82	1.05	1.13	1.32	0.68
96/46	n/a	n/a	n/a	n/a	n/a	1.01	1.02	0.58
96/47	1.38	0.89	n/a	2.48	n/a	0.93	1.19	0.52
96/48	n/a	n/a	n/a	n/a	n/a	0.88	1.11	0.51
96/49	1.57	1.05	n/a	2.31	n/a	0.95	1.15	0.62
96/50	2.72	1.79	3.89	5.02	2.14	1.94	2.02	1.18
96/51	3.71	1.87	4.01	5.31	2.21	2.15	2.21	1.24
96/52	2.34	1.71	3.20	4.15	1.77	1.68	1.74	0.97
96/53	2.79	1.73	3.16	4.42	1.86	1.80	1.86	1.08
96/55	4.23	2.28	4.64	6.55	2.81	2.58	2.69	1.52
96/56	4.43	2.49	5.79	7.56	3.35	3.27	3.51	1.70
96/57	3.17	2.38	4.70	6.12	2.42	2.17	2.48	1.47
96/58	6.98	4.05	7.98	9.91	4.46	4.23	4.63	2.43
BN22	1.52	0.96	n/a	2.38	0.93	0.95	0.96	0.48
BN23	1.68	1.06	2.44	3.12	1.14	1.25	1.43	0.70
BN24	n/a	n/a	1.77	2.42	0.80	1.02	1.12	0.49
BN71	3.52	2.29	4.89	6.61	2.60	2.59	3.03	1.56
BN72	1.95	1.19	2.28	3.03	1.16	1.17	1.35	0.67
BN96	5.32	3.90	6.94	9.20	3.90	3.83	3.92	2.17
BN143	7.34	5.09	9.04	11.42	4.95	4.80	5.58	2.89
BN156	1.49	1.06	2.07	2.58	n/a	0.89	1.11	0.53
BN157	n/a	n/a	2.02	n/a	0.87	0.88	1.19	0.45
BN158	2.43	1.46	n/a	3.57	1.53	1.47	1.62	0.80
BN159	n/a	n/a	2.62	3.66	1.47	1.40	1.62	0.70
BN160	2.40	1.68	2.99	4.20	1.69	1.69	1.73	0.89
BN161	2.80	2.35	3.90	5.03	2.27	2.08	2.26	1.20
BN162	2.54	1.68	2.85	3.80	1.54	1.47	1.70	0.86
BN165	1.66	1.29	n/a	n/a	n/a	n/a	n/a	n/a
BN166	3.81	2.13	4.12	5.32	2.02	2.11	2.32	1.10
BN167	3.06	1.69	3.76	4.82	2.02	2.06	2.14	1.32
BN168	3.46	2.16	3.81	5.33	2.32	2.16	2.27	1.11
BN169	3.03	1.77	3.68	5.02	1.97	1.84	2.07	1.13
BN170	3.55	2.29	4.33	5.74	2.27	2.29	2.41	1.22
BN171	3.01	1.70	3.98	5.19	2.08	2.12	2.35	1.17
BN172	3.03	1.77	3.75	5.10	2.29	1.93	2.16	1.19
BN173	3.43	1.90	4.11	5.25	2.05	1.83	2.12	1.15
BN179	5.34	3.59	6.32	8.38	3.89	3.49	3.93	2.22
BN180	4.79	3.18	6.09	7.61	3.14	3.22	3.51	1.94
BN182	2.91	2.22	3.93	5.02	2.41	2.09	2.23	1.20
BN186	4.06	2.38	4.75	6.53	2.61	2.54	2.91	1.66
BN187	3.56	2.33	4.37	5.79	2.47	2.18	2.50	1.44
BN188	3.47	2.16	3.73	n/a	2.20	2.18	2.39	1.30
BN189	3.56	2.31	3.98	5.44	2.27	2.06	2.45	1.35
BN194	n/a	n/a	n/a	2.27	n/a	0.89	1.05	0.48

Walleye Pollock Comparative Specimens

Specimen	PHA2-1	PHA2-2	HYP3-1	EPB4-1	EPB3-1	VER1-1	VER1-2	VER1-3
BN196	n/a	n/a	1.72	2.18	0.86	0.91	0.98	0.55
BN210	1.44	1.04	n/a	2.27	0.86	1.02	1.04	0.57
BN211	n/a	n/a	n/a	2.25	0.81	0.91	1.08	0.46
TC001	8.17	5.79	9.50	12.80	5.45	5.99	n/m	3.18
TC002	8.99	5.42	10.98	13.47	5.73	5.64	5.99	3.00
TC003	7.15	4.53	8.73	11.11	4.72	4.69	5.00	2.70
TC004	6.51	4.06	8.47	11.39	4.40	3.99	4.60	2.27
TC005	6.46	4.56	8.90	11.07	4.53	4.67	5.37	2.57
TC006	4.85	3.15	6.11	8.02	3.42	3.20	3.55	1.94
TC007	8.29	5.19	9.41	12.48	5.51	4.99	5.53	2.63
TC008	7.22	4.12	8.93	11.96	4.74	4.76	4.97	2.52
TC009	8.47	4.78	9.85	13.10	5.82	n/m	n/m	2.71

Walleye Pollock Comparative Specimens

Specimen	VER9-1	VER9-2	VER9-3	OTOL-1	OTOL-2
93/33	1.73	1.70	1.96	6.92	2.54
95/36	10.58	10.67	8.55	n/a	n/a
95/44	8.60	8.85	8.15	20.93	8.85
96/45	1.17	1.22	1.38	5.29	2.13
96/46	n/a	n/a	n/a	3.88	1.72
96/47	n/a	n/a	n/a	3.82	1.78
96/48	n/a	n/a	n/a	3.85	1.70
96/49	n/a	n/a	n/a	3.74	1.64
96/50	2.30	2.20	2.69	8.79	3.59
96/51	2.40	2.49	2.70	8.82	3.55
96/52	1.90	1.94	2.21	7.43	2.88
96/53	1.99	2.10	2.39	7.54	3.10
96/55	2.96	2.96	3.16	11.42	4.11
96/56	3.59	3.63	3.76	11.82	4.53
96/57	2.76	2.61	2.91	9.55	3.61
96/58	4.83	4.90	4.91	14.27	5.58
BN22	0.97	1.05	1.12	4.05	1.72
BN23	1.42	1.44	1.55	5.24	2.05
BN24	1.28	1.09	1.21	4.49	1.74
BN71	2.99	3.09	3.10	10.72	4.20
BN72	1.24	1.33	1.54	n/a	n/a
BN96	4.33	4.35	4.44	n/a	5.32
BN143	5.51	5.86	5.49	16.58	6.61
BN156	1.06	1.05	1.13	3.89	1.63
BN157	n/a	n/a	n/a	3.76	1.71
BN158	1.54	1.61	1.81	n/a	n/a
BN159	1.44	1.51	1.67	n/a	n/a
BN160	1.76	1.80	2.03	n/a	n/a
BN161	2.38	2.41	2.71	8.30	3.48
BN162	1.62	1.86	1.82	n/a	n/a
BN165	1.12	1.18	1.29	3.79	1.83
BN166	2.39	2.43	2.70	9.44	3.76
BN167	2.42	2.33	2.78	9.01	3.53
BN168	2.50	2.47	2.82	9.05	3.47
BN169	2.13	2.19	2.40	8.21	2.94
BN170	2.56	2.58	2.83	8.80	3.70
BN171	2.37	2.41	2.76	9.04	3.45
BN172	2.25	2.21	2.52	9.02	3.50
BN173	2.24	2.26	2.51	9.14	3.22
BN179	3.81	4.00	4.02	n/a	n/a
BN180	3.55	3.49	3.66	12.25	4.88
BN182	2.39	2.44	2.68	8.97	3.50
BN186	2.89	3.08	3.40	10.24	4.11
BN187	2.54	2.68	2.87	9.65	3.60
BN188	2.54	2.56	2.83	9.10	3.81
BN189	2.47	2.52	2.67	9.44	3.65
BN194	n/a	n/a	n/a	3.70	1.64

Walleye Pollock Comparative Specimens

Specimen	VER9-1	VER9-2	VER9-3	OTOL-1	OTOL-2
BN196	n/a	n/a	n/a	3.47	1.42
BN210	1.15	1.03	1.24	3.74	1.73
BN211	1.04	1.00	1.20	4.05	1.75
TC001	6.40	6.66	6.55	17.78	6.65
TC002	7.13	6.93	7.19	17.52	7.46
TC003	5.17	5.22	5.37	n/m	6.47
TC004	4.98	4.84	5.40	n/m	6.20
TC005	5.41	5.67	6.15	n/m	6.91
TC006	3.97	3.81	4.28	n/m	5.13
TC007	5.91	6.02	6.20	n/m	6.83
TC008	5.35	5.36	6.07	16.09	6.28
TC009	6.22	5.76	6.21	n/m	7.18

www.ingramcontent.com/pod-product-compliance
Lightning Source LLC
Chambersburg PA
CBHW061002030426
42334CB00033B/3327